JAEPL

The Assembly for Expanded Perspectives on Learning (AEPL), an official assembly of the National Council of Teachers of English, is open to all those interested in extending the frontiers of teaching and learning beyond the traditional disciplines and methodologies.

The purposes of AEPL are to provide a common ground for theorists, researchers, and practitioners to explore innovative ideas; to participate in relevant programs and projects; to integrate these efforts with others in related disciplines; to keep abreast of activities along these lines of inquiry; and to promote scholarship on and publication of these activities.

The *Journal of the Assembly for Expanded Perspectives on Learning, JAEPL*, also provides a forum to encourage research, theory, and classroom practices involving expanded concepts of language. It contributes to a sense of community in which scholars and educators from pre-school through the university exchange points of view and boundary-pushing approaches to teaching and learning. *JAEPL* is especially interested in helping those teachers who experiment with new strategies for learning to share their practices and confirm their validity through publication in professional journals.

Topics of interest include but are not limited to:

- Aesthetic, emotional & moral intelligences
- Learning archetypes
- Kinesthetic knowledge & body wisdom
- Ethic of care in education
- Creativity & innovation
- Pedagogies of healing
- Holistic learning
- Humanistic & transpersonal psychology
- Environmentalism and post-humanism
- (Meta)Cognition
- Imaging & visual thinking
- Intuition & felt sense theory
- Meditation & pedagogical uses of silence
- Narration as knowledge
- Reflective teaching
- Spirituality
- New applications of writing & rhetoric
- Memory & transference
- Multimodality
- Social justice

Membership in AEPL is $45. Contact Jonathan Marine, AEPL, Membership Chair, email: jmarine@gmu.edu. Membership includes current year's issue of *JAEPL*.

Send submissions, address changes, and single hardcopy requests to Wendy Ryden, Editor, *JAEPL*, email: wendy.ryden@liu.edu. Address letters to the editors and all other editorial correspondence to Wendy Ryden (wendy.ryden@liu.edu).

AEPL website: www.aepl.org
Back issues of *JAEPL*: http://trace.tennessee.edu/jaepl/
Blog: https://aeplblog.wordpress.com/
Visit Facebook at **Assembly for Expanded Perspectives on Learning**
Production of *JAEPL* is managed by Parlor Press, www.parlorpress.com.

Assembly for Expanded Perspectives on Learning

Executive Board	
Chair	Geraldine DeLuca
Associate Chair	Bruce Novak, The Foundation for Ethics and Meaning
Secretary	Liz DeBetta
Treasurer/ Membership Chair	Jonathan Marine, George Mason University
CCC Standing Group Liaisons	Lisa Blankenship, Baruch College
	Eric Leake, Texas State University
TRACE Website	Elizabeth DeGeorge, University of Tennessee, Knoxville
AEPL Website	Daniel J. Weinstein, Indiana University of Pennsylvania
Advisory Board	Chair: Peter Elbow, University of Massachusetts, Amherst
	Sheridan Blau, Teachers College, Columbia University
	Alice G. Brand, SUNY College at Brockport
	John Creger, American High School, Freemont, CA
	Libby Falk Jones, Berea College
	Richard L. Graves, Auburn University, Emeritus
	Doug Hesse, University of Denver
	Nel Noddings, Stanford University
	Sondra Perl, Lehman College, CUNY
	Kurt Spellmeyer, Rutgers University
	Charles Suhor, NCTE
	Jane Tompkins, University of Illinois at Chicago
	Candace Walworth, Naropa University
	RAsheda Young, Rutgers University
Founding Members	Alice G. Brand, SUNY College at Brockport
	Richard L. Graves, Auburn University, Emeritus
	Charles Suhor, NCTE
Membership Contact	Jonathan Marine, George Mason University
JAEPL Editor	Wendy Ryden, Long Island University

JAEPL is a non-profit journal published yearly by the Assembly for Expanded Perspectives on Learning with support from TRACE at University of Tennessee, Knoxville. Back issues are archived at: http://trace.tennessee.edu/jaepl/.

JAEPL gratefully acknowledges this support as well as that of its manuscript reviewers for their expertise and generosity:

Kati Fargo Ahern, SUNY Cortland
W. Keith Duffy, The Pennsylvania State University
Mara Lee Grayson, California State University, Dominguez Hills
Frank Jacob, Nord Universitet
Keith Lloyd, Kent State University
Mark McBeth, John Jay College of Criminal Justice & The Graduate Center, CUNY
Noor Naga, American University in Cairo
Alexandria Peary, Salem State University
Meg Petersen, Plymouth State University
Maria Prozesky, University of the Witwatersrand
William H. Thelin, University of Akron
Jon Udelson, Shenandoah University
Stephanie Vanderslice, University of Central Arkansas
Stacey Waite, University of Nebraska-Lincoln

The Journal of the Assembly for Expanded Perspectives on Learning

Editor
Wendy Ryden
Long Island University

Book Review Editor
Irene Papoulis
Trinity College

"Connecting" Editor
Christy Wenger
Shepherd University

Copyright © 2022
by the Assembly for Expanded Perspectives on Learning
All rights reserved

(ISSN 1085-4630)

An affiliate of the National Council of Teachers of English
Member of the NCTE Information Exchange Agreement
Member of the Council of Editors of Learned Journals
Indexed with MLA Bibliography
Website: www.aepl.org
Blog: https://aeplblog.wordpress.com/
Visit Facebook at **Assembly for Expanded Perspectives on Learning**
Back issues available at: http://trace.tennessee.edu/jaepl/

Volume 27 • 2022

Contents

Special Section
Creative Writing in Higher Education: Where Are We Going? Where Have We Been?

Wendy Ryden	1	Introduction: Finding Meaning on the Road to Hell
T J Geiger II	3	"Weaving all of them together": How Writing Majors Talk about Creative Writing
Mariya Deykute	21	All Scientists Should Write Poetry: Creative Writing as Essential Academic Practice
Michelle Lafrance and Jay Hardee	39	Werk at Play: Exploring the Creative Play of a Graduate Student Writer to Reimagine Graduate Writing in the Humanities
Erika Luckert	60	A View from Somewhere: Situating the Public Problem in Creative Writing Workshops
James Ryan and Steve Westbrook	79	Toward a Decolonial Creative Writing Workshop: Mbari as a Case Study in Examining Intercultural Models for Arts Education

Essay

K. Shannon Howard	99	Spring Break in Chernobyl: Urbex, Apocalypse, and Materiality in Writing Classrooms

Connecting

Christy I. Wenger	114	Can We Flourish?
Joonna Smitherman Trapp	117	A Meditation: Why Teach?
Jamey Gallagher	119	An Encomium for Community College Students in Five Scenes
Naomi Gades	122	grading
Naomi Gades	123	dear search applicant committee:

Book Reviews

Irene Papoulis	124	The Pandemic Forces Us Back to Our Roots
Matthew Overstreet	125	Wenger, Christy. *Yoga Minds, Writing Bodies: Contemplative Writing Pedagogy*
Madeline Crozier	127	Borgman, Jessie, and Casey McArdle, editors. *PARS in Practice: More Resources and Strategies for Online Writing Instructors*

Kandace Knudson	130	Miller, Richard E. *On the End of Privacy: Dissolving Boundaries in a Screen-Centric World*
Christian Smith	132	Nelson, Steven T. *Teaching the Way: Using the Principles of The Art of War to Teach Composition*
Heidi M. Williams	134	Dively, Rhonda Leathers. *Creativity and The Paris Review Interviews: A Discourse Analysis of Famous Writers' Composing Practices*
Amanda E. Scott	136	Jackson, Rebecca, and Jackie Grutsch McKinney, editors. *Self+Culture+Writing: Autoethnography for/as Writing Studies*
Stan Scott	139	Suhor, Charles. *Creativity and Chaos: Reflections on a Decade of Progressive Change in Public Schools*
	145	**Contributors to JAEPL, Vol. 27**
	148	**Announcement**

SPECIAL SECTION: CREATIVE WRITING IN HIGHER EDUCATION: WHERE ARE WE GOING? WHERE HAVE WE BEEN?

Introduction: Finding Meaning on the Road to Hell

Wendy Ryden

The following is excerpted from a letter I wrote for my 2022 spring semester creative nonfiction class, which met for its last session the day after the leaked document surfaced from the Supreme Court signaling the end of *Roe V Wade*.

It's been a long-standing practice for me to remain relatively silent on the last class meeting when everyone reads their reflections aloud. It's important, I think, for the last words of our course to be the class's words and not mine. After all, you've heard enough of me by this point.

But I'm moved today to break that tradition. I don't know that I'll ever do it again, or that it's a good idea to do it this time. I'm not sure of much these days.

Except this: that our world is not in a good way. Typically, on occasions like these, the facilitator offers words of inspiration and hope and charges everyone to live up to their potential and do great things, to embrace the world, etc. Well, I do want you to live up to your potential, and I can tell you that the time we've spent together has been a great gift. I am moved by your stories, your perspectives, your struggles and the way so many of you have let us in, pushed yourselves, and have progressed with your writing.

But I'm pretty short on offering inspiration and hope. Rather than pretend otherwise, instead I give you the highest level of respect that I know how: to tell you what I really think. This is not a good world that you are going to spend the rest of your lives in, and I see no clear path by which it will get any better.

When I talk to my psychiatrist about the country's, the world's prospects, he, in his eighties, tells me this has never been a good place. "I went to medical school in Mississippi in the sixties," he says. "I know."

And I don't disagree, of course. But it's not nostalgia for a better time from which we've slipped that I'm feeling. It's not that things were once so great, it's that in so many ways they keep getting worse and worse. I don't need to go through the list. The shrink is right: there's never been a great time. But there have been times when we might have glimpsed a way forward, what we might have called progress. I'm not seeing that now. I think of the lyrics from the poet/song writer Leonard Cohen: "everybody knows the fight was fixed; everybody knows the good guys lost." He died in the fall of 2016 at a ripe old age. I wonder what he'd think today.

So in my despair, what keeps me going? The desire to make things better, sure, but—and here's the odd thing—not because I believe it's even possible. I mean, I hope so, to make things better, that is, but that's not why I try. I do it simply because trying is the right thing to do. Trying to make a difference is the only way I know to live something like an authentic and meaningful existence. Notice I don't say happy, but meaningful.

So here's my ask: find out what the right thing is and, please, do it—take action. And here's my elder's statement to you: happiness is transient. It will come and go. It's not a happy life I wish for you all but a meaningful life. If there's one thing I hope that you can take away from learning about creative nonfiction it's that meaningfulness is within our grasp. Why do we write? We write to find meaning; we write to create it. For ourselves. For others.

The rest of my missive finishes with an inside joke that only members of the class would get, so I don't repeat it here (too bad—it's funny—and we probably need all the laughs we can get, because, as we know, things only got worse following that leaked opinion). So here I leave off at the point where I think the essays in this special section of *JAEPL* begin: the question of meaning; the question of "why."

The journalist Nicolas Niarchos, writing about the Russian-Ukrainian war, resurrects the age-old question: "What does art matter when people are dying, starving, and being raped?" (29). It's the vein of question that comes up when we talk about creative writing, for those sympathetic as much as unsympathetic to the arts, both for the general public as well as for academics and administrators, when the institutional push for professionalization is on with a vengeance. (And the cliché seems apt; there does seem something vengeful about the way our universities clamor for the transactional and monetizable almost as though to make up for any time, real or imagined, of an elitist humanistic reign in the academy.) Long before the war started, before *Dobbs V Jackson Women's* was decided, I asked, in the call for papers for this special issue, that contributors consider the role of CW in higher education. Is it a luxury elective with little to no practical value? Or is it a hard-working, performative genre vital to our personal and societal well-being?

As you have probably divined, I *want* it to be the latter. I want to practice and teach creative writing that matters in a world going to hell, and I want to learn more about how I can do that. As you will see, our contributors do, too. I welcome their essays as pieces that help us struggle with that why and that how.

Work Cited

Niarchos, Nicholas. "*Giselle* Goes to War." The Nation, 6 June 2022, pp. 28-31.

"Weaving all of them together": How Writing Majors Talk about Creative Writing

T J Geiger II

Abstract: *The labels "creative" and "creative writing" serve several purposes in the discourses of undergraduate writing majors. In a study of students in two writing major programs, students often exerted significant effort to negotiate among diverse writing experiences and to integrate different understandings of writing. Their efforts mirror scholars' conversations about negotiation and integration at the level of curricula and programs. Writing majors in this study raised issues relevant to the well-established curricular domains of theoretical knowledge, professional expertise, and civic action. They explained their insights using a mix of idiosyncratic, institutional, and disciplinary language that frequently relied on forms of "'not' talk" (Reiff and Bawarshi). One term around which much of their blended-language and 'not' talk centered was "creative." Students used the label "creative" to mean writing fiction and poetry, personal expression, creative nonfiction prose, nonacademic discourse, and flexibility in style and genre. Frequently, these uses were mixed together or slipped casually from one to another. These findings suggest that as students engage with disciplinary purposes for writing in the major, they draw from a range of literacy discourses to negotiate among and to integrate diverse forms of knowledge.*

> I was still really interested in creative writing. I care more about actually being able to take what I learn and being able to produce something rather than just researching things. And so I looked into the writing major. Also, the fact that an internship was expected for students was the biggest deciding factor [in choosing writing as a major]. . . . So, again, it was that issue of being able to take your knowledge and use it to do something.
>
> —*Tyler, senior writing major at Private Research University*

"Creative writing" is a label that circulates within academic debates, professional markets, and popular discourse—carrying with it multiple meanings. In a short piece for *Inside Higher Ed*, Cydney Alexis calls for the abolition of the label "creative writing." She argues that to use the phrase mobilizes a binary with imaginative (creative) literature on one side and all other forms of writing (noncreative) on the other side. To circumscribe creativity as the province of fiction writers and poets, Alexis contends, privileges these forms and devalues other genres. Despite the term's slipperiness and its potential for re-inscribing literacy hierarchies, the academic and cultural ubiquity of the term "creative writing" would suggest that it's not going away anytime soon, making it unlikely that Alexis's provocative call will gain much traction. Indeed, "creative writing"—variously defined—played multifaceted roles among participants in my research into the attitudes, beliefs, and experiences of undergraduate writing majors in two independent writing departments. This term frequently emerged in students' survey responses, interview comments, and writing samples as they articulated the interrelationships among academic discourse, fiction writing, nonfiction prose, and professional writing. For example, in the epigraph above, Tyler, a senior majoring in writing and a research participant, expressed an interest in internships and practical knowledge while also linking that interest with a desire to compose fiction. He connected this interest and this desire through a focus on production. This effort to link diverse writing practices and interests surfaced repeatedly among students in his program and in another independent writing program. Students in these writing major programs often worked toward an integrated understanding of writing expertise.

As writing majors undertook these efforts, they employed a mix of expert, institutional, cultural, and idiosyncratic ways of talking about writing, and they didn't always articulate how or why multiple forms of writing relate, or fail to relate, to each other. Much of the students' blended language made use of discourse akin to what Mary Jo Reiff and Anis Bawarshi call "'not' talk," discussing one form of writing by describing how it's *not* like other forms of writing. One term around which much of this discursively blended 'not' talk centered was "creative." Often this term meant *fiction and/or poetry*, but other times it was a *synonym for personal expression*, a *foil for academic discourse*, and a *flexibility in terms of style and genre*. Students frequently slipped from one apparent meaning to another. This not talk around the label "creative" reveals that the dynamics of negotiation and integration so often described within writing major scholarship at the levels of curricula and programs also operate at the level of student uptake and experience.

Considering what students mean when they employ the term "creative" in reference to writing is a fruitful exercise for developing pedagogical and curricular insights. Others have made similar observations about student use of "creative" and "not creative" labels. For example, Michael-John DePalma and Kara Poe Alexander find an academic versus creative binary at work in students' discussions of multimodal composing, and Tim Mayers asks creative writing students about the view some of them express: that their responses to highly structured prompts are "not 'creative'" ("Notes" 18). Writing majors' discourse around creativity and writing, as explored in the present article, indicates overlaps with, and disconnects from, views about the writing major common within disciplinary scholarship. In what follows, I first briefly describe my research methods. Further details about methods are discussed in a previous publication: "An Intimate Discipline? Writing Studies, Undergraduate Majors, and Relational Labor." I then examine 1) the dynamics of disciplinary and institutional negotiation and integration that exist within writing major scholarship as it relates to curriculum and 2) elements of the historic relationship of writing studies and creative writing. I then examine widely accepted domains for writing major programs and their courses (i.e., theoretical knowledge, professional expertise, and civic action), noting connections between these areas and creative writing. Then, after discussing the methods of research, I analyze accounts from student research participants to demonstrate how writing majors' own words reveal, at the student level, dynamics of negotiation and integration similar to those described within scholarship about curricula and institutions. I focus on student negotiations and integrations within theoretical, professional, and civic domains by attending to how they leverage "not" talk in relationship to the diverse literacy activities they often labeled "creative." Rather than viewing the slipperiness of student discourse about creative writing as primarily a problem to be solved, I, like DePalma and Alexander and Mayers, view it as a rich site for pedagogical and curricular inquiry.

Negotiation and Integration in the Writing Major

Designers of writing major curricula, as well as students within these curricula, find important the negotiation and integration of diverse approaches to writing. Programs frequently perform local and disciplinary negotiations to name their object of study (Langstraat, Palmquist, and Kiefer; Peele). Beyond local negotiation, several scholars actively promote an "integrated" writing major—one that unites rhetorical, literary, professional, and creative concerns. Rodney F. Dick claims the writing major as "a disciplinary 'middle ground' of English studies" (101). Randy Brooks, Peiling Zhao, and Carmella Braniger express a similar view when they witness students form attachments to particular writing identities; they encourage students' integrative efforts to bridge perceived divides between creative and professional writing (41). Student authors in the polyvocal narrative by Bradley et al. endorse this perspective as they learn writing studies disciplinary concepts, write across genres for multiple audiences, read literary texts, compose fiction texts, examine design elements, and study cultural rhetorics for civic purposes. Collie Fulford and Aaron Dial note that they have witnessed faculty across specializations achieve productive curriculum developments for their writing concentration. Other work in the collection *Writing Majors: Eighteen Program Profiles* affirms the ongoing importance of negotiations and integrations at the program-level within English departments or independent units (Giberson, Nugent, and Ostergaard). This work to negotiate and integrate different understandings of writing and writerly identity also appears in the responses of students in the present study. Their invocations of *creative* signal their efforts and the potential difficulties that attend such efforts.

Indeed, while faculty and students in writing major programs may affirm the importance of negotiation and integration, this approach brings with it institutional and disciplinary difficulties, such as departmental marginalization and appeals to divergent traditions. Kelly Lowe and William Macauley found writing major faculty, courses, and students marginalized within a small English department (86-92). Like the challenge Lisa Langstraat, Mike Palmquist, and Kate Kiefer experienced when literature scholars initially objected to the value of writing-intensive internships with "no textual center" for students to master (80), Lowe and Macauley recount how literature faculty devalued writing study (89). Linda Shamoon and Celest Martin report faculty strongly resisting the idea of situating creative nonfiction within a "professional writing" curriculum because a conceptual divide in writing studies casts creative nonfiction as an "a-social, a-political, and a-rhetorical" entity (53).

Tensions described above echo those that have traditionally existed between writing studies and creative writing. Creative writing and writing studies have generally chosen divergent paths: different professional organizations, definitions of writing, and relationships to academic professionalization. Writing studies sought legitimacy through established activities for research-based disciplines. In contrast, Kelly Ritter names an identity-oriented distinction prevalent among creative writers: they are artists rather than academic professionals ("Professional" 208), a distinction that played into the elevation of creative writing and its producers and into the devaluation of rhetorical conceptions of writing, composition teachers, and writing program administers (*To Know* 161). This distinction historically manifested pedagogically, too, as "lore" more than research informed creative writing instruction (Ritter and Vanderslice).[1] Beyond these differences, writing studies scholars often find creative writing suspect because of textual attitudes they perceive among its practitioners. Doug Hesse recounts a history of writing studies practitioners eschewing creative writing because of ideological critiques of imaginative writing, worries over romanticism, and concerns about style as a belletristic, textual, and apolitical domain (37-40). Hesse observes, "When creative writing and composition studies have little to do with one another, the division truncates not only what we teach and research but how writing gets understood (or misunderstood) by our students, our colleagues, and the spheres beyond" (34). My research with writing majors suggests the need to heed Hesse's warning about different directions becoming distorting divisions. Within these different areas, writing studies and creative writing practitioners have articulated shared domains of interest that overlap with goals writing major programs might pursue.

The Writing Major and Creative Writing: Theory, Professionalism, and Civics

Scholars have articulated purpose-oriented domains for writing major curricula based on disciplinary expertise. Rebecca Moore Howard argues for a three-pronged approach to writing major curricula: theoretical knowledge, professional writing, and civic efforts ("History"). These categories come from the 2000 edited collection *Coming of Age: The Advanced Writing Curriculum*, one of the first books to argue for a coherent curriculum of advanced writing instruction, rather than to amass an array of diverse approaches to an advanced course. Students in the two programs I studied also named these areas through discussions of their writing purposes and courses. I briefly overview scholarship about the value of these various approaches and also highlight how they intersect with conversations about creative writing.

Writing studies scholars have argued for the value of engaging undergraduates with disciplinary concepts, and other scholars argue for the value of research-oriented treatments of creative writing. Douglas Downs and Elizabeth Wardle argue that such

---

1. These distinctions may be changing because of the longstanding calls for the development of "creative writing studies" (Mayers "One"; Harper and Kroll). For example, the emergence of certain publication venues, such as *Journal of Creative Writing Studies* and *Assay: A Journal of Nonfiction Studies*, is a promising sign. However, Tim Mayers observed in 2016 that, despite creative writing studies' status as an academic field, the Association of Writers and Writing Programs, the Conference on College Composition and Communication, and the Modern Language Association—major disciplinary conferences with broad constituencies—still did not serve as thoroughly welcoming homes for this field ("Creative").

an approach enables students to produce "genuine, contributive research" that adds knowledge to the field ("What" 174). Laurie Grobman connects the writing major to undergraduate research, contending that the former will fuel the latter (W176). Indeed, writing majors find excitement in working with faculty on projects involving rhetorical analysis and research (Toth, Reber, and Clark). These arguments led me to pay attention to participants implicit and explicit use of theoretical or disciplinary concepts. Even though tensions between "technique" and "theory" have often characterized U.S. creative writing instruction (Myers 168), Mayers argues that creative writing "ought not be conceived as a private preserve" and that scholars can interrogate creative writing's "interrelationships" with "other parts of the English curriculum" ("One" 224). Indeed, students may desire this kind of inter-relational approach (McGaughey, Rentz, and Nastal-Dema). Observing such tensions and interrelationships was a recurrent theme in comments from participants in the present research.

In addition to the place of disciplinary participation and research concerns within undergraduate majors, the role of professionalism in both the writing major and creative writing receives much attention and was mentioned repeatedly by the present study's participants. Widely circulated arguments for the writing major connect it to writing for professional purposes (DelliCarpini; Dick; Franke, Reid, and DiRenzo; Mattingly and Harkin; Murray; Weisser and Grobman). Students in writing majors can themselves see value in linking disciplinary knowledge to professional practices (Sylvia and Michaud). Other scholars express caution regarding a professional writing focus that yields only an auxiliary position for the major, servicing other departments (Moriarty and Giberson 215). As Michelle Smith and Michelle Costello observe about writing majors, undergraduate students themselves are aware of practical/humanistic tensions when considering a major. Among creative writers, tensions can arise—with the frames of "theory" and "professional" opposing the label "creative." Historically, U.S. creative writers in the university actively resisted "'theory'" as an activity undertaken by academic professionals (Mayers, "One" 219). Creative writing has been "a *dissent* from professionalization" (Myers 7). Teaching and composing creative writing are not meant to produce academic commodities. Rather, they should promote a mode of life (Myers 12). However, in *A History of Professional Writing Instruction in American Colleges*, Katherine Adams situates creative writing assignments and courses within the history of advanced composition and professional writing instruction in the US; she documents how creative writing occurred with general advanced composition courses and how more specialized creative writing courses emerged with English departments alongside professional and technical options. Writing majors in the present study raise the interrelatedness of concerns about creativity and concerns about writing as a profession.

Just as with professionalism, strong arguments have been made for the writing major and for creative writing to embrace a civic orientation: "Civic rhetoric . . . has the potential to support vibrant" writing majors (Moriarty and Giberson 215). Writing majors prepare students for undertaking civic action (Jackson 185). The "birthright" of rhetoric students is education for civic engagement (Hauser 52). Similarly, creative writing can "promote more active, engaged citizenship among its students" (Mayers, "One" 224). While some contemporary creative writers assert positively the "'uselessness'" (i.e., the primarily aesthetic rather than rhetorical or political nature) of creative texts (Welch

129), creative writing's mid-century expansion aligned such programs with the belief that cultivating individual voices holds the potential to transform the culture (Cain 231). Students in my study also explore this question of the civic dimensions of creative writing, variously defined. The connection between crafting and using one's voice to transform social conditions and writing that students describe as creative surfaces regularly in study participants' accounts. Numerous recent books have pursued creative writing as a decolonial practice and craft as a rhetorical and cultural practice, with attention to the political implications of decentering the normative identity of the creative writer and *his* mystical craft, in what Ritter calls the "pedagogy of emulation" whereby creative writing students learn through "observation, mimicry, repetition" as opposed to "learn[ing] actively by doing (and reading and theorizing what they see)" ("'How'" 81, 83). Such recent approaches are described in *The Anti-Racist Writing Workshop: How to Decolonize the Creative Writing Classroom* by Felicia Rose Chavez, *A Stranger's Journey: Race, Identity, and Narrative Craft in Writing* by David Mura, and *Craft in the Real World: Rethinking Fiction Writing and Workshopping* by Matthew Salesses.

As students encounter diverse writing orientations across various domains, they negotiate these differences to develop their own understandings and to draw distinctions among kinds of writing work and identities. This negotiation is not an easy or straightforward process. David Franke explains that writing majors in his program "attached themselves with a passion to certain genres and formed . . . an increasingly restricted writing identity" (119). This phenomenon ranged from creative writers desiring character motivation for a technical writing problem, technical writers uncertain about poetry writing, and students unengaged by new media theory (119-20). Brooks, Zhao, and Braniger note that their students invoked a professional/creative binary that worked as a barrier to, or a step toward, their integration of writing knowledge (41). While I did not initially set out to study these specific dynamics, they repeatedly emerged in the context of writing majors' comments about their experiences.

Study Sites and Methods of Research

For my IRB-approved research project conducted in 2011-2012, I collected data from two institutions I am calling Private Research University (PRU) and Liberal Arts College (LAC). These private, non-religious institutions are in New York state. Both schools' writing programs were independent of English departments, and they had their own undergraduate majors; these programs appeared on the CCCC's list of writing major programs. PRU had a writing major that mostly aligned with what Deborah Balzhiser and Susan McLeod call the professional/rhetorical model: a focus on rhetorical theory, writing practices, and some attention to creative nonfiction and professional writing. The LAC writing major, in contrast to PRU, included creative writing and offered optional concentrations in creative writing, nonfiction, feature writing, and professional writing.

Table 1: Study Participants

	Private Research University	Liberal Arts College
Total Number of Majors	75	150
Survey Respondents	42	44
Interview Participants	7	6
Participants Submitting One Writing Sample	1	3
Participants Submitting Two Writing Samples	5	1

The research design for this study employed mixed methods to investigate writing majors' experiences and discourse. As is the case here, researchers may use mixed-methods research when they express the goal of using one kind of data to enhance or complement the other. In this instance a triangulation mixed-methods design was used, in which different forms of data are examined simultaneously and all forms of data are treated as relatively equal in their value. The data collected were survey responses, interviews, and student work. All data were collected in order that they might be considered together and interpreted in concert. Such an approach provides a way to investigate issues of student experience and discourse that one form of research alone might miss. Combining methods allows for the identification of trends between and across data sets and a means for bringing those trends into focus.

The investigation occurred in two phases. In the first phase I administered a cross-sectional survey. As John Creswell reports, cross-sectional survey research solicits information from participants at one particular moment (357). Writing majors responded to mostly closed-ended questions which also had optional comments fields. Survey development began with informal conversations with teachers and students at PRU. Two PRU faculty then provided written feedback on questions. During a pilot period, a small group of PRU students responded to the survey, providing feedback on the questions and design. Finalized questions asked about students' attitudes, opinions, beliefs, and experiences as writing majors. Phase two included contact with students who volunteered for an interview about their undergraduate experiences and/or to submit a sample of their writing that they felt represented their interests and abilities as a writing major. I read all these materials thematically, identifying patterns and anomalies.

At PRU participants were recruited through a listserv for writing majors, and I also visited three upper-division classes in person and distributed paper copies of the survey. Of those forty-two survey respondents, I conducted interviews with the seven students who were willing to be interviewed. At LAC the survey was distributed through a listserv. Three days after that e-mail went out, forty-four responses came in from students in that program. I conducted interviews with six of the seven students who volunteered. Scheduling conflicts prevented an interview with the seventh participant.

My approach to interviewing was informed by semi-structured interviewing techniques and feminist methodological principles as articulated by Andrea Fontana and James H. Frey. Interviews were structured through the use of a guide with set questions asked to all participants in an established order. The goals of the interviews were to learn about students' attitudes, beliefs, and experiences related to life and work as writing majors. I asked about their experiences and motivations across several areas: their schools, their major programs, the classes they took, what they had learned from their writing classes, their reasons for majoring in writing, and meaningful writing experiences.

As I read the data, I saw that students used the term "creative" to cover diverse discursive territory. Potentially suggestive of the negotiation and integration occurring at the curricular and program levels, this ubiquity likewise indicates the kinds of integrations students themselves perform. Study participants sought to be "agents of integration," writers who "*perceive* as well as . . . *convey effectively to others* connections between previously distinct contexts" (Nowacek 38). Their integrative efforts often relied on prior knowledge and identity concerns. In their efforts to integrate writing insights and experiences, students also mobilized what Reiff and Bawarshi label "'not' talk," defining a genre or practice by describing how it's *unlike* another genre or practice. Students also employed 'not' talk in terms of identity (e.g., being a fiction writer, not an editor), institutional location (e.g., being a senior, not a first-year student), and program content (e.g., a writing program is not a journalism program) as well as genres. Specifically, the term "creative" served as a catchall term for much of the language that blended students' interests in, and sources of knowledge about, writing.

Three thematic categories from Howard's introduction to *Coming of Age* ("History") organize my examination of writers' purposes and writing's functions: theoretical, professional, and civic. Even as several more recent efforts to classify writing major programs provide productive categories for analysis (Balzhiser and McLeod; Campbell and Jacobs; DelliCarpini), after multiple readings of the student-generated data, Howard's older analytical framework seemed best suited to the ways students talked about writing purposes and writing occasions. In my approach, I hope to honor both institutional concerns as articulated in writing major curricula and individual concerns as named by students within writing major programs. In so doing, I aim to follow the example of Mark McGurl, who insists that to understand the intimate relationship between institutional schooling in creative writing programs and the production of post-World War II US literary culture "need not entail any avoidance of the pleasures of charisma and eccentricity" (xi). If the study of creative writing has, as McGurl suggests, focused more on the individual than the institution, the study of the writing major has largely seen the reverse. Howard's three-part framework provides a way to keep both individual and institutional concerns in view. Understanding the creative-invoking, individuality-exploring, personal-saturated, and integration-seeking discourse of writing majors within a context shaped by longstanding programmatic arguments and concerns is not to lose track of the students' particularity. It is to explore the intersection of individual, as well as institutional, negotiation and integration. In what follows, I seek to give primacy to students' voices through significant quotation.

Interests in Writing Theory

Theoretical concerns about how to understand the nature and function of different kinds of writing surfaced repeatedly in participants' accounts. These accounts echo Howard's argument that advanced students should acquire disciplinary knowledge, including "history, theory, research, and practice," so that they "understand the nature of writing" ("History" xvi-xvii). Students also employed this knowledge to articulate "a reflective sense of themselves as writers" (xv). Many of the theoretical discussions about writing among study participants 1) take up Mayers's charge to consider the interrelations of different kinds of writing in connection with creativity and 2) resemble the interrelational approach enacted by faculty and student in work by Barbara Jayne McGaughey, Aleyna Rentz, and Jessica Nastal-Dema.

Students in the present study viewed theoretical concepts as productive frameworks for invention and as aids for thinking about their writing in their courses as well as other contexts. For example, a junior at LAC, Jennifer, said that there were many "chances to practice [her] writing" in workshop courses, but she highlighted the one required course that wasn't focused only on producing creative writing. She desired more chances to learn about "the theory behind writing." Across both sites, writing majors' efforts to integrate writing theories and practices often centered around a strong interest in genre and qualities they termed "creative."

Frequently, "creative" meant a quality of flexibility in genre and style and it was seen in opposition to academic writing. One student tried to determine how two apparently different kinds of writing—poetic, "playful" creative nonfiction and efficient, "serious" academic discourse—interacted. Gina, a PRU junior, discussed a course on the "lyric essay," which she defined as "sort of a blurring of the lines between standard creative nonfiction and a more poetic form of writing. Really playing with all your resources." She shared and discussed her final reflective essay from that course, demonstrating how she engaged with models that put creative nonfiction and academic discourse into dialogue. Gina's final course essay "was about trying to find this balance between academic writing and more poetic writing." In the essay, Gina wrote, "I plan the structure of an academic essay, whereas I feel the structure of a poem. The lyric essay requires a hybrid of these approaches." She consulted other texts while also reflecting on her own composition, a process that was both cognitive and affective (i.e., "plan" and "feel"). While Gina called this process "play," it involved significant work: ongoing reading, practicing a new form, and blending knowledge of different genres.

Gina provides an example of genre-involved 'not' talk providing scaffolding for literacy integrations. In her essay's conclusion, Gina acknowledges how her piece is not what she intended: "I do not believe I have written a lyric essay. I have incorporated both poetry and academic writing, but each style is distinct.... [This piece] is both an explanation and a demonstration of the issues and ambiguities I am working through in my writing." Her piece is not the creative nonfiction form she intended to write. It draws on poetic and academic discourses, which she views as unlike each other. This reflection about the perceived difference between creative and academic elements, with its author embracing ambiguity and limitations, suggests a writer not content to settle for simple answers to challenging writing problems. Gina is not self-satisfied or even text-satisfied. Rather, a sense of accomplishment follows work on a writing problem.

Other students similarly saw creative nonfiction and academic writing as existing in tension, if not outright opposition, while they also wondered about the possibilities of these domains sharing common ground. Lisa, a first-year writing major at PRU who reflected on her extracurricular experiences writing fiction and on a first-year creative nonfiction course, sought to escape a felt confinement within a creative/academic binary: "If you could see academic writing and creative writing kind of mesh together, I would love to do that.... But right now they're just polar opposites.... But I think you could try to mesh them together." Academic writing, for Lisa, appeared to be a circumscribed set of rhetorical resources for creating polished texts:

> I've been told by teachers, 'Try it again. Look it over. You never know what you missed.' [The writing major] really has helped me look at my own writing. And that's kind of where the academic and, I think, the creative mesh because when I write my own stories, I find myself looking at them to make sure they're grammatically correct, to see if it's cohesive enough. And I feel like that's academic writing in itself.

In this account, "academic" meant practices and knowledge that enabled her to make her scholarly prose "correct" and that serviced her fiction and creative nonfiction work, a perception supported by how she understood previous teachers' feedback. For Lisa, teachers' invitations apparently fed a conception that wed academic issues with mechanical correctness. However, Lisa also attempted to leverage previous knowledge and experience for her own writing purposes. She employs "creative" to indicate fiction writing, lively nonfiction, and nonacademic prose.

Reflecting on class experiences and instructor feedback, Gloria, a graduating senior double-majoring in writing and English, leveraged 'not' talk to link the *creative* with the *personal*. In so doing, she also raises questions of authorship and the interrelationships between academic, nonfiction, and fiction writing. Given a perceived lack of models for integrating writing experiences from creative nonfiction and literature courses with her understanding of academic discourse, she wrestled with how to make use of her senior-year "discovery" that academic writing may incorporate the personal:

> Gloria: In creative nonfiction, we did a lot of creative stuff.... I thought if you added creative elements to your writing it wasn't—it wasn't academic anymore. And even a lot of our academic papers were creative in a sense.
>
> Researcher: What made them creative?
>
> Gloria: I think if I use "I" in an essay, then it's creative.... I think you have to completely remove yourself from your academic papers a lot of the time.... I had an English [literature] professor freshman year—she went through and crossed out all the parts where I put "I" in a paper.... So I never did it again. When I came to write my thesis, my advisor said, "Oh, you can put your point

of view in the introduction and talk about what you think specifically." And it was so difficult doing that I because I'd never had a chance to do that before.... But I realize when you get higher up—as a freshman you're told not to do that because they're trying to get you to write sophisticated and professional, whatever. *But then as a senior* they'll tell you, "Oh, it's fine. Do it sometimes." I don't know why that is.

For Gloria, the "creative" part of creative nonfiction equaled the "personal," understood initially as *nonacademic*. That creative/personal association stemmed from the license to use first-person pronouns in a senior-level creative nonfiction (writing) course and in her English literature undergraduate thesis, an experience starkly contrasted with her first-year literature (English) course. It might be tempting to cast the English instructor from Gloria's first year of college as a current traditionalist guardian of propriety and culture. Such a characterization might make it possible—even predictable—to celebrate this student's recent embrace of the personal in academic writing. However, the issue for Gloria was not manipulating surface textuality or reveling in the previously impolite insertion of a unique personality into academic discourse. The issue was the sense she had of herself as a writer with greater or lesser degrees of institutional authority to make authorial choices and the role of coursework in developing this sense.

Such an account shows how students' prior coursework can haunt later efforts to understand and practice new forms of writing, influencing their sense of writerly identity. At stake for Gloria was the apprehension of an authorial hierarchy in which she gradually acquired greater authority through her institutional identity *"as a senior"* to make composing choices. As a first-year student, a perceived lack of authority led her to excise first-person pronouns from school writing. First-person pronouns were later explicitly allowed by her thesis advisor and a creative nonfiction instructor as graduation neared. With the recognition of this differential treatment (i.e., how a first-year student is not treated like a senior) came an interest in knowledge about writing and how students are prepared to approach barriers that often deny authorship to first-year students.

In short, Gloria discerned an authorial hierarchy (i.e., seniors have options first-year students do not) and a writing binary (i.e., academic-as-objective and creative-as-personal). This discernment occurred as Gloria learned conflicting visions of literacy from, on the one hand, advanced literary and creative nonfiction study and, on the other hand, introductory literary instruction. Her efforts to reconcile insights about language registers, discourse community membership, and situated authorship support the idea, following Grobman, that students should explicitly learn how authority and authorship function as a spectrum rather than discrete states. Such explicit instruction might support students who keenly feel the differences that attend diverse writing situations, but who may not have a framework for mapping how these experiences work together.

Similar to instructor feedback, graded assessment enabled students to explore the differences they perceived between what they called *academic* and *creative* writing. Two first- year students provided two writing samples: Lisa at PRU and Jane at LAC. Each paired an academic essay with, respectively, an imagined college commencement speech and a short story. While they did not view their shared texts as similar to each other, both of these first-year writing majors linked their academic submissions to the grades they received—that is, they raised the matter of grades unprompted. Lisa wanted to demonstrate that she "got A's on both" fiction and analytical texts. She went on, though, to explain that academic writing is not where she feels most engaged. Jane said, "For Writing about Fiction, . . . that paper was my last effort to do something about my grade." These students viewed more traditionally academic efforts as performances for teachers rather than as satisfying personal goals. At the same time, Jane and Lisa wanted to represent the range of writing they undertook, indicating an appreciation for diverse writing tasks and situations.

Professional Interests

Howard argues that advanced writing curricula should equip students "with tools for entering the profession of writing" ("History" xv). Study participants likewise expressed an interest in broadly defined professional concerns related to writing. They communicated an interest in being theoretically astute, working writers. One PRU survey respondent made this comment regarding internships and "'hands on'" learning: "There is a breadth of genres we explore. It's very diverse." For this respondent, a connection existed between engaged learning (often associated with "real world" and practical, if not necessarily professional, situations) and theoretical knowledge about—as well as practice with—genre. Tyler, a senior-level student who spoke directly and frequently about his practical orientation and employment concerns, described a sequence of varied writing assignments in one course, his interest in fiction writing, and how genre awareness benefited his job search. Tyler described how he composed definitions, a narrative, and a researched essay. By working across genres to communicate about a range of subjects, Tyler believed he possessed positive resources in his job search. This sequence, its felt benefits, and his linking both fiction writing through an attention to production all pointed to a kind of integrative *phronesis*—that is, Tyler points toward a concern for theoretically informed action, for practical wisdom that moved across life domains (i.e., school and work). In the first epigraph to my article, Tyler's attentiveness to rhetorical theory (i.e., the simultaneously practical and theoretical consideration of what he called "the mechanics of writing") manifested itself in relationship to internships and fiction writing. Tyler brought into focus the intersection of conceptual knowledge about writing, composing practice, and situated rhetorical action.

Students' own writing identities were often at stake in how writing as a profession included—or didn't include—creative, professional, or academic writing. Even as Tyler expressed a concern about employment in the first epigraph to this piece, he also claimed a desire to write creative work. He connected these interests through a focus on production. Mark provided another manifestation of this concern. A LAC junior, Mark spoke of how access to models and curricular opportunities to practice professional writing may not always confirm an interest. Access and opportunity may, in fact, lead students to disavow an interest (and an attendant identity):

> I've always told people I wanted to be a writer...of fiction.... I wanted to work on my creative writing, rather than journalism, which I'd burned out on high school.... Later, I thought I might work in publishing, but an internship at a

university press and my Editing and Publishing class helped me realize that wasn't for me.

In this account, a student's writing education was filled with professional opportunities, and each encounter confirmed a primary identity as a creative writer. While early foreclosure on various lines of writing work might suggest the kind of overinvestment in specific writerly identities that concerns Franke as well as Brooks, Zhao, and Braniger, a sense of writing investments is surely useful and important for students to discern.

Civic Dimensions

Students demonstrated a concern for writing as a public or civic enterprise. Writing concerned with public purposes appeared in a few written submissions (e.g., a political speech and a position paper) and in students' survey and interview comments about texts and classes that mattered to them. Again, civic writing is a central purpose Howard named for advanced writing curricula ("History"). As indicated earlier, many scholars have considered the connections among rhetorical education, creative writing, and politics (Adams *A Group*; Mattingly; Welch). Undergraduates themselves also take up civic efforts within the writing major and do so in relationship to creative writing.

One student reported how work at the intersection of rhetorical analysis, creative writing, and civic aims promoted an integration of theoretical concepts, goals for written products, and plans for social action. For example, Laura, a PRU sophomore, took a "civic writing" course where students "analyzed a lot of nonprofit organization documents. It was really interesting to try to figure out how they got their message across." According to Laura, analysis of texts from local organizations cultivated students' critical capacities. They also composed digital and non-digital multimodal materials for particular groups with socially conscious missions: "We did one project where we got into groups and were assigned an organization to work with. My group worked with a wildlife rehabilitation center.... My group, we made a Twitter account for them and a children's book. So we talked a lot about how to get their message across to different audiences." In Laura's description, rhetorical analysis and production mutually informed each other. With an attention to varied digital and creative composing tasks (e.g., creating a social media account and a children's book), Laura highlighted how the course created an opportunity to consider how genre, audience, and purpose interrelate in ways that enable purposeful writing.

Jane, a first-year student at LAC, reported an instance where she undertook creative writing for civic purposes and, in so doing, integrated personal and familial connections, essayistic literacy, and the craft of fiction. A sense of creativity as involved with the personal, as expressed below, may well develop from fiction writing exercises that try to capture sensory experience or from creative nonfiction readings that craft a persona. Family history and personal observation informed a short story Jane discussed during her interview, and her comments demonstrate the power in everyday literacies, in the dynamics of family and friends. Jane chose to carry a copy of that story in her backpack for several days after completing it. During her interview, Jane commented on her sense of the creative as connected to the personal. When asked to elaborate, she retrieved that story and said,

> In high school, I did community service for something called Angel Island Immigration Station.... It's a very big deal from where I'm from. But coming to the east coast, seems nobody has heard of it.... I've done interviews with people who have emigrated here from China. My own grandmother came through Angel Island, apparently the West Coast version of Ellis Island. [In this piece,] I've tried to weave in stories of what I've heard.... And there was something called "paper names." People would basically sell their names...and bring other people's children to the U.S. My auntie had a paper name and for the longest time she couldn't be her real name.... The piece has historical essay-like qualities, and I felt it had poetic sentences in it. So it's weaving all of them together. I'm learning how to work with it.

This account exploring perceived connections between creative writing and the personal may not describe how writing studies scholars typically imagine public and civic writing. It did, however, engage with issues of how material access and discursive forces beyond the individual have historically shaped communities' opportunities and their ways of confronting restrictive conditions. Jane spoke of composing creative—i.e., personally expressive and fictional—work that explores a history of resourcefulness in the face of immigration barriers. Moreover, Jane wrote herself into a national narrative and sought to expand the nation's possibilities. For example, Ellis Island is surely a readily accessible image in U.S. cultural memory, but Jane found that none of her college peers knew about an important aspect of Asian American immigration. She used Ellis Island to contextualize the historical weight, cultural importance, and personal significance of Angel Island. Forging these connections created space for Jane to craft new narratives about Americanness and citizenship. Additionally, paper names, the tactic employed by her forebears to facilitate immigration to the U.S., required a complex system of rhetorical, literate, and material practices. Representing this collective experience, Jane sought to write a fictional piece that brought her family into U.S. cultural memory and that responded to her peers' lack of historical awareness.

Comments from Jane and Laura illustrate some of the ways writing majors think about the relationship between writing labeled creative and civic concerns. For Laura the connection emerged in part through the context of production (that is, a course dedicated to civic writing). For Jane, even though she did not use the words *civic*, *public*, or *political*, her fictional piece and her description of how it came about surely point to how one writing major conceived of creative work as drawing on research, experience, and genre awareness to respond to pressing social needs.

Conclusion

The widespread emergence of *creative* as a ubiquitous and multi-purpose term across both Private Research University and Liberal Arts College surprised me. Even though I certainly anticipated that students might connect creative writing with fiction writing, especially at LAC, I was surprised by the range of territory the label covered overall. Given that Howard describes the function of composition pedagogy as dialogic with regard to its capacity to mediate between disciplinary expertise and lay values ("The

Dialogic"), perhaps it should be expected that the writing major would create space for student discourse that blends expert, institutional, popular, and idiosyncratic elements. These findings point to a few considerations for future research and teaching.

First, studies of instructor feedback and students' use of that feedback hold a valued place within writing studies, and my findings suggest that future researchers might fruitfully investigate how students in the writing major perceive and use the feedback they receive. While teachers might intend for their comments to serve as an invitation to experience revision as a more robust and holistic endeavor, leading to new choices—choices that might produce a new text, choices that ask the writer to follow an intuition about what's possible—students may or may not perceive this invitation. For example, regardless of what teachers meant, Lisa easily placed her experiences within the broad cultural frame that treats writing instruction as functional skills. Gloria's account suggests the forceful ways genre and feedback affect student work and attitudes, leading students to identify and work with genres in ways that are distinct from the ways disciplinary professionals do. She recounts how previous experiences with feedback may have a chilling effect: "no first-person" and slashes through every I—injunctions and marks from prior coursework that haunt the work of undergraduate writers.

Second, participants' comments point to ways metacognitive reflection, especially in regards to identity, might increase the likelihood of writing majors achieving the literacy integrations they seek. Jane addressed family history and Chinese-US immigration in relationship to fiction writing that had personally important and civic exigencies. Gloria raised issues of institutional and school-based identity in relationship to creative nonfiction and academic writing. For some students, these identity matters manifested in *writing identities*: Mark was a fiction writer and Tyler was a marketable writer who saw opportunities for creativity across writing domains. Participants mobilized 'not' talk to establish writerly identities: Mark was *not* an editor or journalist, Jeremiah was *not* a fiction writer, Gail the creative nonfiction writer was *not* primarily an academic writer. Through class discussion and writing exercises, teachers might aid and enrich this kind of reflection.

Even if they are not always certain how to integrate their insights across forms and inquiries, students—through their comments and texts—insist on a capacious understanding of writing. These understandings affirm Howard's claim that a writing major "asserts presence, not absence, for writing pedagogy" because "instruction in writing responds not to the absence of students' skills but to the presence of expertise" ("History" xxii). And attending to their presence, the *students'* presence, helps teachers and researchers better understand how undergraduates craft points of connection with, and divergence from, the way disciplinary professionals perceive writing and writing programs. The prevalence of *creative* as an important term among writing majors is not a distraction from disciplinary conceptions or an enactment of hierarchies that diminish theoretical, professional, civic, or other forms of writing. Indeed, viewing students' discourse as a positive presence led me to observe the multifaceted ways *creative* was leveraged to negotiate and integrate different experiences with purposes and understandings of writing within writing majors.

Works Cited

Adams, Katherine H. *A Group of Their Own: College Writing Courses and American Women Writers, 1880-1940*. SUNY P, 2001.

—. *A History of Professional Writing Instruction in American Colleges*. Southern Methodist UP, 1993.

Alexis, Cydney. "Let's Banish the Phrase 'Creative Writing.'" *Inside Higher Ed*, 3 Jan. 2017. https://www.insidehighered.com/views/2017/01/03/we-should-stop-distinguishing-between-creative-and-other-forms-writing-essay.

Balzhiser, Deborah, and Susan McLeod. "The Undergraduate Writing Major: What Is It? What Should It Be?" *College Composition and Communication*, vol. 61, no. 3, 2010, pp. 415- 33.

Bradley, Erin, Melissa Davis, Michelle Dierlof, Keith Dmochowski, John Gangi, Laurie Grobman, Kristy Offenback, and Melissa Wilk. "Coauthoring the Curriculum: Student Voices and the Writing Major." *Composition Studies*, vol. 43, no. 2, 2015, pp. 172-76.

Brooks, Randy, Peiling Zhao, and Carmella Braniger. "Redefining the Undergraduate English Writing Major: An Integrated Approach at a Small Comprehensive University." Giberson and Moriarty, pp. 32-49.

Cain, Mary Ann. "'To Be Lived': Theorizing Influence in Creative Writing." *College English*, vol. 71, no. 3, 2009, pp. 217-28.

Campbell, Lee, and Debra Jacobs. "Toward a Description of Undergraduate Writing Majors." Giberson and Moriarty, pp. 277-86.

Chavez, Felicia R. *The Anti-Racist Writing Workshop: How to Decolonize the Creative Writing Classroom*. Haymarket Books, 2021.

Creswell, John W. *Educational Research: Planning, Conducting, and Evaluating Quantitative and Qualitative Research*. 2nd ed. Prentice Hall, 2004.

DelliCarpini, Dominic. "Re-Writing the Humanities: The Writing Major's Effect upon Undergraduate Studies in English Departments." *Composition Studies*, vol. 35, no.1, 2007, pp. 15-36.

DePalma, Michael-John, and Kara Poe Alexander. "A Bag Full of Snakes: Negotiating the Challenges of Multimodal Composition." *Computers and Composition*, vol. 37, 2015, pp. 182–200.

Downs, Douglas, and Elizabeth Wardle. "What Can a Novice Contribute? Undergraduate Researchers in First-Year Composition." Grobman and Kinkead, pp. 173-90.

Fontana, Andrea, and James H. Frey. "Interviewing: The Art of Science." *The Handbook of Qualitative Research*, edited by Norman Denzin and Yvonna S. Lincoln, Sage Publications, 1994, pp. 361-76.

Franke, David. "Curriculum, Genre and Resistance: Revising Identity in a Professional Writing Community." Franke, Reid, and DiRenzo, pp. 113-30.

Franke, David, Alex Reid, and Anthony DiRenzo, editors. *Design Discourse: Composing and Revising Programs in Professional and Technical Writing*. Parlor P, 2010.

Fulford, Collie, and Aaron Dial. "Stone Soup: Establishing an HBCU Writing Concentration." *Composition Studies*, vol. 43, no. 2, 2015, pp. 177-81.

Gail. Personal interview. 31 Mar. 2012.

Geiger II, T J. "An Intimate Discipline? Writing Studies, Undergraduate Majors, and Relational Labor." *Composition Studies*, vol. 43, no. 2, 2015, pp. 92-112.

Giberson, Greg A., and Thomas A. Moriarty, editors. *What We Are Becoming: Developments in Undergraduate Writing Majors*. Utah State UP, 2010.

Giberson, Greg, Jim Nugent, and Lori Ostergaard, editors. *Writing Majors: Eighteen Program Profiles*. Utah State UP, 2015.

Gina. Personal interview. 8 Aug. 2011.

Gloria. Personal interview. 5 Apr. 2012.

Grobman, Laurie. "The Student Scholar: (Re)Negotiating Authorship and Authority." *College Composition and Communication*, vol. 61, no. 1, 2009, pp. W175-97.

Grobman, Laurie, and Joyce Kinkead, editors. *Undergraduate Research in English Studies*. National Council of Teachers of English, 2010.

Harper, Graeme, and Jeri Kroll, editors. *Creative Writing Studies: Practice, Research, and Pedagogy*. Multilingual Matters, 2008.

Hauser, Gerard. "Teaching Rhetoric, Or Why Rhetoric Isn't Just Another Kind of Philosophy or Literary Criticism." *Rhetoric Society Quarterly*, vol. 34, no. 3, 2004, pp. 39-54.

Hesse, Doug. "The Place of Creative Writing in Composition Studies." *College Composition and Communication*, vol. 62, no. 1, 2010, pp. 31-52.

Howard, Rebecca Moore. "History, Politics, Pedagogy, and Advanced Writing." Shamoon and Martin pp. xiii-xxii.

—. "The Dialogic Function of Composition Pedagogy": Negotiating Between Critical Theory and Public Values." *Under Construction: Working at the Intersections of Composition Theory, Research, and Practice*, edited by Christine Farris and Chris M. Anson, Utah State UP, 1998, pp. 51-64.

Jackson, Brian. "Cultivating Paideweyan Pedagogy: Rhetoric Education in English and Communication Studies." *Rhetoric Society Quarterly*, vol. 37, 2007, pp. 181-201.

Jeremiah. Personal interview. 5 Apr. 2012.

Langstraat, Lisa, Mike Palmquist, and Kate Kiefer. "Restorying Disciplinary Relationships: The Development of an Undergraduate Writing Concentration." Giberson and Moriarty, pp. 50-66.

Lowe, Kelly, and William Macauley. "'Between the idea and the reality . . . falls the Shadow': The Promise and Peril of a Small College Writing Major." Giberson and Moriarty, pp. 81-97.

Mark. Personal interview. 4 Apr. 2012.

Mattingly, Carol. *Well-Tempered Women: Nineteenth-Century Temperance Rhetoric*. Southern Illinois UP, 1998.

Mattingly, Rebecca de Wind, and Patricia Harkin. "A Major in Flexibility." Giberson and Moriarty, pp. 13-31.

Mayers, Tim. "Creative Writing Studies: The Past Decade (and the Next)." *Journal of Creative Writing Studies*, vol. 1, no. 1, 2016, pp. 1-7.

—. "Notes Toward an Inventive, Process-Oriented Pedagogy for Introductory Multigenre Creative Writing Course." *Creative Writing Innovations: Breaking Boundaries in the Creative Writing Classroom*, edited by Michael D. Clark, Trent Hergenrader, and Joseph Rein, Bloomsbury, 2017, pp. 7-19.

—. "One Simple Word: From Creative Writing to Creative Writing Studies." *College English*, vol. 71, no. 3, 2009, pp. 217-28.

McGaughey, Barbara Jayne, Aleyna Rentz, and Jessica Nastal-Dema. "The Evolving Identity of an Undergraduate Major in Writing and Linguistics." *Composition Studies*, vol. 43, no. 2, 2015, pp. 190-92.

McGurl, Mark. *The Program Era: Postwar Fiction and the Rise of Creative Writing.* Harvard UP, 2009.

Moriarty, Thomas A., and Greg Giberson. "Civic Rhetoric and the Undergraduate Major in Rhetoric and Writing." Giberson and Moriarty, pp. 204-16.

Mura, David. *A Stranger's Journey: Race, Identity, and Narrative Craft in Writing.* U of Georgia P, 2019.

Myers, D. G. *The Elephants Teach: Creative Writing Since 1880.* Prentice Hall, 1996.

Nowacek, Rebecca S. *Agents of Integration: Understanding Transfer as a Rhetorical Act.* Southern Illinois UP, 2011.

Peele, Thomas. "What Do We Mean When We Say 'Writing'?" *Composition Studies*, vol. 35, no. 1, 2007, pp. 95-96.

Reiff, Mary Jo, and Anis Bawarshi. "Tracing Discursive Resources: How Students Use Prior Genre Knowledge to Negotiate New Writing Contexts in First-Year Composition." *Written Communication*, vol. 28, 2011, pp. 312-37.

Ritter, Kelly. "'How the Old Man Does It': The Pedagogy of Emulation in Creative Writing Programs." *Composing Ourselves as Writer-Teacher-Writers: Starting with Wendy Bishop*, edited by Patrick Bizzaro, Alys Culhane, and Devan Cook, Hampton, 2011, pp. 81-96.

—. "Professional Writers/Writing Professionals: Revamping Teacher Training in Creative Writing PhD Programs." *College English*, vol. 64, no. 2, 2001, pp. 205–27.

—. *To Know Her Own History: Writing at the Woman's College, 1943-1963.* U of Pittsburgh P, 2012.

Ritter, Kelly, and Stephanie Vanderslice, editors. *Can It Really Be Taught? Resisting Lore in Creative Writing Pedagogy.* Boynton/Cook Heinemann, 2007.

Salesses, Matthew. *Craft in the Real World: Rethinking Fiction Writing and Workshopping.* Catapult, 2021.

Shamoon, Linda K., and Celest Martin. "Which Part of the Elephant Is This? Questioning Creative Non-Fiction in the Writing Major." *Composition Studies*, vol. 35, no. 1, 2007, pp. 53-54.

Smith, Michelle, and Michelle Costello. "English Majors are Professionals, Too: Liberal Arts and Vocation in the English Writing Major." *Composition Studies*, vol. 43, no. 2, 2015, pp. 193-96.

Sylvia, Cami, and Michael J. Michaud. "Looking into Writing." *Composition Studies* vol. 43, no. 2, 2015, pp. 186-89.

Tyler. Personal interview. 11 May 2011.

Toth, Christie, Mitchell Reber, and Aaron Clark. "Major Affordances: Collaborative Scholarship in a Department of Writing and Rhetoric Studies." *Composition Studies*, vol. 43, no. 2, 2015, pp. 197-200.

Weisser, Christian and Laurie Grobman. "Undergraduate Writing Majors and the Rhetoric of Professionalism." *Composition Studies*, vol 40, no. 1, 2012, pp. 39-59.

Welch, Nancy. "No Apology: Challenging the 'Uselessness' of Creative Writing." *JAC*, vol.19, 1999, 117–34. Print.

All Scientists Should Write Poetry: Creative Writing as Essential Academic Practice

Mariya Deykute

Abstract: *Creative writing in undergraduate academia has often been regarded as an elective practice that has benefits primarily for students who plan to pursue creative or literary majors. However, poetic inquiry specifically offers crucial benefits to STEM students, owing both to the transformative nature of poetic process and to the way poetic inquiry can stimulate innovative, ethical, multilingual and interdisciplinary growth. The author frames the issue through individual experience of teaching poetry to STEM undergraduates in the context of a rich multilingual environment, in which many students are fluent or proficient in several languages. The author argues that due to the commonalities poetry writing shares with the scientific process, as well as the essential skills it requires of the practitioners, poetry writing is an essential techne in academia rather than a "quirky elective."*

Creative Writing in Academia: Past and Future Revolutions

Creative writing in academia has a relatively recent history. That is, of course, if one is to consider such history from the perspective of official course offerings and departmental recognition rather than student writers' clubs, journals, and creative writing in the university community, which doubtlessly existed prior to creative writing's official entry into the academic purview. Sources differ on when this entry occurred, but even if one were to take the early date of the 1880s (Myers 278-279) rather than the 1910s, (Radavich 109) one can argue that creative writing in academia is still among the nascent disciplines—as much change as it underwent after the first writer's workshop opened in Iowa in the 1950s (Radavich 110). Initially, creative writing courses were introduced as an attempt to revolutionize the study of literature: to show the benefit of the living process of creating poetry and fiction, rather than reserve the scope of literary studies to only the final product, the published text (Myers 279). And while the current state of creative writing courses and programs and their continual growth has long surpassed this initial aim, the revolutionary potential of creative writing education for the academic community, I would argue, is yet to be fully actualized.

This is unfortunate. Creative writing education is capable of producing a generative paradigm shift, a fundamental change in how we think about arts education and education in general. I will focus here on one aspect of all such possible revolutions: establishing creative writing, specifically poetic inquiry, as a routine companion and collaborator to the sciences and STEM education, particularly in the context of a multilingual student body. I review literature on the false dichotomy between creative writing practice and research as well as the complementary and often parallel natures of poetic and scientific inquiry. In addition, I discuss my experience of teaching a rigorous poetry and research seminar at a STEM university in the Republic of Kazakhstan to establish poetic inquiry as beneficial practice in STEM contexts.

My argument owes much to the commonalities creative writing shares with the scientific process and the neurobiology of inquiry. Creative writing, with its ability to "explore the interconnections between the world of ideas and the world of our lived experience" is truly a natural companion to the sciences (Watkins and Tehrani 33). The skills required of practitioners (namely, in the form of accessing difficult questions; persevering through adversity and the unknown; synthesizing knowledge from a variety of disciplines; and establishing a personal, ethical and integral relationship to the product of one's own scholarship) further establish poetry writing as an essential practice rather than the dilettante's prerogative. While undoubtedly beneficial for humanities students, poetry writing also forms a way for those outside the humanities to establish a holistic, intentional, and integrated relationship with their language(s), which will inevitably serve to inform their work as scientists, engineers, computer programmers and mathematicians. Here I will also argue that in order to accomplish these goals and fully capitalize on these benefits, poetry courses that seek to bridge the perceived gap between the fine arts and the concrete disciplines must involve not only individual work or poetic craft, but also research, collaboration, and frequent in-depth exposure to the languages of others through reading and writing multilingual poetry, translation, in-depth peer workshop, and peer editing.

The Poet or the Scientist: The False Dichotomy

As someone who has been involved with creative writing in academic settings for more than a dozen years—as a student, a secondary school teacher, a university instructor, a program coordinator—I have been continuously surprised by very distinct aspects of the practice as it currently appears in academia. Some benefits students derive from creative writing are well-documented, such as developing a deeper connection to language and expression that can support marginalized or disadvantaged voices (Kinloch 96); creating meaning, finding relevance, power and authentic self-expression in the midst of their educational experience (Ostrom 81; Hunt 75, 83); forging a cross-disciplinary community and thus maintaining resilience, engagement with scholarship, and a closer tie to school or university (Philip, Doolan, and Wilson 2-3).

However, some of the other benefits are perhaps not quite so obvious or well-researched and may even seem of dubious value in a course that is supposed to impart some kind of certainty onto the student-scholar. I am speaking here of the ability to embrace what the poet John Keats termed "negative capability," namely, "when a man is capable of being in uncertainties, Mysteries, doubts, without any irritable reaching after fact and reason" (Hebron). While Keats was frustratingly brief in his exploration of this term, in undergraduate creative writing students this essential negative capability manifests as the ability to live with, interrogate, and find joy in exploring difficult questions, ambiguities, the undiscovered; to pursue with intellectual rigor queries and obsessions that originate within themselves and that perhaps do not find a quick wrap-up by the end of the semester but instead continue to generate ever more questions and instigate a journey that lasts through their years at university and beyond.

This ability to tolerate and illuminate the unknown and the unresolved (Peary 68) and the ability to constantly generate new questions are also ones that find relevance not only in writing or the pondering of philosophical or humanitarian questions, but in biology, computer science, engineering, linguistics and fine art classrooms (Watkins and Tehrani 33). The capacity to tolerate the unknown is recognized by social constructivist pedagogical theories as one of the necessary steps in the epistemological and personal development of an undergraduate student and scientist. In particular, Baxter Magolda's "epistemological reflection" (ER) model is not only closely tied to the development of young adult identity but also shows a progression between "absolute knowledge" and "transitional," "independent," and "contextual" knowledge (Hunter, Laursen and Seymour 38). Each successive step in epistemological development necessary to conceive of oneself—and become—a successful scientist is impossible without developing tolerance and appreciation of ambiguity, the unknown, and the unresolved. This faculty—to remain curious and persistently open in the face of staggering, failing drafts and no clear directions or instructions—often sets apart those students who go on to become innovators, inventors, the meaning-makers in STEM disciplines (Edwards and Ashkanasy 168; Alexander, Berthod, Kunert, Salge, and Washington 84; Root-Bernstein 267-268; Webb and Lee 193). And this is where the revolutionary potential of creative writing instruction fully emerges, not only for the field of literary study but for cross-disciplinary academic environments, an idea I will return to.

The less pleasant surprise that I encountered as a creative writer and an academic was how often the general university environment perceived creative writing courses as fashionable but niche (McVey 290), optional, or "easy": in other words, an elective that conveyed some benefits but was certainly less "rigorous" or "academic" for students of practical disciplines like the sciences. And even within English and creative writing departments housing the burgeoning MFA, major and minor programs, the backlash against the "MFA factory" and the increasingly impractical creative writing degrees meant that creative writing courses, according to David Radavich, were more and more seen as an investment in personal rather than professional development (110-111). While Radavich is optimistic about the direction of creative writing studies, in our present climate of increased budget cuts and elimination of humanities departments, creative writing courses yet again occupy a precarious position.

This issue is prevalent not only in the U.S. or the broadly-termed "Western World," but within international Western-style STEM universities. In my own institution in the Republic of Kazakhstan, writing across the curriculum, and specifically creative writing across the curriculum, is viewed by most STEM educators and students as a fairly useless concept. However, in the context of a multilingual, multicultural university in which students must navigate additional layers of identity formation in order to conceive of themselves as scientists, scholars, writers (especially in English), creative writing and poetry writing is even more crucial in developing what Leonardo Da Vinci called "a complete mind," the creation of a scholarly identity steeped in connections among disciplines, between ideas and work and lived experience (Watkins and Tehrani 30).

Ultimately, the view of creative writing courses as an elective practice is as pervasive as it is mistaken—and falls out of line with the scientific community's finding that creative writing (among other arts) is not only aesthetically pleasing but also intellectually stimulating. More and more, creative writing is recognized as a valuable tool in the greater scientific and technological communities as well as in pioneering pedagogy—as a way to encourage creative thinking (Charon, Hermann, and Devlin 346); to raise levels of engagement with content (Krom and Williams 235); to communicate complex ideas to the public (Januchowski-Hartley, Sopinka, Merkle, Luz, Zivian, Goff and Oester 905); to encourage scientists, engineers, and doctors to consider ethical, humanistic, and cross-disciplinary effects of their work (Atkinson 33). Stephanie Januchowski-Hartley et al. begin their exploration of the use of poetic inquiry in conservation studies by citing diverse examples of the way science is communicated through art, such as the 2018 Linwood Pendleton's plenary, "Rethinking marine conservation science in three acts," that brought together poems, music, video, and dance to demonstrate how creative approaches can help to achieve and celebrate breakthroughs in marine conservation science (905-906). Robert Root-Bernstein in his chapter on creativity, polymaths, and innovation cites numerous examples of scientists, engineers, mathematicians (such as Jonathan Kingdon, Robert Bakker, Kack Coulehan, Santiago Ramon y Cajal, Rorscharch, Alexander Graham Bell, Desmond Morris, Kenneth Clark) who were or are also accomplished artists (and while it is important to note that the majority are visual or musical artists quite a few are novelists and poets) (268-272). Root-Bernstein further asserts that proficiency in an artistic or literary pursuit is a significant and reliable predictor of scientific productivity, interdisciplinary thinking, and innovation (267).

Of course, some academic contexts have also recognized this—from courses that engage accounting students in writing fairy tales (**Krom and Williams 238**) to undergraduate chemistry students writing horror stories (Nicholes) to professors using haikus and creative nonfiction to stimulate greater engagement and understanding of their content across disciplines (**Januchowski-Hartley et al. 906-907**). However, as Root-Bernstein notes, the general educational trend is still to propagate the rift between the arts and the sciences, to separate rather than to merge, and concludes that "we need a new kind of education that fosters interaction between disciplines rather than divisions between them.... [T]he future of innovation will reside, as it has always resided, in the minds of multiply talented people who transcend disciplinary boundaries and methods.... [W]e ignore this profound truth at our own peril" (276). Root-Bernstein's new kind of education that normalizes and establishes creative writing as an essential academic practice is exactly the kind of education that would allow CW to transcend its niche, trendy status and fully bestow its benefits upon the interdisciplinary student collective.

Poetry in particular has long been recognized as useful in developing empathetic, reflective, and innovative skills in research and inquiry, particularly in qualitative research (Brown, Kelly, and Finn 258). However, the specific usefulness of poetry in the case of reconciling various linguistic realities and what this means for a STEM student is not as widely explored. In this sense, the poetry course that I taught at Nazarbayev University worked most urgently through multilingualism and the meticulousness of poetic language with the dual developments of an epistemological and personal identity of the writers, what Anne-Barrie **Hunter, Sandra L. Laursen, and Elaine Seymour** call the self-authorship (38) necessary for the conception of oneself as a scholar, a scientist, a thinker. However, STEM students were reluctant to recognize themselves as poets—to own and author as meaning-makers and language-shapers rather than spectators—and to align their lived experiences with epistemological inquiry. Added to the existing rifts between their private languages and their public, professional language was the often greater rifts among their identities as scientists, scholars, and human beings.

Alas, what lies at the core of this rift are false dichotomies: the opposition of theory with research and practice (Webb and Lee 190) and of the arts and sciences (Snow 4-5). These false dichotomies have long plagued academia in addition to the lack of recognition of the necessary interplay and the similarities that may very well exist between the neurocognitive processes of engaging in creative writing and the neurocognitive processes involved in scientific research (Liu, Erkkinen, Healey, Xu, Swett, Chow, and Braun 3361). Researchers remark that, whether in their scholarship or through their own experience as students and educators, educational systems continue to support artificial divisions of knowledge, neither serving the learner nor the educator particularly well (Petersen). Taken further, the continual adherence to this false dichotomy is a failure to recognize the unique skill transference that takes place when students of creative writing (in the case of this article, poetry) engage in other disciplines that require critical thinking. As Maria Fernandez-Gimenez, Louise B. Jennings, and Hailey Wilmer note, when describing the advantages and applications of Arts Based Research (ABR) using poetic inquiry to interrogate and find solutions to natural resource issues, ABR in general and poetic inquiry in particular possess distinct advantages, including provoking new insight and learning; forging micro-macro connections; raising critical consciousness; elevating marginalized voices; challenging dominant ideologies; promoting dialogue as well as participatory research and advancing public scholarship (1082).

Such skills and dispositions may be even more essential for the scientific disciplines than the humanities, in part due to the ever-increasing pace of technological innovation (Berman and Dorrier) and the continual difficulty scientists encounter in both finding ways to connect their research holistically and communicate this research to the general public (Retzbach and Maier 430-432; Blythe, Grabill, and Riley 290-293). While the kind of thinking creative writing embodies does not offer solutions or clear-cut avenues of research, or even readily accessible and generalizable knowledge, it nonetheless "directs attention to questions that need to be asked, and understandings that need to be formulated" (Webb and Brien 192) which lie at the heart of scientific inquiry. As novelist and scientist Richard Mueller writes, "art may be a necessary condition for constructing the new consciousness from which future science gets its structural realities" (320). While Mueller's book *The Science of Art* was first published more than 50 years ago, his sentiments are perhaps even more applicable to our contemporary realities.

Establishing Context: Teaching Poetry in a Multilingual STEM University

The focus of my article is not on the broad discipline of creative writing in general, but specifically on the teaching of a strenuous elective course (300-level) in poetry writing at Nazarbayev University (NU), the leading English-language STEM university in the Republic of Kazakhstan. The student body, while largely Kazakhstani, includes students from a wide range of cultural, socioeconomic, and linguistic backgrounds. The latter, of course, is of crucial importance to the teaching of creative writing and requires elaboration. While the English-language creative writing courses in the US (and in the UK, Australia, and New Zealand) certainly contain a sizeable number of students who are bi- tri- or multilingual (and, as I will later argue, all contain students who speak multiple Englishes), the students at Nazarbayev University are unique in that none of them are monolingual. English for many is a third language, if not a fourth or a fifth. Most grew up speaking Russian and Kazakh; many know Turkish, Chinese, Arabic or Uighur; others learned French, German, Italian and Polish at school before coming to university. As such, their studies at Nazarbayev University are a near-constant navigation of linguistic contexts and translations with students code-switching constantly as they move among the university classroom, their social life, their family lives, and the private language of their own thoughts and creativity.

Over the course of designing and teaching this course, I was fortunate to teach students with a diversity of future aspirations: engineers, biologists, geologists, historians, computer programmers, robotics and neuroscience scholars as well as economists, anthropologists, and literature majors. As the course has no prerequisite requirements save for an application and a portfolio, students self-selected by interest, but also formed a more diverse cohort than in other, more traditionally integrated humanities courses. In creating this course, I was confronted with its status as an interdisciplinary outlier. I wanted to focus on the production of creative writing through a lens of rigorous research and systematic inquiry as well as systematic practice. After all, poetic inquiry, as mentioned above, is uniquely fitted to provide the necessary skill transference in STEM fields. Thus, while the observations made do apply to other branches of creative writing (based on my prior experience teaching fiction and memoir), the scope of this paper will be limited to discussing the specific benefits and influences of poetry specifically, including poetry written in English, a non-native language to the vast majority of this student population.

Multilingualism and translation are important to this approach of teaching poetry in a research-based, upper-level course. While some creative writing courses in monolingual contexts do introduce some aspects of multilingualism or translation into their syllabi, in an English-medium university in an officially trilingual country (and, as shown above, with students speaking a wide variety of language), there is an even greater urgency to give students the necessary tools to intimately connect to their languages, their stories and their unanswered questions, as well as create a relationship to English and their scholarship that goes beyond the performative or merely pragmatic. NU students are navigating multiple linguistic realities, certainly, but also shifting sociopolitical and semiotic contexts that are uniquely tied to language—from changing street and city names, to the weight and prestige put on one language over another, such as the decolonization campaigns to reclaim Kazakh as the national language in an effort to subvert Russian language hegemony in the post-Soviet era. Of course, the real language politics and linguistic experiences are not quite so clear-cut.

Poetry writing gives these students the ability to reconcile, or at the very least get to know and accept, their many languages—and develop and strengthen their private language, a semiotic expression that is uniquely their own, populated with symbols and linguistic choices distinct from the social/public languages surrounding them. This move supports not only their academic education, but their mental health, their individuated meaning-making, and their ability to be aware local and global citizens. Of course, these pursuits and needs are not unique to students in Kazakhstan: one could say they form a pervasive universal, even in so-called monolingual contexts. In fact, this capacity of poetry to foster communication across and build awareness of different linguistic landscapes is not one that is unique to a multilingual environment. I argue that any environment is by its nature multilingual, as students even within a monolingual environment have to navigate a variety of socioeconomic, political, and usage differences that make awareness of the many languages we speak essential (Marshall, Hayashi, and Yeung 33; Piller 26). The poet Oana Avasilichioaei writes about this fact, exposing monolingualism as a myth, and speaking about her English, which "revels in its bastard status because [its] context has never been and will never be monolingual." She further postulates that any language is "an ecosystem, complex, alive, unstable, and struggling in a fraught environment" and less static than we believe.

 Scientific communication largely utilizes formal, academic English, and an important dimension of future scientific practice will be the translation of scientific knowledge into existing monolingual or multilingual communities and the promotion of scholarship in minority languages (Ludi 214-215). Regardless of one's language background, fluency occurs with the knowledge of how language shapes meaning; the attention to detail that poetry invites highlights the subtle, crucial shifts that mark this function. Fluency is achieved precisely through mending the rifts between the false split of research and practice; between the creative and the scientific; the personal and the academic. The fact that monolingualism is, perhaps, a myth, does not mean there are not important contextual differences between the multilinguistic context of NU and a traditionally conceived monolingual classroom. The students arriving in my poetry classroom arrive with complex relationships with their language that are often already recognized, even formulated. Such relationships are not theoretical but derived from lived experiences that create firm divisions in the student's understanding of themselves, the world around them, and the future's possibilities. The language of childhood (for many, Russian or Kazakh), the language of interpersonal relationships and daily life (often, Russian), and the language of achievement and the future as they report it (English) are compartmentalized and shared among students. Thus these preconceived divisions become important starting points for the revolution that multilingual poetry can create in a shift towards integration rather than separation of their multiple literacies. This cohesiveness may facilitate the development of advanced empathy for others through attention to language, as well as deepen their self-knowledge, reflective practice, and meaning-making. This kind of linguistic cohesion contributes to personal as well as epistemological growth, shown as inextricably linked in undergraduate learners (Hunter, Laursen, and Seymour 39). And while students everywhere confront this process, the students who entered my poetry classroom faced a unique set of challenges and opportunities due to the fact that their personal and professional identities resided on separate linguistic isles. The recognition of English as a potential private language, not just as the language of their professional disciplines, facilitated necessary personal and epistemological growth.

When students entered my course, I asked them whether they thought of themselves as poets and, if so, what role poetry occupied in their scholarship—whether they came from a humanities background or a STEM background. Many found both questions perplexing. Certainly, they all submitted a portfolio to be considered for the course; however, few considered themselves "poets" and even fewer saw any connection between their impassioned verses and the experiments they conducted in the lab, the code they wrote in Python, or the historical inquiries they conducted into Russian Imperial interaction with the Kazakh tribes. They generally agreed that there are criteria to be considered a poet—seriousness of pursuit, inborn talent, a kind of manic dedication to poetry—and that there are criteria to be considered a professional in their fields, including seriousness of pursuit, inborn curiosity, a kind of manic dedication to inquiry and the production of knowledge. While some of these commonalities were not lost on them, even students who did consider themselves poets viewed their poetic self as wholly and necessarily separate from their scholarly self: two reluctant roommates, as it were, working opposing shift schedules, never truly meeting, let alone considering combining their efforts and learning from each other.

At the root of this individual divide lies the same aforementioned dichotomy that even creative writers adopt in academia when discussing creativity in relation to their own poetic work and the creativity involved in their research (Webb and Brien 190). Dominique Hecq outlines in *Towards a Poetics of Creative Writing* that research in creative writing has been considered by many to be highly problematic, fraught with unanswered fundamental questions and lacking in any clear models and concepts. The greatest impediments for conceptualizing creative writing practice and research may be the epistemological character of the research itself, as by nature subjective and grounded in individual practice rather than verifiable patterns and shared methods and patterns. This is coupled with a resistance in academia to theorizing creative writing within the constraints of a traditional model of theory formation, expansion, and diversification. This resistance has compounded creative writing's inferior status as a discipline, relegating it in the romantic binary to the wild, unknowable feminine epitomized in Nigel Krauth and Tess Brady's figure of the rude girl who "sits in the senate…out of place amongst all that beige and grey" (qtd. in Sparrow 78). For some, the problem stems from the mode of production of creative research and the indivisible link to the subjectivity of the researcher, thus bringing the "objective" aspect of research into question (Sparrow 2).

Few students have been invited to see their poetic creativity as anything other than a private fancy; almost none of them saw the "rude girl" of their creative craft having bearing on their scientific research, despite the fact that, as Meg Petersen writes, "good scientific writing…draws on a wealth of details and specific language. Meticulous distinctions… require precise language" (98) in the same manner as attention to poetic language does. These convictions, then, obscure the opportunities of integrated multilingualism that are potentially so valuable for students. As mentioned earlier, students' relationship to language is often fragmented with regard to sense of self and authorship. The academic environment appears as its own linguistic landscape in which students feel compelled to cast aside languages and speech patterns from previous studies or daily life in order to fully commit to the conventions and mores of academic English. For my students, their rich multilingualism mentioned previously is often set aside and sacrificed to that false dichotomy separating the personal and the academic/public worlds. Poetry here is a dangerous, transgressive interloper, a rebel matchmaker that, if not bound to a specific paddock by the instructor, will run wild, much like Jen Webb and Donna Brien Lee's bowerbird (198) that takes material promiscuously to create its unique nest. This, in truth, is poetry's ontological power, to seek that which it needs in order to create new meaning irrespective of disciplinary boundaries. Students see this power when they incorporate research into their poetry writing; when they use poetry to illuminate research, theoretical concepts, and to create new paths of meaning in the STEM fields. This is poetry's great gift—that of creation and connection, making bridges among the human researcher, the research itself, and then, loftily, the greater humanity that can benefit not merely from the fruits of that research but by understanding it as well.

The Unique Power of Poetry in the Context of Scientific Innovation

Poetry, more than any other genre, is at its core a reimagining and remaking of a private language. In the case of this course, it's the creation of one's own English, even as it works in conjunction with "public" or "commonly accepted" English. Poetry is not private. As the poet Ilya Kaminsky writes, "In his or her privacy [a] poet creates a language in which he or she is able to speak, privately, to many people at the same time." This creation of the private-public language is a way of reimagining symbolic reality in much the way the scientific disciplines must imagine alternative futures, solutions, pathways of meaning, and knowledge creation. And much like scientists who must translate their discoveries into meaning outside of the immediate scientific community, poets plant new symbolic roots and establish new linguistic connections: creating, thus, new ways that dialectically inform the private and public languages (as suggested in the currently understood less deterministic version of the Sapir-Whorf hypothesis where spoken language influences thought and cognitive processes) (Ottenheimer 8). Poetry, "not an argument but a way of seeing," just like science, creates new modes of thought and perception, deriving from "a hypothesis about experiential reality" (Webb and Brien 191).

A significant number of scientists and science educators use poetry in their work, sometimes writing their own or leveraging poems to illustrate connections, teach content, and create engagement for their students (Atkinson 35; Fernandez-Gimenez et al. 1080-1083; Charon et al. 348). Likewise, when my students drew on their primary disciplines to create and analyze poetry, they found ways in which their poetic language— and thus, their integrated, personal, private language—was enriched by the concepts hitherto siloed in their professional worlds. Thus, one student finds his voice through writing poem-programs in Python; another subverts her essay on the Communist Manifesto and gains new understanding of her own language and her own material through remaking it into a black-out poem; another takes a leaf out of Amy Catanzano's *Quantum Poetics* and considers through their work the "question of what defines the present and the parameters of language, spacetime, and reality" (6). In time, the false dichotomy falls away to reveal, as Octavio Paz claims, that "poetry is a form of knowledge, of experimental knowledge" that, despite its subjective nature, similar to science holds "a respect for the autonomy of the phenomenon being investigated."

Beyond the structural similarities of poetic and scientific inquiries, poetic language remaking has tangible benefits for the scientific community, such as fostering resilience, communication, innovation, interdisciplinary connections, ethical integrity, as well as the ability to view and accept the world as messy, multidimensional, and multivocal. For example, the earlier mentioned negative capability of Keats highlights the remarkable resilience that the intentional, rigorous practice of poetry can ingrain in the practitioner who dwells with questions rather than immediate answers through desire and drive to produce the worthwhile, something true to the poet's hypothesis of reality. Poetry is always and inevitably an act of translation; and translation always and inevitably is as frustrating as it can be surprising and gratifying. The translation that happens is, of course, from the aforementioned private language or nonverbal image into a language whose truth reaches a reader. The process of such a translation, from the vague notion of hypothetical ideas; to the bowerbird-like gathering of materials in order to express a complex synthesis of ideas; to the numerous experiments that need to be conducted, scrapped, reflected on, tried again; to the final presentation of an often surprising product (and sometimes, too often, an admittance of failure—that no matter the drafts, the hypothesis, the approach was simply not sufficient) imparts the kind of resilience that is personal, passionate— not unlike that of an impassioned scientist (Webb and Brien 199)— revealing the "self to the self" (Hunt 17). This journey provides practice in confronting that with which all risk-takers must routinely contend: failure (Fernandez-Gimenez et al. 1083; Hunt 100) and familiarity with the uncertainty humans tend to find threatening (Stillman and Baumeister 249-250).

While teaching multilingual poetry and encouraging students to engage with numerous multilingual poets (Anuar Duisenbinov, Eugene Jolas, Anne Tardos, Rhina Espaillat, Kaveh Akbar, to name a few), I pushed back against the rigidity they were taught and emphasized a different ethos: they should aim not for separation of their languages but rather unity among them, the kind that, as poet Antoine Cassar, author of the multilingual book *Muszajk*, notes "allows mutually distinct voices to coexist in harmony and interact to different degrees" (3). Cassar insists that writing in multiple languages "allows [him] to listen to the voices within and around…without the pressing need to translate all thoughts, ideas and emotions into a single tongue" (4-5).

My students produced work that not only synthesized their own languages but also explored the languages of others through collaboration, translation, extensive peer workshops and collaborative editing. In order to foster the kind of resilience and comfort with the unknown and the "other" that I believe is essential in any kind of education, my course relied far more than is usual on the practices of multilingual writing, translation, and collaboration. This challenged my students perhaps more than simply creating their own work would have (collaboration is difficult even for seasoned poets), but it also allowed them to demystify the process of writing early on; to disengage from the particular draft as "truth" (as one must disengage from a particular experiment as "the only possible experiment") and instead work with the greater truth of intention, of articulating both their private language and understanding the language of their peers and, ultimately, to gain the resilience necessary to embrace this process as a whole.

This process of community practice increased their ownership of their epistemological journey and increased their confidence in themselves as poets as well as knowledge-creators and thinkers, whether that practice was scientific or creative (Hunter, Laursen, and Seymour 38). One of the exercises ended up being a telling celebration of the private language of each multilingual individual. The exercise was two-fold. The students wrote down seven words that held deep emotional and semiotic significance for them in one or more of their first (or second or third languages). Then they wrote an English-language poem that would incorporate and give further elaboration, context, rhythmic, or tonal interplay to the words. The students had the option of revising the poem into one of the established forms we practiced in class, or into a traditional form in either Kazakh or Slavic poetry. What emerged, especially in cases where students chose to house their language in formal structures, whether Western or Eastern, was that their poems were much better than poems written only in English – and not only because of the exotic incrustations of Kazakh or Turkic or Russian. The English also became more nuanced as they thought about the importance of reaching often into their childhood to choose the seven significant words and of using English to bring out the emotional and personal significance of non-English words while then setting these poems into the beautiful constraints of formal poetry. The fact that the cohesive rather than fragmented linguistic identity can give great benefit to their writing and their thinking was perhaps most obvious when they wrote multilingual poems themselves and entered into the practice of multilingual poetry and a multilingual community of practice. This ability to take and restructure their private language and make it public, make it understandable and accessible to themselves and to others, is something that can inform their work as scholars and scientists as well. Science, like poetry, emerges from the "mind's magic lantern" (Jenkins 1095), the imagination's leap of faith that brings together the disparate parts to create the new.

More than just the imaginative leap that both poetry and science require, the ability to look at all of their languages and consider both their emotional importance and their interplay through initial generative drafts and subsequent revisions contributed to an important skill of stepping away from an emotionally charged or significant problem—what scientists call an incubation period—a period of reflection and gathering that is just as important for the arts as it is for the sciences (Januchowski-Hartley et al. 906). Students found revising poetry very difficult, especially poetry that integrated such deeply held emotional truths as the use of one's childhood language. The labor of revising something in which the creator is deeply self-invested is important not just for the artist but for the scientist, for the engineer, for the mathematician.

I assigned a number of exercises that were aimed at achieving this resilience and cognitive flexibility through several kinds of translation. Students engaged in "classical" translation; the act of taking a text from a language they know well (usually Kazakh or Russian) and translating it into English. Likewise, they tried their hand at translating one of the poems we read during class into Kazakh or Russian. However, the two weeks we spent on translation introduced several variations on this relatively straightforward exercise. The first was aimed at showing how private language of association, imagery, and linguistic nuance shone through the public, or translated language. I asked student working on translation to work on the same poem, and then compare their translations in class, using both free observations and a few guided questions, such as interrogation of specific imagery, form, and word choices. The target poem for one semester was a difficult one to translate, Elizabeth Bishop's "One Art." Before translation students read excerpts of Bishop's letters about the work and responded extensively to the poem through free writes and their own formal poetic compositions to become familiar with the intricacies of the work. Their translations showed clear evidence of choice and nuance. For example, the synonyms for "loss" showed how those synonyms play with vastly different grammatical structures in Russian and Kazakh (some chose to translate into one language versus the other). Students had to consider the choice of rhyme and the villanelle form and whether rhyme and form were preserved in the translated version, or sacrificed to preserve image and literal meaning. Some students fell away entirely from Bishop's lists ("lost door keys, the hour badly spent") and elected to bring others in their place that seemed more poignant to them in terms of communicating this narrative of snowballing loss. The veracity or skill of the achieved translation is not necessarily of interest here; it is the act of making a linguistic choice that demonstrates how one's own private language and private understanding of language influenced the act of translation.

This translation exercise drives home the similarity of poetic discourse to scientific by bringing attention to the subtleties marking private and public language (Petersen 98). In addition, it continues to promote writing as a transferable, or "travelling" skill, as a "flexible method for communicating knowledge and experience" (Stephens 69). This was particularly valuable in the context of a multilingual classroom, because along with looking at the flexibility of language within translation (and the choices the translator must make), students were able to reconcile with and interrogate the translations they undertook in their own lives—the translations that formed a core of their lived experiences and that necessarily made their way into their learning as well.

The second exercise drew on this. Students were asked to translate one of their own poems from English to another language, or vice versa. This exercise (which students found incredibly difficult) went hand-in-hand with our discussion of the different ways the students viewed themselves in their respective languages. For many, English was the academic respite from the emotional language(s) of childhood. Poetry, in this way, occupied an interesting territory. Many said it was difficult to access poetry in English because they associated poetic language with emotion; and yet others discovered liberation in a language free from emotional or childhood association. The act of translating oneself showed precisely how varied that self can be across linguistic landscapes (and hearkens back to Cassar's argument for multilingualism and simultaneous expression in multiple languages). Certain things, students found, were simply untranslatable, or much more explanation, both for themselves and their peers. The occasional failure to explain the translation; to explicate the "private" language as it turned public; the difficulty in rendering an emotional reality of one language onto another proved useful when discussing with them the diverse and, it would seem, divergent aspects of their lives as poets, scholars, scientists, human beings. It also set the stage for being comfortable with the untranslatable, the liminal, the only privately understood.

The third set of exercises was designed to demonstrate the gulf between the inner, unformed, preverbal language of image and association and the word itself: the translation from the unknown. In class I took a poem from a language none of them knew (most recently, a Lithuanian poem by Salomea Neris, though I have used German poems by Rainer Rilke and readings of the Old Norse beginning of Beowulf to similar effect) and read it aloud to the students. I then asked them to make a "sound" translation—to create a poem that translated the original simply by virtue of sound. We discussed their translations, commonalities, associations—how at times they were able to grab onto a similar Sanskrit root word like *neshti* in Lithuanian (nesti or, to carry, in Russian) and other times rendered a completely divergent reading of the text by personal associations and sounds. The second part done at home was a "translation" of a dance or a contemporary painting/sculpture. I purposely assigned them images and videos from my own private stores without releasing the author's name or location to prevent them from reading what others had said about the works.

Finally, the students completed an exercise they submitted for a mini-workshop with a group of students specifically selected from other disciplines. I asked them to take a text that was in some way seminal in their discipline (whether a historical document; a C++ manual; a set of laws in Newtonian physics; a logic proof, etc.) and translate it into a poem. We looked at Amy Catanzano's *Quantum Poetics* as an example of taking concepts unique to physics and transforming them into a poetic language or interweaving academese and the text of formulas and textbooks with a language of emotion, connection, and image; ultimately, I left the interpretation of the assignment up to them. Already prepared for the unknown, for strange connections and how they may manifest in their work, the students ended up creating found love poems out of the Communist Manifesto; a computer program that was trying to make the user a poet; a narrative of writing a paper on geologic strata and mourning a breakup; an ode to the word *mother* as seen through the linguistic prism of language families and loan words. Crucially, in the context of this essay, students reported in our reflective sessions gaining not only an increased understanding of poetry and the leaps of faith required to produce a fresh image or a clear connection but also an increased appreciation for their major and a novel way to relate to the concepts they once considered unrelated to their emotional life, private language, or poetic inquiry.

While these last exercises were perhaps not true "translations" but closer to ekphrastic pieces inspired by other art forms or explanations of the viewer/listener experience, this kind of exercise forced students to think in ways that were unconventional, expanding their understanding of what was possible in creative writing and in crossing genre and discipline platforms as well, especially with regard to collaboration. Unfortunately, in my many years as a student in undergraduate and graduate workshops, I have never worked with collaboration, collaborative editing, or translation. My multilingualism, while a feature of my own poetry, was never something beyond an exotic curiosity. However, pushing students to engage in collaborative creative practices not only creates a writing community that is uniquely linked but also prepares students for facing uncertainty generally when working with others. In both poetry and science, the language of passion, the language of criticism and reinvention is crucial—and so is the ability to develop not only one's own vision, but contribute authentically to a larger work, as well as the ability to recognize the value and beauty in the complex, nuanced and often difficult to comprehend languages of others (Avasilichioaei).

This quality goes hand-in-hand with interdisciplinary curiosity and the ability to embrace knowledge creation and academia in its sometimes contradictory, multidimensional incarnations. Interdisciplinary curiosity and collaboration are essential to the sciences (Root-Bernstein 269); my experience suggests that a research-based poetry class that exposes students to investigative poetics, multilingual, experimental, documentary, historical and science-based works is at its core an exercise fostering such interdisciplinarity and engagement not only in one's own field or concern, but in that of others. Students gain admiration for the execution of a well-framed inquiry. At its core, just like the work of a scientist, the work of a poet is that of inquiry (Webb and Brien 190).

Ethics and Prophetic Technocreativity: Using Poetry Writing to Shape the Future

The main concern of this essay is the idea that teaching poetry in higher education, especially in STEM contexts, is an essential rather than elective practice. With regard to the former, I would like to draw attention to the orientation of progress and innovation in the sciences: namely, the often one-way, rapid-fire launch towards the future that typifies the trajectory of technological progress and the increasing pace of technological and scientific advancement (Berman and Dorrier). The students who are becoming scientists, engineers, innovators today are not simply working within established parameters that change comfortably. The speed with which industry develops is sometimes deeply uncomfortable, both for the practitioners and the bystanders, leaving little room for reflection or course correction or consideration of implications (Alexander et al. 6). Of course, this is not new, as reflection on and recognition of technology's place in the human world has often lagged behind its implementation. But I would argue that as the world grows and becomes ever more interconnected and these advances increase in speed, the ability of the innovators at the helm to connect to their work holistically, with the questions of larger humanity and ethics in mind, is not only essential, it is imperative (Atkinson 33).

This, then, is where the crucial piece of the puzzle emerges: the ability of poetry to foster the exact kind of self-reflection that works with difficult questions of new meanings, new realities, and how this may impact the collective as well as the individual (Lehmann and Gaskins 4). The speed of technological change inevitably brings to the forefront a need for scientists and innovators not only to be aware of their role as meaning-makers, but to ask difficult questions of the technology itself. We can use poetry and creative writing to help us navigate the ethics and the personal in the processes of invention and innovation, rather than compartmentalize such questions or leave them in the hands of philosophers or scholars of scientific history. Who we are as human beings is at the core of poetry and indeed, I would argue, should be at the core of scientific progress and innovation. In fact, this concern with our shared humanity lies at the heart of understanding science and technology, a task all the more important as distrust in scientific thought is at a high point (Iyengar and Massey 7656) and as we face new global challenges. We make and remake meaning through language; our symbolic worlds are shaped in how we use, perceive, and manipulate language. It is thus essential that this awareness of meaning-making through language is central to the innovation and progress of science and technology: for therein lies the ability to bridge the gap between the scientist and the layman; the mind and the heart; the future and the present.

The pathetic appeal of poetry is not, contrary to how it may be perceived, a weakness and should not be excluded from our understanding of science and its communication. As cognitive scientist Theodore Rees-Cheney notes, "even the most conscientious and intelligent reader may soon forget the factual content of a piece if material [has] entered the brain with little emotion wrapped around it [and] humans remember best what enters the brain in an envelope of emotion" (qtd. in Webb and Brien 36–7, 197). This means that learning is enhanced when the content is connected to the emotional human core of the learner and that the objectivity of scientific communication or thought can benefit from consideration of the emotional core forming human associations with facts and discoveries.

Finally, it is important to say something about creativity itself. Excellent research has already been done to show that the intersection between the arts and the science leads to transformative creativity fostering innovation (Root-Bernstein 283; Lehmann and Gaskins 2-3; Januchowski-Hartley et al. 906-907). But looking forward, I want to mention an exceptional feature of poetry, namely, what Roland Barthes terms "prophetic technocreativity" (qtd. in Webb and Brien 67, 192). As Webb and Brien describe it, prophetic technocreativity refers to the idea that "knowledge innovations emerge first in art works, and only subsequently emerge in philosophy" (192). This sentiment is echoed by Paul Magee who postulates that "a modern poem is not a knowledge-report, nor even a mode of self-expression, so much as a device for generating creative desire—the desire for meaning, for resolution, for further aesthetic experience, for an infinite number of things—in others" (qtd. In Webb and Brien 192). This creative desire, this need to formulate questions, synthesize disparate approaches, remake language, meaning, and embrace divergent theories and understandings is the great contributor to creativity in STEM that poetry can offer.

Of course, some recognition of this approach already exists: many universities like Stanford and MIT have courses and interdisciplinary pathways of study that combine science and the arts; a number of initiatives (like the recent Science, Technology and the Arts program in Europe) dedicate their efforts and resources to establishing an exchange of ideas and methodologies between artists and scientists. However, the kind of institutional recognition I argue for in the future would be routine rather than exceptional; an intuitive conflation rather than a rare experimental approach—the establishment of poetry writing (and creative writing at large) as a necessary companion to the world of technological and scientific innovation at the undergraduate level and beyond. Because, in truth, and selfishly, not only science stands to benefit from this companionship. For the maintenance of the false dichotomy is often mutual; creative writers often see their worlds as woven from different cloths than their science/techno colleagues. But the benefits to poetry are enormous if the connection between the rigor of scientific inquiry and the rigor of poetic inquiry and research are stressed in creative writing classes; if negative capability is truly embraced rather than just talked about; if the languages of others and the kind of knowledge and questions that come from multidisciplinary inquiry gain a central rather than peripheral place in the creative writing classroom. This can allow students to explore new subjects as well as eliminate many of the unhelpful and damaging biases/blocks that exist in the mind of a creative writing student, such as the bias/block against multilingualism; or the reluctance of a creative writer to undertake research as an integrated academic rather than one who must be "two-headed" (Webb and Brien 188) and necessarily separate practice from research in a ghostly echo of New Criticism. Breaking down these self-imposed barriers pushes poetry to continue to do its vital work of shaping language and transforming the private language of individuals into the public language of human ethics, consciousness, and empathy.

Works Cited

Alexander, Allen and Olivier Berthod, Sebastian Kunert, Torsten Oliver Salge, Anne L. Washington. *Failure-Driven Innovation.* artop, 2015.

Atkinson, Timothy N. "Using Creative Writing Techniques to Enhance the Case Study Method in Research Integrity and Ethics Courses." *Journal of Academic Ethics,* vol. 6, 2008, pp. 33–50.

Avasilichioaei, Oana. "Linguistic Alter Ec(h)o." *The Town Crier,* 12 October 2016. http://towncrier.puritan-magazine.com/language-ecosystem/

Berman, Alison and Jason Dorrier. "Technology Feels Like It's Accelerating — Because It Actually Is." *Singularity Hub* 22 March 2016. https://singularityhub.com/2016/03/22/technology-feels-like-its-accelerating-because-it-actually-is/

Blythe, Stuart, Jeffrey T. Grabill and Kirk Riley. "Action Research and Wicked Environmental Problems: Exploring Appropriate Roles for Researchers in Professional Communication." *Journal of Business and Technical Communication*, vol. 22, no. 3, 2008, pp. 272–298.

Brown, Megan E.L, Martina Kelly, and Gabrille M. Finn. "Thoughts that breathe, and words that burn: poetic inquiry within health professions education." *Perspectives on Medical Education,* vol. 10, 2021, pp. 257–264.

Cassar, Antoine. *Muzajk, an exploration in multilingual verse.* Edizzjoni Skarta, 2008.

Charon, Rita, Nellie Herman, and Michael J. Devlin. "Close Reading and Creative Writing in Clinical Education: Teaching Attention, Representation, and Affiliation." *Academic Medicine,* vol. 91, no. 3, 2017, pp. 345–350.

Edwards, Marissa and Neal Ashkanasy. "Emotions and failure in academic life: Normalising the experience and building resilience." *Journal of Management and Organization,* vol. 24, no 2, 2018, pp. 167-188.

Fernandez-Gimenez, Maria. E., Louise B. Jennings, and Hailey Wilmer. "Poetic Inquiry as a Research and Engagement Method in Natural Resource Science." *Society and Natural Resources,* vol. 32, no 10, 2019, pp. 1080-1091.

Hebron, Stephen. "John Keats and 'Negative Capability.'" Free Resources from the British Library, 15 May 2014. https://www.bl.uk/romantics-and-victorians/articles/john-keats-and-negative-capability

Hecq, Dominique. *Towards a Poetics of Creative Writing.* Multilingual Matters, 2015.

Hunt, Celia. *Therapeutic Dimensions of Autobiography in Creative Writing.* Jessica Kingsley, 2008.

Hunter, Anne-Barrie, Sandra L. Laursen, and Elaine Seymour. "Becoming a Scientist: The Role of Undergraduate Research in Students' Cognitive, Social and Professional Development." *Science Education,* vol. 91, no. 1, 2007, pp. 36-74.

Iyengar, Shanto and Douglas S. Massey. "Scientific communication in a post-truth society". *Proceedings of the National Academy of Sciences of the United States of Americ*, vol. 116, no. 16, 2019, pp. 7656-7661.
Jenkins, Bill. "The Mind's Magic Lantern: David Brewster and the Scientific Imagination." *History of European Ideas*. vol. 47, 2021, pp. 1094-1108.
Januchowski-Hartley, Stephanie et al. "Poetry as a Creative Practice to Enhance Engagement and Learning in Conservation Science." *BioScience*, vol. 68, 2018, pp. 905-911.
Kaminsky, Ilya. "Of Strangeness That Wakes Us." *Poetry*, October 2013.
Kinloch, Valerie F. "Poetry, Literacy, and Creativity: Fostering Effective Learning Strategies in an Urban Classroom." *English Education*, vol. 37, no. 2, 2005, pp. 96–114.
Krom, Cynthia L. and Satina V. Williams. "Tell Me a Story: Using Creative Writing in Introductory Accounting Courses to Enhance and Assess Student Learning." *Journal of Accounting Education*, vol 29, no 4, 2011, pp. 234-249.
Lehmann, Johannes and Bill Gaskins. "Learning Scientific Creativity from the Arts." *Palgrave Communications*, vol. 5, no. 96, 2019, pp. 2-6.
Liu, Siyuan, Michael G Erkkinen, Meghan L Healey, Yisheng Xu, Katherine E. Swett, Ho Ming Chow, and Allen R Braun. "Brain Activity and Connectivity during Poetry Composition: Toward a Multidimensional Model of the Creative Process." *Human Brain Mapping*, vol. 36, no. 9, 2015, pp. 3351-72.
Ludi, Georges. "Monolingualism and Multilingualism in the Construction and Dissemination of Scientific Knowledge." *The Multilingual Challenge: Cross-Disciplinary Perspective*, edited by Ulrike Jessner-Schmid and Claire J. Kramsch, Walter de Gruyter and Co KG, 2015, pp. 213-238.
Marshall, Steve, Hisako Hayashi, and Paul Yeung. "Negotiating the Multi in Multilingualism and Multiliteracies: Undergraduate Students in Vancouver, Canada." *The Canadian Modern Language Review*, vol. 68, no. 1, 2012, pp. 28-53.
McVey, David. "Why All Writing is Creative Writing." *Innovations in Education and Teaching International*, vol. 45, no. 3, 2008, pp. 289-294.
Mueller, Richard. *The Science of Aart*. John Day, 1967.
Myers, David. "The Rise of Creative Writing." *Journal of the History of Ideas*, vol. 54, no. 2, 1993, pp. 277–297.
Nicholes, Justin. "Lab Reports and Horror Stories: Leveraging Chemistry Majors' Writing Interests for Student Engagement and Retention." *Journal for Learning through the Arts*, vol. 16, no. 1, 2020.
Ottenheimer, Harriet. *The Anthropology of Language: An Introduction to Linguistic Anthropology*, 2nd ed., Cengage, 2009.
Ostrom, Hans. "Hidden Purposes of Undergraduate Creative Writing: Power, Self and Knowledge." *Teaching Creative Writing. Teaching the New English*, edited by Heather Beck, Palgrave, 2012, pp. 80-85.
Paz, Octavio. "Modern Poetry and Science." *Canadian International Youth Letter*, 2002.
Peary, Alexandria. "Spectators at Their Own Future: Creative Writing Assignments in the Disciplines and the Fostering of Critical Thinking." *Writing Across the Curriculum Journal*, vol. 23, 2012, pp. 65-77.
Petersen, Meg. "The Atomic Weight of Metaphor: Writing Poetry Across the Curriculum." *Writing Across the Curriculum Journal*, vol. 12, 2001, pp. 97-100.

Philp, Alexandra. "The Writing Collective: A Cross University Collaboration between Undergraduate Creative Writing Students." *Creating Communities: Collaboration in Creative Writing and Research,* special issue of *TEXT: Journal of Writing and Writing Courses,* vol. 24, no. 2, 2020.

Piller, I "Monolingual ways of seeing multilingualism," *Journal of Multicultural Discourses,* vol. 11, no. 1, 2016, pp. 25-33.

Radavich, David. "Creative Writing in the Academy." *Profession,* 1999, pp. 106–112.

Retzbach, Andrea, and Michaela Maier. "Communicating Scientific Uncertainty: Media Effects on Public Engagement with Science." *Communication Research,* vol. 42, no. 3, 2015, pp. 429–456.

Root-Bernstein, Robert. "The Art of Innovation: Polymaths and Universality of the Creative Process." *The International Handbook on Innovation,* edited by Larisa Shavinina, Elsevier, 2003, pp. 267-278.

Snow, Charles Percy. "The Two Cultures." *The Two Cultures.* Cambridge UP, 2008, pp. 1-21.

Stephens, Gregory. "Transferable Skills and Traveling Theory in Creative Writing Pedagogy." *New Writing,* vol. 15, no. 1, 2018, pp. 65-81.

Stillman, Tyler F. and Roy F. Baumeister. "Uncertainty, Belongingness, and Four Needs for Meaning." *Psychological Inquiry,* vol. 20 no. 4, 2009, pp. 249-251.

Watkins, Adam and Zahra Tehrani. "Brave New Worlds: Transcending the Humanities/STEM Divide through Creative Writing." *Honors in Practice,* vol. 16, 2020, pp. 29-51.

Webb, Jen and Donna Lee Brien, "Addressing the 'Ancient Quarrel': Creative Writing as Research." *The Routledge Companion to Research in the Arts,* edited by Jen Webb and Donna Lee Brien, Routledge, 2010, pp. 186-203.

Werk at Play: Exploring the Creative Play of a Graduate Student Writer to Reimagine Graduate Writing in the Humanities

Michelle Lafrance and Jay Hardee

Abstract: *This nontraditional essay poses the imaginative possibilities of fostering creative, intellectual play in graduate classes in the Humanities. Exploring the case study of a vlog produced by a student in a graduate seminar, the essay traces how the hybrid, multimodal writing—writing that meshes the digital conventions of creative and scholarly genres—in the course enabled this student to "reimagine" the purpose and stock moves of effective "scholarly" writing as the student blended voices, identities, and genres in his work. Creative play can be understood as an important pedagogical tool that allows graduate students to resist coercive and exclusionary processes of socialization, the co-authors argue. Such assignments encourage powerful interventions into traditional models of academic preparation, opening literacy landscapes of reimagined "world-building" and belonging.*

This essay explores creative play as a pedagogical tool that allows graduate students to resist coercive and exclusionary processes of socialization, as it opens a literacy landscape of "world-building" and belonging, where difference and activism may become rhetorical assets.

More accurately, this project began in two moments of "fuck it."

But let's not begin there.

We begin instead by putting three quotations into conversation. We ask you to read them as a call to reimagine graduate student writing, the subject of this essay.

> Play is not in excess to writing. . . Writing as play means that fictional elements are valid aspects of critical writing. Play involves performance, critical engagement with texts, considerable rhetorical skill, audience awareness, capacity to negotiate voice and tone, and an understanding of social relations–pragmatic, rhetorical knowledge, in other words. In addition, though, play entails wonder, curiosity, idealism, hyperbole, and imaginative leaps—an expansive horizon that purposefully exceeds predetermined limits." (Micciche 182)

> [I]nspired play (even when audacious, offensive, or obscene) enhances rather than diminishes intellectual vigor and spiritual fulfillment.... As long as words and ideas exist, there will be a few misfits who will cavort with them in a spirit of *approfondement*—if I may borrow that marvelous French word that translates roughly as 'playing easily in the deep'—and in so doing they will occasionally bring to realization Kafka's belief that a novel should be an ax for the frozen seas around us." (Robbins 61)

> Under certain circumstances failing, losing, forgetting, unmaking, undoing, unbecoming, not knowing may in fact offer more creative, more cooperative, more surprising ways of being in the world. (Halberstam 2)

Play. Performance. Curiosity. Imaginative leaps. Experimental. Approfundament. Unmaking. Undoing. Unbecoming. Creative. Cooperative. Being in the World. These are not terms typically associated with pedagogies that support graduate student writers.

Indeed, a cursory glance at the proliferating resources available for graduate students and those who support, mentor, or study them shows that graduate student writing is often characterized by deficiency, anxiety, and struggle, posed as a problem to be solved, or reduced to pragmatic how-to's and/or "hacks" (see, for instance, Brooks-Gillies, Garcia, Kim, Manthey, and Smith; Simpson, Caplan, Cox, and Phillips; Allen). Rarely in field literatures or texts do we see writing characterized as joyful, comforting, or playful.

Because graduate studies is a highly politicized site upon which many of the larger discussions of the value, purpose, and outcomes of education and professionalization play out, Burford, Amell, and Badenhorst argue, graduate student writing inevitably indexes the thorny disciplinary complexities, interpersonal challenges, and institutional hierarchies that give shape to other highly prescribed aspects of graduate professionalization. We would be remiss if we did not also acknowledge the ways that the shrinking academic job market and the continuing adjunctification of higher education provide an ominous backdrop for graduate degree-work, lending a sense of gravity to graduate study, urgency toward training in formal written conventions, and weighting professional publication. Conversations about graduate-level writing are often subsequently highly instrumentalized, producing overly generalized, meritized, and institutionalized conceptions of writing. We join these authors, along with the growing cadre of writing studies scholars who center the mentoring, support, and studying of graduate student writers in their professional projects, in asking how such writing might be reimagined within these 21st century contexts. As Burford, Amell, and Badenhorst note, the invitation to reimagine the writing graduate students produce is also an invitation to blue sky thinking about what "might enliven our ideas of what doctoral writing may be and how it might be researched" (6).

Hey y'all, can I just sneak in for a minute? It's me, the Irreverent Rhetorician, here to spill the tea about vlogs I created during a pandemic-era summer sesh with Michelle. I'm so excited for the opportunity to revisit that project, that I'm having a hard time waiting my turn. Sorry, Michelle. This playful project was key to helping me unlock my identity as a queer academic and finding a scholarly voice that feels both suitably authoritative and satisfyingly subversive, a voice I want to deploy in future text-based scholarship as well as in this newfound videographic side gig.

Who knew four vlogs about fetish porn, ethical riots, bisexual Barbies, and gay-sounding voices could do so much? It was liberating to have the space to explore such spicy subject matter; like Stacey Waite, I also have "a kind of mission to illuminate [the world's] queerness to others" (113), and my vlogs certainly did that. Yet, while it was devilishly fun to bring gay porn into the classroom, I was most profoundly—approfondely?—impacted by the encouragement in Michelle's class to eschew traditional academic prose in favor of creative writing play. In this play, I not only illuminated dark corners of the queer world out there to be explored by us learned academics, but also shined a light on my own queer presence within academia itself. I'll say more, in due time, don't you worry, but I need to let Michelle back in to set shit up.

This essay, which alternates between genres of traditional academic narrative and other forms of personal and academic storytelling, teases out the value of centering graduate study in the Humanities around creative, intellectual play. The imperatives are all around us: a global pandemic that has remade the spheres of schooling and work, the increasing impact of global climate change which requires dramatic, immediate, and creative working solutions, and the undeniable persistence of systematic, dehumanizing social inequities—as Naomi Klein notes, institutions often perpetuate the problems they were created to address, and institutions of higher education have been integral to the perpetuation of each of these issues.

It is no time to play small. Inseparable from the other unsettling futures we have called up, the future of graduate study must, necessarily and unabashedly, be creative.

Ohmygod, yes! Now is not the time to play small, y'all.

Reflecting on the vlogging of the Irreverent Rhetorician (the nom de plume of coauthor Jay Hardee), we explore the ways that one graduate student embraced creative play as his primary intellectual undertaking in a summer graduate seminar. In the Irreverent Rhetorician's discussion about how hybrid and multimodal forms opened queer being-in-the-world and self-making, we see the possibilities for both reimaging what "writing" and writing assignments look like for graduate students in the humanities *and* for more effectively supporting these students' diverse goals, identities, and needs. In our reflections about what Jay gained in his experiments, we re-see graduate preparation in the humanities as the training ground for emergent professionals who are ***empowered toward Jack Halberstam's "being in the world," a form of change-making and purposeful activism conceptualized and realized in their writing projects.***

Inspired by the feminist, queer, and literary scholars we cited in our opening, we see our piece as purposefully modeling the types of play with voices, genres, and conventions that we advocate be more central to graduate preparation in humanities. In our text, the Irreverent Rhetorician uses *italics* and other markers to interrupt, share, and theorize his story. Michelle continues in the straight-man role, making the necessary academic linkages across and through the Irreverent Rhetorician's reflections. **Dr. LaFrance interrupts, using bold and brackets—a clear indicator of her authority—to advise, caution, and carefully socialize Jay and his work into institutional norms.** Many of these insertions are pulled directly from comments, communications, and endnotes Dr. LaFrance provided graduate students in the summer course, including Jay. These interventions demonstrate the powerful stakes for those who bend or refuse academic conventions within the contexts of graduate study.

With these moves, we intend to explore and explode the expectations of traditional academic forms for writing and knowledge making practices and to play with conventions and traditional scholarly registers to adopt strategies of refusal, dis-ordering, assemblage, "braiding," and constellating that have been integral to many nonacademic forms (see for instance Cixous; Deleuze and Guattari; Waite; LaFollette; Powell et al.). As such, we do not intend for this text to read seamlessly but instead present moments where readers grapple temporarily with the meanings they make across seemingly unrelated moves and assembled parts.

Our Story Begins: That First Moment of "Fuck It"

Pandemic summer, 2020. People were dying—first in distant places, then in "our" cities and neighborhoods and families. Business as usual seemed a tone-deaf response to so much social turmoil.

And yet, Emergent Pedagogy, a summer grad class that treated the newest conversations about teaching, learning, and academic writing in writing and rhetoric, was impatient to be designed. How to conjure an antidote, an escape hatch, Tom Robbins' "ax for the frozen seas" of endless zoom classes, masking, social distancing, no vaccine in sight? The thought of assigning the usual—drafts of literature reviews, conference presentations, journal articles—was weighty and colorless.

It had been such a hard year. Where was the joy?

"Surprise me," she typed. "Delight yourself," a more genteel way of saying, "Fuck it."

The semester's readings were richly interconnected and provocative, covering the embodied teacher and student, material rhetorics such as disability, queerness, contingency, emotional labor, as well as the deep work of listening, mindfulness, and reflecting on community. Why shouldn't the writing assignments offer ways to shake off the languishing of the previous months as well?

The description for the summer's writing assignments began with a reminder that genre choices are often deeply intertwined with ideals of character and embodiment. Students were asked to choose a character, persona, argument, or topic to "embody." The goal was to "take up and explore the concepts, themes, and conversations presented in our readings and class sessions," while encouraging "*fun*, creativity, character play, and VISION," in ways that fostered audience- and genre-awareness, but also pushed against those conventions (see appendix for full text of assignment).

In response to the invitation to write big and write weird, co-author Jay Hardee proposed a series of "vlogs" that would take up queer theory and "unruly rhetorics" (Alexander, Jarret, and Welch). Running with this assignment, he scripted humorous, highly individualized, and cross-audience video-treatments of his responses to course themes and readings.

The Possibilities of Play

> "On a basic level, we learn through play about the ball, the labyrinth, the dance, the mask, the drum, and about sport. Through play, we test our relation to the world, to others, and to ourselves"
>
> –Eichenberg, *Questioning Play*

While "play" itself is "is a complex, overdetermined term fraught with contradictions and ambiguities" (Rouzie 629), so "notoriously difficult to define," (Daniel-Wariya 118), educational theorists, psychologists, philosophers, and Writing Studies specialists alike have enshrouded the generative and developmental functions of play for writers and learners in decades of scholarship, often posing play as inseparable from crucial forms of personal and professional development (Sutton-Smith; Fergusson). "Play has resisted definition mainly because it is difficult to render dynamic relationships into language," Scott Eberle writes, grounding his own working definitions of the term in the "pleasures" of imagination, anticipation, and expectation, as well as surprise, curiosity, inquiry, discovery, delight, satisfaction, joy, happiness, and/or fun: "an ancient, voluntary, emergent process driven by pleasure that yet strengthens our muscles, instructs our social skills, tempers and deepens our positive emotions, and enables a state of play that leaves us poised to play some more" (231).

Right, who's not down for some more hedonic humanities? Embrace the value of pleasure-seeking in knowledge-seeking, y'all.

Similarly, Patrick Sullivan argues the benefits of centering writing pedagogies on creativity, as a crucial component of effective writing, "If we theorize creativity as a highly sophisticated and valuable form of cognition, it must also, then, by definition, be regarded as a necessary and indispensable part of any curriculum in a writing classroom" (19). Sullivan notes that recent paradigmatic shifts have seen creativity (and its related cousin "curiosity") gain greater value as it is increasingly associated with problem solving, critical thinking, and other well-valued higher order cognitive processes. Similarly, Spencer Jordan re-imagines "creativity" as a "tactical intervention," particularly into "affective change, [or] what Donna J. Haraway calls 'troublemaking'" (2). "Creativity is not just the production of physical artifacts or performances," according to Jordan, but "is also an inherent part of cognitive psychology, the ongoing sense-making process of our brains" (34).

Scholars in rhetoric, composition, and literacy studies have used both terms to denote and study classroom spaces that encourage curiosity, exploration, experimentation, risk-taking, and crucial reflection on the self and other, the rhetorical situation, and composing practices (see for instance Sirc; Gee; Batt; Shipka; Oleksiak). The benefits of play for learners in many contexts, then, lies in its ability to encourage identity exploration/formation, self-directed problem solving, skill development, and rhetorical awareness, as play is argued to make implicit or unrecognized rules or boundaries more explicit, tap the imagination, and (potentially) lower the stakes of experimentation. Play with genre and hybridity has also been central to discussions of the overlaps and differences between the texts enshrined by creative writing and those central to composition (Hesse; Graff), the nature of "experimental writing" (Patricia Sullivan), as well as multimodal approaches in writing studies pedagogy (Arola and Wysocki; Rhodes and Alexander).

Re-conceiving graduate student writing as a form of creative play amplifies a number of similar interventions into rote conceptions of academic writing—especially via the intentional or exaggerated use of transgeneric forms (LaFollette), transrhetorical storytelling strategies, "constellating" or assemblage (Powell), purposefully unconventional writing processes and forms (Waite)—and aligns with feminist critique, indigenous storytelling methods, and queer world building that highlight the "messy, complicated, embodied, intimate…matrices of oppression that complicate privilege and marginalization" (Oleksiak 307). (For example, Timothy Oleksiak's goal in embracing queer world making and slow process is to move writing classes away from what he names "the improvement imperative" (307), an additionally crucial component of reimagining the surrounding contexts and stakes for graduate student writers.) The resulting reconceptualizations of self, the messiness of meaning making, the unbinding of the composing process, and other conventions offer emergent writers the opportunity to stretch, flex, and remake texts.

Speaking of which, I'm over here strecht, flext, and ready to run with some text. Can I tap in now?

Playing with Your "Self" Online

When my good Judy, Michelle, asked me to write this with her, I gotta be honest, I wasn't that well versed in Creative Writing Across the Curriculum (CWAC) scholarship. So sis dug in, reading all about the potential for CWAC to deepen students' engagement with course material. Like, Alexandria Peary defines CWAC as an "enactive" pedagogy that enables students to "learn by doing" (352). This, in turn, stimulates a richer engagement with course material as students creatively put concepts "in action" and show how an idea is "subject to change in a particular context" (353). First person narrative assignments, for example, "in which the student becomes a character effectively activate course concepts" (359). Cool, I get that. And, werk, activating course concepts is totally awesome, but my experience in Michelle's class leaves me with firsthand experience in the deeper knowledge of *self* that CWAC offers. Y'all, *I* was activated.

Michelle instructed us to take up our chosen genre as "a character" to "embody" through our deliverables; and "[c]ostumes, characters, . . . and ensembles [were] encouraged" for vid-casts (syllabus). This direction required me to pay careful attention to the mise-en-scene of my vlog, which in turn made me think more deeply about a genre that was entirely new to me as a writer/creator. But the Irreverent Rhetorician was not just a vlog; it was a character, so I had to think about who that character would be and get to know him. How to become him? Sure, he's me, but how do I want to perform myself in academic contexts? Which parts of Jay get revealed in journal articles like this one? How would I creatively construct a hybrid-persona that cited, commented upon, and extended or applied scholarship? And how would I speak and embody myself on camera?

Ultimately, if you'll pardon my trip back to the 90s (which are totally making a comeback, so get over it), the Irreverent Rhetorician is like a Jim Carrie Bradshaw. In other words, I try to exude a sense of style that extends from my wordplay to my wardrobe, but I deliberately undermine this cool influencer-before-influencers-were-a-thing vibe with the cartoonish malleability of my face that I deploy with all the subtlety of a silent film star. Some might see a Randy Rainbowishness to the Irreverent Rhetorician, and that would not be wrong, but I actually think he's more like *The Kids in the Hall's* Buddy Cole, if Buddy were to trade the barstool for grad school.

Attention to character in the Irreverent Rhetorician allowed me to rehearse the persona of a queer scholar, mined from my own personality and life experience (and clearly a bunch of Gen X cultural references), and to put it on its feet in an academic setting. However, I am less interested in the way these vlogs deepened my understanding of course concepts. I am more excited by the way that playing a character—playfully—and approaching the vlogs as a multimodal storyteller allowed me to discover my voice and ethos as a queer scholar, and to make some space for my own brand of subversiveness in academic contexts.

> [I give this project a HUGE greenlight and two thumbs up, Jay, it's exciting and fresh work. But I do want to caution you that there may be people in our class and field who may not understand why your work is important and timely, or who may be offended by the topic you take up. Let's keep talking about how to manage these situations and audiences as you prepare to share your work in class sessions. –Dr. LaFrance]

Fuck It, We're Writing About Porn

The Irreverent Rhetorician kicked off with "Lance Hart's PervOut," about my high school friend who is now an award-winning Renaissance man of hardcore pornography. Lance is an occasional contributor to mainstream publications, like Cosmopolitan, where he discusses the ins and outs of pegging, but I wanted to celebrate his construction of a sexual identity that refuses easy labeling, developed in his website and blog PervOut. As I note in the opening of the episode, I set out "to dig into the dark recesses of the internet to unearth some seriously counterpublic discourse"—and, gurl, I found it.

My exploration of Lance's corpus drew inspiration from one of the readings that framed the class: Jonathan Alexander and Jacqueline Rhodes' "Queerness, Multimodality, and the Possibilities of Re/Orientation," which advances "a theoretical approach to the multimodal construction of queerness that situates such a figuring as a challenging possibility for queering sexuality, for queering our understanding of the queer and heteronormative, and for queering our interaction with multimedia and multimodal texts" (189). Alexander and Rhodes argue that multimodal compositions have the potential to complicate representations of queerness, playfully enacting queer modes of being; to connect the "queer diaspora" scattered across cyberspace (192); and to resist the disembodiment and desexualization of "queer," which they note has become "'safe,' or at least legitimate, institutionally" (206). We are here for the queering, y'all! And grateful for the opportunity to follow the Irreverent Rhetorician's prurient curiosities and to playfully render the queerness of fetish porn scholarship that is both unflinchingly frank and funny.

Figure 1.

[For this class exercise, work that is "hybrid" seeks to balance academic and non-academic conventions, demonstrating deep and attentive reading of our core texts, cross-audience awareness, and a clear exigence. I love how you've pushed the envelope, but I also want to encourage you to lean a little more into common academic conventions–citing, summarizing, and paraphrasing from our core texts more frequently. –Dr. LaFrance]

Undoing Limits through Play in Queer Worlds

You know who else is here for queer and I'd like to think would be down for my brand of irreverent rhetoric? Stacey Waite. I found myself nodding and "yas qweening" to her "Queer Literacies Survival Guide." She writes, "the world is a queer place, and as I grew up and left home it became a kind of mission to illuminate its queerness to others, to ask that others see the queerness in this world, and even imagine the possibility of queerer worlds" (113). My own desire to spotlight the subversive and urge to erect queer worlds led me out of the gate to fetish pornography. Natch. What can I say? I wasn't looking "to queer" some esoteric academic shit; I wanted "to academic" some kink that was patently queer to begin with. Like the foremother of porn studies Linda Williams, I find pornography fascinating as a "discourse of limits" (36)—the rhetorics of what Williams dubs the "on/scene," what mainstream culture deems obscene but nonetheless finds its way onto screen (37). This desire to provocatively transgress the limits of academic discourse—as well as the limits of public discourse—and to make room for queerness motivates the Irreverent Rhetorician. And that's what Michelle's Emergent Pedagogies enabled me to do.

Right, but you might ask, did I really *need* CWAC to write about porn? Why not just write like Linda Williams? OK, smarties, sure, I could have waxed old-

school-scholarly about porn or any of the other queer shit I explored in my vlogs but the playful premise of Michelle's assignment was wonderfully disinhibiting, and the creation of my scholarly queer alterego propelled me, fuck it, compelled me toward naughty queer worlds ripe for rhetorical analysis. And so the direction to play and experiment with genre and character enabled me to bring my queer world and the world of my queer friends into the classroom, undoing the boundary between my academic self and my queer self and allowing me to be fully embodied and engaged in both worlds at once.

> [Be sure to balance the citations you include with your chosen voice, so that the work you compose centers on the academic texts at the center of your interest, even if your unpacking of those texts is about illuminating or demonstrating your lived experience. –Dr. LaFrance]

My Queer "Aesthetic Artifact" and Sense-Making Affects

The Irreverent Rhetorician wasn't just here to explore queer worlds, but to engage in some queer world-making of my own, so I was deeply invested in my vlog as a queer "aesthetic artifact" (Peary 355). I wanted to demonstrate to my professor and peers (and anyone else who finds my vlogs on YouTube) what a queer academic world might look like. As the first episode opens, I speak directly into camera—the gender plural "y'all" of my address—introducing myself and aligning my project with Alexander and Rhodes' queer rhetorical scholarship. I try to affect the tone of your sassy gay bestie, playfully gossiping about some queer shit. To create a sense of intimacy and camaraderie with my viewers in a queerly affected space, I frame my head and shoulders in the shot, as I sit on a cushy chair in front of a bright pink and deep blue backdrop and allow myself room to lean into the camera to emphasize certain moments. Although I adhere to the language and moves of standardized academic prose and popular/scholarly video essays, I sprinkle naughty words and queer vernacular idioms throughout the script like pixie dust. I elaborate a scholarly conversation, citing and visualizing quotes from esteemed authors, before using this framework to analyze a text, but the text I analyze is porn and I see fit to include a clip and graphic images of it, along with some hopefully hilarious reaction shots and delightfully bonny bon mots. ("Lance got his foot fetish in the door of the porn industry" is a good one, ya gotta admit.)

> [Even as I encourage you to push that envelope as far as you can, let's also be sure to touch base about the stakes of this sort of work for you all. How do some exigencies encourage us to confront audiences that may not be ideal? –Dr. LaFrance]

Consummate performer that I am <wink>, I aimed to evoke viewer pleasure in my vlog about PervOut—like when I intercut a scene from an outré sci-fi porno (in which a bound and naked Lance Hart comically gets electrocuted with CGI space lasers) with closeups of my face making clownish reactions of surprise and disgust, and I ask the camera, "Gurl, what the fuck are we watching?!" It was important to me to include clips of Hart's work; I wanted to communicate that even gay fetish porn has something valuable to teach us if we're bold enough, queer enough to see it—opening rhetorical scholars' eyes to performances of sexual identity that simultaneously confirm and resist the very notion of sexual identity itself, and to the generative tension between fantasy and honesty that exists in Hart's world of fetish porn. But I was also aware that my mixed audience would include people who do not share my penchant for a pedagogy of porn. Therefore, I selected a deliberately campy scene that was X-rated but also extremely absurd and I incorporated myself to function like a Greek chorus, channeling the response of my audience and humorously giving permission to the discomfort that I had deliberately provoked. In this way, I use the humor of this particular porno scene and my ludic looks to camera to introduce BDSM to the rhetoric classroom and to then manage my audience's discomfort; thus, through creative cheekiness I prime my not-queer audience to engage with the queer academic world I wish (us) to (co)inhabit.

> [Is some/most/all academic work "activist" by nature? What does it mean when we blend the two identities, scholar and activist? What about other personas often embodied by popular authors–comedian, influencer, detective, adventurer, politician, boss, witness, visionary? What balances must be struck for these roles to claim a scholarly center? –Dr. LaFrance]

Playing with Discomfort

At times, I didn't want to diffuse the unease my audience might be feeling and preferred instead to lean into uncomfortable affects. As a professional actor I can tell you that some scripts are comedies and others are tragic, but play can find the truth in both. In the final episode I produced during the semester, I experimented with form to emphasize the sonic rhetoric of gay-sounding voices, as I put forth my idea that the materiality of queer voices creates intimate sonic publics. Citing both Eric King Watts and Frank J. Macke, I argue in the vlog "that the queer voice 'announces [the queer speaker's] idiosyncratic presence in the world'" (Watts 181); "it is his 'sensual bodily insertion'" (Macke 136) into the public sphere, and this 'resonant encounter' between queer and normative sounding bodies can affect a strong response" ("Irreverent Rhetorician 1.4").

To make this argument, I played with an aesthetic approach that foregrounds the sound of my voice. Atop a high-key B/W still image of my face, I overlay a pulsating pink circle, providing the only visual movement on the screen as it vibrates to the hum of my voice. I deliver the scholarly monologue slowly, deliberately, in a seductive voice that might seem more apt for the bedroom than the classroom. I intend to intone a frisson of eroticism as I almost moan: "Jesus, I can't count the times I've been ridiculed for the sound of my voice, but I'm lucky; I've never been violently attacked for sounding funny as some gay men have" ("Irreverent Rhetorician 1.4"). In this vlog, I wanted to perform the idea that sound and sonic rhetoric are inherently intimate, and that this intimacy renders queer sounding speakers vulnerable to phobic violence because of the ways sexuality gets read in the mate-

riality of voices like mine—even when I'm not whispering sweet nothings in your ear. I want viewers to draw a connection between their discomfort at the sound of my voice and the humiliation and violence that gets redirected at speakers who sound like I do, and I attempt to achieve this through creative forms of writing and performance.

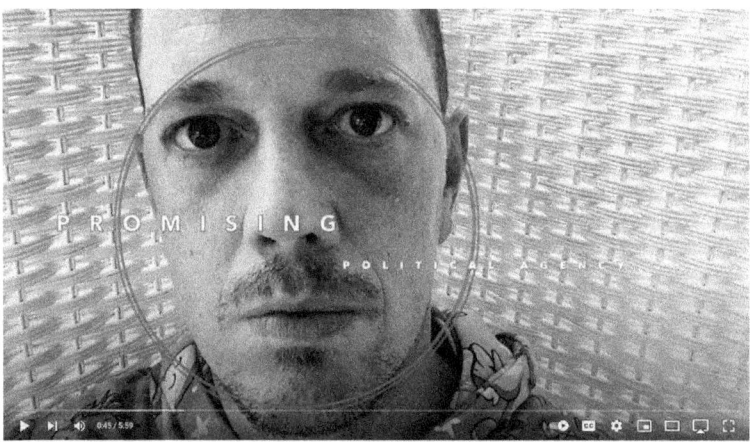

Figure 2.

[Jay Hardee's fantastic "Irreverent Rhetorician" Vlog will be the topic of our first student-led class discussion. It is both impressively engineered AND a brilliant piece of new scholarship. But the Vlog does also contain explicit content and, while tastefully compiled and very well argued, I want to recognize that some viewers may find the material discomfiting. The questions central to how we handle difficult, uncomfortable, and potentially fraught topics in our classrooms is crucial for all teachers and scholars to sit with. I know we'll have a very productive, classroom-as-community-building conversation. –Dr. LaFrance]

Creativity Is Inherently Political

Jordan reminds us that the storymaker is "troublemaker," and "creativity becomes a tactical intervention whose end is affective change" (2). The troublemaking Irreverent Rhetorician thus seeks to make a world of "alternative modes of thought, both transgressive and resistant to social or economic norms" (36), such as the norms of White cisheteronormativity. In Episode 1.2 of the Irreverent Rhetorician, my queer worldmaking project takes aim at my own, holding other White gay men accountable for the loss of queer ethos from our supposedly queer community. In "Stonewall and the Rhetorical Riot," I use chapters from Unruly Rhetorics: Protest, Persuasion, and Publics *to argue, as Nancy Welch does, that "civility…may be a virtue, but not one in service to democracy" (110), and to suggest the possibility of ethi-*

cal riots working "in service not of the mob (ochlos) but of the demos" (Alexander and Jarratt 15). I was moved by anger to create this vlog after I saw a White gay friend share a story on Facebook about graffiti on the Lincoln Memorial during the riots sparked by the murder of George Floyd. This friend called the desecration of national monuments "disgraceful," and that pissed me off.

I open the vlog with a montage of images from the riots and other reactions to George Floyd's extrajudicial killing, and I set the montage to an upbeat version of "June is Busting Out All Over" that Leslie Uggams heroically soldiered through on live television after a cue card fiasco left her without the words. Uggams resorts to nonsense lyrics, but she does so without missing a note or a beat and with style and showmanship that is nothing short of inspirational. I worry that playing with this song as I do toes the line of acceptably irreverent discourse from a White gay man; my intention, however, is to creatively underscore a poignant irony that I develop in the episode, which laments the seeming loss of radical ethos from the annual celebrations of gay Pride busting out all over June.

Episode 1.2 quickly moves from discussing the BLM riots of June 2020 to a history of the Stonewall riots of June 1969, which catalyzed the gay liberation movement that fateful night Marsha P. Johnson and Sylvia Rivera led a multi-racial crowd of young radical queers in violent protest against a frustratingly familiar police raid of queer spaces. The ensuing riots were "the death knell for mannerly" politics of earlier homophile organizations like the Mattachine Society and Daughters of Bilitis (Faderman 176). Within a year of Stonewall, the Gay Liberation Front and other radical gay groups had spread across the country with a revolutionary message of gay pride—a tactic, Lillian Faderman notes, that was inspired by "militant black groups" and their defiant declarations of Black pride and beauty (179). Thus, given the radical roots of Gay Pride, I find it dispiriting to see Pride coopted by the kind of conservative respectability politics that dominated pre-Stonewall gay organizing. And I get real pissed when I see White gays with their rainbow-branded corporate merch policing Black anger. So, I conclude with a reminder to pearl-clutching gay men upset about uncivil BLM protests that the gay civil rights they currently enjoy (however tenuously) are indebted "to the embodied rhetoric of a catalytic riot" ("Irreverent Rhetorician 1.2").

> [I want to note again that the video does include a few explicit images borrowed from gay porn videos and websites. —Dr. LaFrance]

Gaiety and Utopia in Grad School–Who Knew?

My most nakedly political vlog was about the rhetoric of riots, but even my most playful episode of the summer was nonetheless a queer world-making endeavor that tapped the "critical-utopian capacity of storytelling" (Jordan 36); it just did so with dolls. The vlog "Tiggy Upand & 'Queer World-Making'" analyzes the bisexual themed webcomic Upland, about a pink-haired bi activist who works at a Boston hostel, as well as the companion webcomic Tiggy Goes to Jail, about Tiggy's experience volunteering for the Massachusetts Bail Fund. Tiggy and all her friends in both webcomics are played by an array of dolls and so I thought it fitting to stage my discussion of this work as a play with dolls as well. I searched online for queer dolls and surprisingly/unsurprisingly I found quite the cache, including Barbie-adjacent dolls with some killer looks—one doll I dub "Gay Spicoli" for his pastel tie-dye tank-top and long blond hair; a guy fashionista (fashionisto?) rocks stylish shades and a manbun to make my bald head envious; and an androgynous boy doll serves 90s club-kid realness in platform trainers and cropped green hair fabulousness. A shirtless werewolf from Twilight, who I jokingly dub "Wolf Trade," makes a cameo, and I enlisted my friend to voice Billie Jean King Doll—but she never leaves her original packaging because "you never know what a ground-breaking lesbian Barbie could be worth one day" ("Irreverent Rhetorician 1.3").

I staged the vlog as a play with queer Barbies not only to pay tribute to Tiggy Upland's doll dioramas, but also to creatively engage with Sara Warner's Acts of Gaiety, *elaborated in Londie T. Martin and Adela C. Licona's chapter in* Unruly Rhetorics, *"Remix as Unruly Play and Participatory Method for Im/Possible Queer World-Making."*

Figure 3.

Martin and Licona contend that play creates a space where "cheeky, irreverent, and spontaneous fun works collaboratively with a vulnerable, deadly serious insistence on a queer presence" (251-252). My vlog argues that Tiggy Upland's multimodal compositions use this form of play and the queer affects of gaiety in a utopian world-making project. Warner describes acts of gaiety as "comical and cunning interventions that make a mockery of discrimination and social exclusion" (xi). She argues that the "positive affects" of queer gaiety "involve pleasurable sensations and foster jubilant practices of life, art, and activism" (4), and have played "an integral part in the establishment and maintenance of LGBT public cultures" (6). I see this utopian gaiety in Tiggy Upland's bi webcomic, and I want to enact this politically potent affect in my own work. And so, I roped in my friend, her tweenage daughter, and my almost-eight-year-old twins for a gaily subversive play with dolls, which you can now view on YouTube and TiggyUpland.com (Ya know ya wanna see it for yourself).

> [Let's think about where you can take these videos for publication, Jay–they're so impressive, cogent, timely, and provocative. I want them to gain a wide viewership! A multimodal/online journals may be interested in them as video-texts, but we'll also want to think about fit for your content. –Dr. LaFrance]

Shablam!

Having the space in Emergent Pedagogies to exercise this creative gaiety in an academic context was incredibly empowering. Like Martin and Licona and Warner, I am deeply committed to José Esteban Muñoz's sense of queerness as a utopian world-making project in which "representational practices help[] us to see the not-yet-conscious" (3). Muñoz's Cruising Utopia *contends that "we can glimpse the worlds proposed and promised by queerness in the realm of the aesthetic" (1), and tips us off to the power of these aesthetic "wish-landscapes" to imagine and summon into being "the territory of [queer] futurity" (5). Creative compositions, like the Irreverent Rhetorician's vlogs, have the power to destabilize institutionalized thinking "through the more nuanced avenue of feelings," and so enable us to rethink identities and modes of being that challenge cisheternormativity (Warner 3). Thus, Martin and Licona urge us "to risk pursuing the pleasure and transformative potential of a playful orientation [to scholarship] because it provides us with a way to imagine" new forms to "resist hetero/normative logics and neoliberal imperatives" (245). In other words, the playfulness I experienced, and which is encouraged by these creative opportunities, creates space within the academy to challenge the norms of institutionalized cisheteronormativity and other systems of domination.*

<tongue pop!>

> [I want to pause here and ask again about your audience. Who are you imagining your ideal viewer to be? –Dr. LaFrance]

The Stakes: Who Gets to BE in Academic Worlds?

> *"We will wander, improvise, fall short, and move in circles. We will lose our way, our cars, our agenda, and possibly our minds, but in losing we will find another way of making meaning in which…no one gets left behind."*
>
> —J Jack Halberstam, *The Queer Art of Failure*

Though we came to this project about reimagining graduate student work through our own moments of exasperation, questioning, exhaustion, and the desire for freer movement as writer and mentor, we quickly realized that we do not stand alone in this effort. We are neither the first to make calls for nor to explore the possibilities of creative play for graduate student writers at many different stages of study, nor the first to challenge rote and overly professionalizing ideas about graduate preparation in the Humanities. In a *Chronicle of Higher Education* opinion piece that laments the creative opportunities missing from traditional graduate study in the Humanities, Grace Lavery wonders whether the teaching goals of graduate programs, teachers, and mentors adequately recognize the highly creative backgrounds or the imaginative and nontraditional aspirations of her students, particularly in light of the collapsing academic labor market. Graduate students come to the humanities with a thirst for innovation, social change, and creative exploration of critical work, Lavery writes, yet, professionalization into academic standards and preparation for the dismal realities of academic career paths seem to sap "the magic" from process, product, and student. "These structures may very well help students communicate their ideas," Lavery writes, "but they also supply them with the mystifying delusion that all good writing is good in the same way, and that the best writing is that which abides most fully by the established rules."

In this essay, we've joined a growing chorus of scholars, researchers, and graduate students interested in what creative forms (essays, life writing, constellated rhetorics, ethnographic fiction, and storytelling methodologies) lend academic work and academic writers. As Aja Martinez demonstrates in her work on counterstories and critical race theory, many of our students must write their way into an academy that has little interest in seeing them for who they are; countering the stories that would silence, disenfranchise, erase, or remove them is not just a means to resist, but also offers opportunities to reimagine, remake, and reform the structures and epistemic patterns of academic culture, creating more spaces for authentic belonging (8). Shawn Combs argues similarly that an embrace of creative writing often gives a graduate writer "liberty to live, move, and have [their] being on the page" (137).

But the stakes are high indeed, even for those students, like Jay, who find a natural affinity for experimental and boundary-breaking graduate work. As Julia Molinari writes, academic circles still lean toward quite closed epistemic understandings of academic production—graduate students who do not have the support of a close academic advisor may face severe consequences for rule-breaking or diverging from expected norms. Keith Rhodes laments "the current paradigm of readerly hegemony" (50) in scholarly writing and composition instruction:

> In Bakhtin's term, we've made scholarly writing, too, increasingly "monologic," focused on having authors prove that they partake of the "conversation in the field," fluent in all the latest genre conventions, jargon, and (ahem) affordances. . . It's almost as if the most successful writer will be one who surprises us the least, conforming most expertly to the model we already imagine, constructing readers as masters to be served in precise, settled ways. (48)

We hear the urgency Waite, Martinez, Malea Powell and others—*who argue they are often writing for their very lives, writing so that they may "be in the world"*—bring to our understandings of the stakes of this conversation for graduate students learning to write. Waite confides in her "Queer Literacies Survival Guide" that "Without the ability to develop and cultivate alternative ways of reading and composing, I might be dead" (111). Powell invites us to "play language games lovingly, tenderly, remembering that 'all acts of kindness are lights in the war for justice' (Harjo...), all acts of scholarship are battles in a war of words, and of worlds" (21). Adapting playful and experimental writing pedagogies, as Waite points out, "is deeply political work—feminist and queer work," but it is "work we must do as scholars in composition and work our students must do in order to be more complicated thinkers and better writers....[W]e must find ways to blur the boundaries, so that we can push them, so that we can take our field and our students outside the bounds of where we think we can go, outside the bounds of what kinds of knowledges we can access, and how" (54).

We've argued above that these types of explorative exercises can lead graduate students to greater understandings of the self, of others, of the social world, of audiences and readers, and of the many factors that lead to rhetorical awareness and effective writing. Jay's experience creating the Irreverent Rhetorician affirms the possibilities we point out of expanding our ideals of creative play via writing to open such spaces and restructurings. We recognize that not all projects may be playful—some may be healing, angry, grief-stricken, sad, or reconciling. Some, like Jay's, may be about the current work of a former classmate-turned-porn-star. But the opportunity to narrate lived experience, to break with conventions, and explore texts as a representation of an emergent scholarly self can lead to a greater sense of belonging to and *being in* academic worlds that see and support all those who wish to dwell within them. Our active remaking of graduate student writing in the humanities establishes many of the foundational conditions for reimaging graduate studies at large.

On this note, we end with the Irreverent Rhetorician's own words:

> *Authoring the Irreverent Rhetorician empowered me to speak in my own vernacular and communicate through queer affect, while I channeled my life experiences, my queer interests, the materiality of my voice and body, and even my friends and children into my scholarship. Creative academic play opened the gates to a classroom literacy landscape where I was able to locate my ethos as a queer scholar and to experience that ethos as a rhetorical asset. Rather than leaving those parts of myself at the boundary of the classroom, I was able to locate all of me within the geography of my discipline, and Michelle's CWAC approach to the semester showed me that these various parts of myself have power and that my ethos as a queer academic is a rhetorical virtue.*
>
> *Werk!*

Appendix

Choose Your Own Adventure Assignment

Game ON!: What adventure (persona) do you choose this summer?

Choose from one of the following. Though your work may take on many different shapes/actions/qualities this semester, please be sure that **the readings, materials, and discussions of the course remain the root content for what you produce**. I want to discourage any "pure" reflection or traditional "responses." That is, what you produce should (creatively) take up and explore the ideas and conversations presented in our readings and class sessions. I encourage *fun*, creativity, character play, and VISION, even as I ask you to offer audience- and genre-appropriate attention to scholarly ideals in your work.

Vid-Cast Master: Get your 21st c School House Tiger King Rock on! With this adventure you will create 4 videos (of at least five minutes). Like any self-respecting YouTube star, you may even want your own online channel. Be sure to compose your vid-casts in ways that change up, model, extend, or challenge the many different genres of vid-play for educational and infotainment purposes. Costumes, characters, interviews of classmates and others, and ensembles encouraged. (You may wish to supplement your vids with a "script," to demonstrate the time and attention you paid to production values.)

Captain Pod-Cast: Get your Fresh Air, Kojo Nnamdi, Serial, or Cult of Pedagogy on! With this adventure you will create 4 Pod-Casts (of at least 10 minutes. Like any self-respecting audio producer, you may even want your own online channel. Be sure to compose your pod-casts in ways that change up, model, extend, or challenge the many different genres of audio-play for educational and infotainment purposes. Points here for guests, interviews, creative audio, and other neato sound landscapes. (You may wish to supplement your vids with a "script," to demonstrate the time and attention you paid to production values.)

Social Media Influencer: What's on your mind FBuser?! Here, you will use a range of different social media tools (images, texts, vids, shares, conversations, events, etc.) to create a *four-week social media blast* (of at least two posts every other day—or at least 20 posts that mix media and up to 250 words of text). The goal is to change up, model, extend, or challenge the many different genres/constraints of social media for educational and infotainment purposes.

Auteur *Extraordinaire*: *Can you not see I'm working here?* This very serious solo genius will craft a long form creative nonfiction piece (of 15 or more pages) that draws on the course themes and readings. If you opt for this form you must complement our course readings with independent research and a bit of peer review/revision. (Plainly, this is to beef up the requirement, because the other options require that students sink time into work with fussy tech.) Be sure to identify your venue in advance: *The Atlantic*? *The New York Times* Sunday? *Peitho*? *College English*? The new public and cultural rhetorics journal, *Rhetoric, Politics & Culture*? *Longreads*?

That Upstart Blogger: Here Comes Everybody! I *dare you* to yawn yourself to death as you blog this one out. Create, revive, or retool a blog that takes up an issue a week for six weeks. Posts must be 850 words or more in length, citing from readings and making connections to other blogs, news stories, and online content. Your blogs should bring in all the best of blogging—pithy and/or experimental expression AND juicy, nuanced, well-evidenced/cited content.

My GRRL Friday News Writer: Extra! Extra! Your goal here is to share the scoop with *a series* written for a popular news source such as Inside Higher Ed or the Chronicle's pedagogical "blog." Your series should entail five weekly installments. Essays must be 950 words or more in length and make academic concepts central to our readings accessible for a broad academic audience. Your news articles should adhere to the highest ethical standards for journalist writing—that is, your content must be well evidenced, supported and reasoned.

I Dropped the Map. We Didn't Need It: You tell me what set of assignments you'd like to produce this semester. I'm looking for 20plus total pages and/or around 40 hours above our reading and writing activities. Go for it!

Notes: 1) All deliverables *must be public*. We will "show and tell" these via the BB discussion Forums over the course of the semester. 2) **POST ALL DELIVERABLES TO THE DISCUSSION BOARD. All other work comes to me via email**. 3) Please watch your time, closely—I worked to "even out" the time commitment and workload expectations for each option, but there's just no way to tell how long some of these projects might take. ***Go simple, go small, and go lower-tech, when in doubt.*** 4) If you miss a deadline or need to change your plan, please submit your work with a brief *description of your re-alignment and the "penalty" that you have incurred*. 5) Submit all work to me via email, because BB is the worst and we're only using it because we are required to. I will post sharing areas for us to "view" and/or share and comment on your deliverables.

Works Cited

Allen, Jan E. *The Productive Graduate Student Writer: A Guide to Managing Your Process, Time, and Energy to Write Your Research Proposal, Thesis, and Dissertation, and Get Published*. Stylus Publishing, LLC, 2019.

Alexander, Jonathan, Susan C. Jarratt, and Nancy Welch, editors. *Unruly Rhetorics: Protest, Persuasion, and Publics*. U of Pittsburgh P, 2018.

Alexander, Jonathan, and Jacqueline Rhodes. "Queerness, Multimodality, and the Possibilities of Re/Orientation." *Composing Media Composing Embodiment*, edited by Kristin L. Arola and Anne Frances Wysocki, UP of Colorado, 2012.

Alexander, Jonathan, and Susan C. Jarratt. "Introduction." Alexander et al., pp. 3-23.

Arola, Kristin L., and Anne Frances Wysocki, eds. *Composing (Media) = Composing (Embodiment): Bodies, Technologies, Writing, the Teaching of Writing.* Utah State UP, 2012.

Batt, Tom. "Using Play to Teach Writing." *American Journal of Play,* 2010, pp. 62-81.

Badenhorst, Cecile, Brittany Amell, and James Burford. *Re-imagining Doctoral Writing.* The WAC Clearinghouse; University Press of Colorado, 2021.

Brooks-Gillies, Marilee, Elena G. Garcia, Soo Hyon Kim, Katie Manthey, and Trixie G. Smith. *Graduate Writing Across the Disciplines: Identifying, Teaching, and Supporting.* The WAC Clearinghouse; University Press of Colorado, 2020.

Burford, James, Brittany Amell, and Cecile Badenhorst. "Introduction: The Case for Re-imagining Doctoral Writing." Badenhorst, Amell, and Burford, pp. 3-28.

Cixous, Hélène. "The Laugh of the Medusa." Translated by Keith Cohen and Paula Cohen, *Signs,* vol. 1, no. 4, 1976, pp. 875-893.

Combs, Shane. "The Me I Don't Meet Unless: Life Writing, Play Studies, and an Untested Story." *How Stories Teach Us: Composition, Life Writing, and Blended Scholarship,* edited by Amy E. Robillard and D. Shane Combs, Peter Lang Verlag, 2019.

Daniel-Wariya, Joshua. "LUDIC RHETORICS: Theories of Play in Rhetoric and Writing Chapter." *Reinventing (with) Theory in Rhetoric and Writing Studies: Essays in Honor of Sharon Crowley,* edited by Andrea Alden, Kendall Gerdes, Judy Holliday, and Ryan Skinnell, University Press of Colorado; Utah State University Press, 2018, pp. 116-132.

Deleuze, Gilles and Felix Guattari. *A Thousand Plateaus.* University of Minnesota, 1980.

Eberle, Scott G. "The Elements of Play: Toward a Philosophy and a Definition of Play." *American Journal of Play,* vol. 6, no. 2, 2014, pp. 214-33.

Fergusson, Misty. "Harnessing Play for Mutual Humanization in the Classroom." *The English Journal* vol. 107, no. 6, 2018, pp. 43-47.

Halberstam, Jack. *The Queer Art of Failure.* Duke UP, 2011.

Hardee, Jay. "Irreverent Rhetorician 1.1: Lance Hart's *PervOut*." *YouTube,* 9 June 2020, https://youtu.be/6iOyAt5RFcY.

—. "Irreverent Rhetorician 1.2: Stonewall and the Rhetorical Riot." *YouTube,* 19 June 2020, https://youtu.be/YmvBdHt8Rgc.

—. "Irreverent Rhetorician 1.3: Tiggy Upland's Queer World-Making." *YouTube,* 12 July 2020, https://youtu.be/WnVb9RIm1wk.

—. "Irreverent Rhetorician 1.4: Intimate Sonic Publics and the Queer Voice." *YouTube,* 23 July 2020, https://youtu.be/PzMf3Q8brg8.

Hesse, Douglas. "The Place of Creative Writing in Composition Studies." *College Composition and Communication* vol. 62, no. 1, 2010, pp. 31-52.

Klein, Naomi. The Shock Doctrine: The Rise of Disaster Capitalism. Toronto: Alfred A. Knopf Canada, 2007.

Gee, James Paul. *Good Video Games and Good Learning: Collected Essays on Video Games, Learning and Literacy.* Peter Lang, 2007.

Graff, Gerald. "What We Say When We Don't Talk about Creative Writing." *College English* vol. 71, no. 3, 2009, pp. 271-79.

Jordan, Spencer. *Postdigital Storytelling: Poetics, Praxis, Research.* Routledge, 2020.

LaFollette, Kristin. "Constellating Arts-Based and Queer Approaches: Transgenre Composing in/as Writing Studies Pedagogy." *The Journal of Multimodal Rhetorics,* vol. 5, no. 2, 2021.

Lavery, Grace. "Making Graduate School Work for the Weirdos." *The Chronicle of Higher Education,* February 3, 2022.

Macke, Frank J. "Communication Left Speechless: A Critical Examination of the Evolution of Speech Communication as an Academic Discipline." *Communication Education,* vol 40, 1991, pp. 125-143.

Martin, Londie T. and Adela C. Licona. "Remix as Unruly Play and Participatory Method for Im/Possible Queer World-Making." Alexander et al., pp. 244-260.

Martinez, Aja. *Counterstory: The Rhetoric and Writing of Critical Race Theory.* NCTE, 2020.

Micciche, Laura. "Writing as feminist rhetorical theory." *Rhetorica in motion: Feminist Rhetorical Methods and Methodologies,* edited by Eileen Schelle and K. J. Rawson, University of Pittsburgh, 2010, pp. 173-188.

Molinari, Julia. "Re-imagining Doctoral Writings as Emergent Open Systems." Badenhorst, Amell, and Burford, pp. 49-69.

Muñoz, José Estaban. *Cruising Utopia: The Then and There of Queer Futurity.* New York UP, 2009.

Oleksiak, Timothy. "Queer Praxis for Peer Review." *College Composition and Communication,* vol. 72, no. 2, 2020, pp. 306-332.

Peary, Alexandria. "The Pedagogy of Creative Writing Across the Curriculum." *Creative Writing Pedagogies for the Twenty-first Century,* edited by Alexandria Peary and T.C. Hunley, Southern Illinois UP, 2015, pp. 342-389.

Powell, Malea. "2012 CCCC Chair's Address: Stories Take Place: A Performance in One Act." *College Composition and Communication,* vol. 64, no. 2, 2012, pp.383-406.

Powell, Malea, Daisy Levy, Andrea Riley-Mukavetz, Marilee Brooks-Gillies, Maria Novotny, and Jennifer Fisch-Ferguson. "Our Story Begins Here: Constellating Cultural Rhetorics." *Enculturation,* vol. 25, 2014.

Rhodes, Jacqueline and Jonathan Alexander. *Techne: Queer Meditations on Writing the Self.* Computers and Composition Digital Press, 2015.

Rhodes, Keith. "Seeing Writing Whole: The Revolution We Really Need." *Journal of the Assembly for Expanded Perspectives on Learning,* vol. 25, 2020, pp. 47-57.

Robbins, Tom. "In Defiance of Gravity." *Harper's Magazine.* Sep 2004, pp. 57-61.

Rouzie, Albert. "Beyond the Dialectic of Work and Play: A Serio-Ludic Rhetoric for Composition Studies." *JAC,* vol. 20, no. 3, 2000), pp. 627-658.

Simpson, Steve, Nigel A. Caplan, Michelle Cox, and Talinn Phillips. *Supporting Graduate Student Writers: Research, Curriculum, and Program Design.* University of Michigan Press, 2016.

Sirc, Geoffry. *English Composition as a Happening.* Utah State University Press, 2002.

Shipka, Jody. *Toward a Composition Made Whole.* University of Pittsburgh Press, *2011.*

Sullivan, Patricia Suzanne. *Experimental Writing in Composition: Aesthetics and Pedagogies.* University of Pittsburgh Press, 2012.

Sullivan, Patrick. *The UnEssay: Making Room for Creativity in the Composition Classroom. College Composition and Communication,* vol. 67, no. 1, 2015, pp. 6-34.

Sutton-Smith, Brian. "Evolving a Consilience of Play Definitions: Playfully." *Play and Culture Studies*, vol. 2, 1999, pp. 239–56.
Warner, Sara. *Acts of Gaiety: LGBT Performance the Politics of Pleasure*. U of Michigan P, 2013.
Watts, Eric King. "'Voice' and 'Voicelessness' in Rhetorical Studies." *Quarterly Journal of Speech*, vol. 87, no. 2, May 2001, pp. 179-196.
Welch, Nancy. "Informed, Passionate, and Disorderly: Uncivil Rhetoric in a New Gilded Age." Alexander et al., pp. 244-260.
Williams, Linda. "Pornography, Porno, Porn: Thoughts on a Weedy Field." *Porn Archives*, Eds. Squires, David, et al. *Porn Archives*. Durham, NC: Duke University Press, 2014. pp. 29-43

A View from Somewhere: Situating the Public Problem in Creative Writing Workshops

Erika Luckert

Abstract: *This essay is an effort to better situate the creative writing workshop in the diverse perspectives of its participants, by drawing on parallels between critiques of the writing workshop and critiques of the idealized public sphere. Habermas's idealized public sphere has been critiqued for privileging dominant identities, much as creative writing workshops have been critiqued for privileging white writers like me. In this essay, I begin by listening to the critiques and testimony of BIPOC writers, which reveal that workshops are hegemonic spaces that reproduce and magnify racist, sexist, and classist systems. By reading these testimonies in conversation with critiques of the public sphere, I underscore the structural nature of this problem: when issues of race and culture are ignored in writing workshops, not only do we fail to achieve the ideal of an equitable space, we actively reinforce the power imbalances that we insist on overlooking. If, instead of trying to create a culturally neutral space, we welcome the complex identities of our students into our workshops, many parts of our pedagogy may need to change. To begin this work, I use Donna Haraway's theory of situated knowledge to consider how we might workshop not with a pseudo-objective view, but with a "view from somewhere" instead. I suggest ways that author's notes and workshop letters may be used to practice a more situated workshop, where participants reflect on their own positionings and learn to be accountable for the feedback they give.*

I cannot think of any space in which I have learned more about writing, and about myself as a writer, than I have in writing workshops.

In my first creative writing workshop in college, the desks stretched in a horseshoe shape around the room so we could all see each other as we gave feedback on each other's writing. It was my only class that semester where every single student spoke, and the atmosphere was invigorating.

I loved workshops—so much so that I went on to pursue an MFA in creative writing. I loved sitting in a room talking with other writers; I loved reading the drafts of my peers and, around a seminar table, grasping for the words that could describe what it was that their writing did, and could do. As I talked my way through my peers' writing, I developed a vocabulary that would help me to better describe my own.

I loved listening too—even in workshops where the silence of the writer was not required, I would refrain from speech—a rare thing for me as a student who always thrived through active participation. Instead of speaking, I would fill the margins of my drafts with notes, sifting through the different opinions of my peers, working my way towards a fuller understanding of what I wanted my revisions to be.

In my thesis workshop, where six of us sat around the table for hours, sometimes workshopping past midnight, I relished those moments when our discussion, often meandering, veered towards consensus—that sense that we had solved something, arrived at the perfect revision, understood a piece of writing more completely.

I gained so much from workshops that even when I finished my MFA, even as I began to teach workshops myself, I kept at it—meeting with fellow writers in their living rooms, their kitchens, whatever corners of our small apartments could accommodate a handful of writers and their words.

I loved workshops, but as Matthew Salesses points out, what made workshops effective learning spaces for me are what can make them harmful spaces for others: "So many of the advantages workshop offers break down when a writer is in the workshop minority" ("Who's at the Center"). For me, a white, third-generation college student accustomed to speaking frequently in class, it was a new and productive educational experience to remain silent while my work was discussed. Over the years, I learned to jockey my way into male-dominated classroom conversations, interrupting, countering, and crafting authority in ways I learned from my own professor father at the dinner table. Listening during workshop was a valuable change for me. For a student who is often sidelined in classroom environments, though, it's easy to see how the workshop's "gag" rule could become an act of silencing that devalues the writer's authority over their own work rather than a productive exercise in listening (Kearns 794). As Salesses puts it, "The person who thinks she is in charge of her story is made to listen to other people telling her what her story is or should be" ("Who's at the Center"). Under these circumstances, the consensus of a workshop that I relished as a student might, to someone else, feel less thrilling and more like dismissal of an alternate view.

A workshop may feel impressively equitable, even ideal to a student in my position—after all, what other pedagogy has such active participation from all students? But problems arise when we fail to acknowledge and address the power structures at play. Salesses reminds us that "the workshop is incredibly persuasive, as power usually is" ("Who's at the Center"), but the powerful benefits for students like me can be harmful for queer students, students of color, or others in the minority. This is a problem that BIPOC writers have been talking about for years, but that those of us in the workshop majority—white, cis, abled, moneyed writers and teachers of writing—have not adequately recognized or addressed. It's a problem of power, which is always unequally distributed, and the way that power influences what each student can say and learn. This, of course, is not a problem unique to the workshop space. It is, however, a problem that is uniquely critical to address in these contexts, where many of our basic pedagogical habits and assumptions make it easier to sideline or even ignore the dynamics of race, gender, sexuality, class, and culture.

Many of these pedagogical habits and assumptions are rooted in the workshop's American history and the students it was made to serve in the early 1950s: predominantly white, male students returning to school on the GI Bill (Bennett). Though centered in a U.S. context, this history is influential enough that it shaped the workshops of my undergraduate education in Canada. In the Afterword of Anna Leahy's *Power and Identity in the Creative Writing Classroom,* Graeme Harper and Stephanie Vanderslice consider some of the differences among workshop traditions in different anglophone creative writing contexts, suggesting that we have a great deal to gain by mutual understanding and cooperation on a more global scale. With that in mind, I focus here on the North American workshops that have informed my own writing and teaching, contexts where, as Vanderslice notes, there is a need for the writing workshop to "respond to the educational landscape in which it currently exists instead of the one in which it was conceived over half a century ago" (30). We need to consider a much more diverse educational landscape: the students we are teaching now.

But what does it look like for the workshop to respond to more diverse populations? In D.G. Myer's 1996 history of creative writing, the question of responding to diverse students barely even makes it into the afterward, where he describes the "dilemma" as he sees it: "if the pronouncement of literary verdicts is really the social campaign to assign dominant status to a particular perspective, then any writing teacher who praises and faults student effort is surreptitiously trying to silence young ethnic writers in his [sic] class" (177). The history of creative writing that Myers tells is inherently white and predominantly male, bearing little resemblance to the contexts where I began teaching as a young woman poet and educator in New York City's public schools and colleges. Myers' response to the "dilemma" is not only inherently defeatist, absolving the (naturally, white male) teacher of responsibility, it also trivializes the experience of writers who may feel silenced in a writing workshop. In Tim Mayers' 2014 *Rewriting Craft*, minoritized writers in the workshop garner slightly more acknowledgement, but he stops his inquiry with the question: "Where, precisely, does one draw the lines between students' poems and their lives? Is it possible to do so in harmful or detrimental ways?" (146).

The short answer to Mayers' question is yes. But a more thorough answer is that creative writing teachers and facilitators need to listen to BIPOC writers' testimonials that describe the damaging or dangerous ways workshops have functioned. As a student and teacher who has thrived in these environments, it's a problem I need to reckon with. It's a problem all of us who rely on workshop pedagogy, regardless of genre, need to understand. Any time we gather a group of writers in a room, any time student writing is discussed by a group of peers, it's a problem that we become responsible for. Taking responsibility and responding to the current educational landscape means understanding the ways writing workshops are connected to structural systems of inequality. Philip Gross suggests that "a workshop is a small world, which reflects and refracts worlds outside" (61). In this "small world," I see reflections and refractions of the idealized public sphere as proposed by Jürgen Habermas, widely critiqued for its privileging of dominant identities, much as the workshop has been critiqued for privileging white students like me. This essay, then, is an effort to understand the parallels between critiques of the writing workshop and critiques of the idealized public sphere, and to use that understanding to remake a workshop responsive to the perspectives of its diverse participants.

Critiques of the Writing Workshop

While in many places I discuss, through critical discourse and my own experiences, the inequities in the writing workshop in terms of race, it is important to note that these injustices—like any experience of power—are intersectional. Junot Díaz's much-cited essay, "MFA vs. POC," drew public attention to the question of race in the writing workshop, and yet, reports by women of his misogyny and allegations of his sexual misconduct (Rivera; Alter, Bromwich, and Cave) remind us to interrogate the many ways that power may be used and abused in our workshops. What Díaz calls "the standard problem of MFA programs" might also be described as the standard problem of the university institution: "that shit was *too white*." In his essay, Díaz addresses two audiences: one who experiences this whiteness, and one that is unaware: "Some of you understand completely. And some of you ask: *Too white* . . . how?"

A chorus of other writers explain. In the November 2016 issue of *Acentos Review*, a special feature gave voice to the workshop experiences of Latinx writers in MFA programs. A student from Arizona writes, "when you are introduced to your cohort/ you start to see how colored you are/ contrasted against this background." From New Jersey, a student writes, "I wonder about the social class of my writing and readers." Another writes, "Everyone liked the story about the queer women, but didn't comment on their brown skin. These stories, my MFA says, are not for everyone." A Vermont Student describes "Cautiously picking workshops to minimize micro-aggressions,/ Insisting POC limit rant time about comments by other student or faculty so we can/ talk about our craft." Another in Texas writes, "you fear your implication in our pain, and so you deny it exists, and divorce your responsibility because to do so is easiest" ("Our MFA Experiences").

Many critiques of whiteness in the workshop, or accounts of the harm experienced by minority writers, come in the form of testimonial, of story. And so, even as they move us, they may seem too easy to dismiss—*that's not how it was in the workshops I took*, or, *that's not how it is in the workshops I teach*, I might tell myself. The work of scholars like Amy Robillard and Aja Martinez, though, remind me of the power that stories hold to expose the intersectional oppressions that are built into the very structures of our departments and classrooms. Martinez explains the critical role these stories play: "experiential knowledge of people of color is legitimate and critical to understanding racism that is often well disguised in the rhetoric of normalized structural values and practices" (3), (i.e., practices like the writing workshop). As we listen to the experiences of writers of color in the workshop, then, it's also important we hear the echoes of these stories in our own pedagogies. We need to consider the ways that our workshops are constructed to allow for, and even invite, these harmful experiences. To Díaz's description of the problem with the writing workshop—"that shit was *too white*"—I make this vital addendum which we must address to produce change: *This shit is structural.*

Salesses asks that we "think about the way in which the workshop mirrors the minority experience in real life" ("Who's at the Center"), while Díaz describes how his workshop "reproduced exactly the dominant culture's blind spots and assumptions around race and racism." While we may like to think of our workshops as safe spaces for nurturing creativity, or as pre-publication "test audiences," grappling with oppression in the workshop means understanding how such classes reproduce, mirror, and even magnify systemic racism, sexism, and classism. If a workshop reproduces structural racism, then we need to make counter-hegemonic choices that resist this. How do we stop replicating oppression and instead reconstruct a more equitable space? While our inclination as teachers may be to try and keep power dynamics out of our workshops, or to construct a neutral space for discussion, this pseudo-objectivity can mask dangerous and hegemonic pedagogies and prevent us from making ethical changes in our practice.

Critiquing the Workshop as an Idealized Public Sphere

To understand what is so dangerous about constructing workshops this way, it is useful to consider, as Rosa Eberly does, the parallels between writing classrooms and the idealized public sphere (171-172). The public sphere, proposed by Habermas, describes an idealized space in which private people discuss issues that concern them collectively. It is characterized by three institutional principals: first, a disregard of status in favor of "the parity of 'common humanity'"; second, a "domain of 'common concern,'" which forms the basis of the collective discussion; and third, a level of inclusivity and accessibility that allows everyone to participate (Habermas 36-37). As Eberly points out, "this model of public sphere can fit writing classrooms rather well" (171-172), and it may be especially illuminating in how well it fits the writing workshop, where we purportedly aim for an inclusive environment in which differences in power and status are "set aside" so that everyone might participate in the discussion of a topic of common concern: the writing itself. When put this way, the workshop, like Habermas's public sphere sounds ideal. But as public sphere theorists have pointed out, there is a profound flaw in this idealized construction.

Nancy Fraser explains it this way: "declaring a deliberative arena to be a space where extant status distinctions are bracketed and neutralized is not sufficient to make it so" (60). While the deliberative arena that she describes is much larger than a classroom, this premise applies equally to the smaller space of a writing workshop. As Salesses and Díaz suggest, a writing workshop is not separate or safe from the power imbalances of our larger society. Just like the public sphere Fraser describes, we may intend our workshops to be "open and admissible to all" (59), but simply arranging the desks in a horseshoe shape, and giving each student time to speak, as I experienced in my first undergraduate workshop, is not enough to create parity. That vision—of everyone sitting in a circle, on equal footing—while often constructive can also reinforces a false view: that we all come to the workshop from the same position, and with the same amount of power, or that power can be neutralized by mere intent and arrangement. But ignoring race and culture and leaving identity at the door in attempts to depoliticize our classes and make them safe not only fails to achieve the ideal of a space "open and admissible to all" it actively reinforces those power imbalances that we insist on overlooking. As Fraser reminds us, "bracketing" inequalities "does not foster participatory parity,"—instead, it "works to the advantage of dominant groups in society, and to the disadvantage of subordinates" (64).

The attempt to "bracket inequalities" is closely linked to another fundamental feature of the idealized public sphere for Fraser. It's worth considering her critique in full, for every instance of the words "public sphere" in Fraser's critique, we might equally read the word "workshop":

> The misplaced faith in the efficacy of bracketing suggests another flaw.... This conception assumes that a public sphere is or can be a space of zero degree culture, so utterly bereft of any specific ethos as to accommodate with perfect neutrality and equal ease interventions expressive of any and every cultural ethos. But this assumption is counterfactual, and not for reasons that are mere-

ly accidental. In stratified societies, unequally empowered social groups tend to develop unequally valued cultural styles. The result is the development of powerful informal pressures that marginalize the contributions of members of subordinated groups. (64)

In a writing workshop, those unequally valued cultural styles become what Rosalie Morales Kearns refers to as "implicit aesthetic norms" (797), unspoken yet influential ideas of what a poem or a story should be. In my MFA workshops, I relished those moments when we all came to agree on a revision to a poem—but Kearns asks me to consider what implicit aesthetic norms we enforced in order to reach that point of consensus: "When people have an aesthetic expectation that they have not examined or articulated but nevertheless use in judging others' works, they do not have to explore the implications of their historically and culturally specific expectations; rather, they can believe that their judgements merely reflect universal standards of what constitutes good art" (798). Felicia Rose Chavez puts it more sharply: such people "wield bias as a weapon, mistaking ego for objectivity" (134). In other words, just as in the idealized public sphere that Fraser critiques, these unarticulated, normalized cultural styles can act as an oppressive force in the workshop. As in the idealized public sphere, these dominant styles or norms in classrooms are often denied through the universalizing impulse Fraser identifies. The result of pretending neutrality is the further marginalization of those we would claim to accommodate. The workshop Díaz describes was effectively race-blind: "we never explored our racial identities or how they impacted our writing—at all." Octavio Pimental, Charise Pimental, and John Dean explain how "the myth of the race-neutral writing classroom" is based on logics of colorblindness and meritocracy which "usually translates into classroom practices that build upon and bestow neutral [white] students' cultural, linguistic, and racial knowledge."

Even without any explicit mention of identity or race, Tim Mayers echoes this experience: "nearly all the creative writing courses I have taken have focused so sharply on the student text as to obscure any questions about whether, and how, the individual student text might fit into a larger textual network." This focus on the text as isolated from author and context is rooted in the ideas of the New Critics. In the U.S. in the late 1930s, at the same time as the Iowa workshop was forming, New Criticism was taking hold in English Studies, and the feeling among the New Critics, many of whom were poets too, was that creative writing and this form of criticism went hand in hand (Myers 132-133). The idea that we should treat writing "objectively," discussing only the text, without consideration of its histories, identities, or culture, has persisted in English Studies and influenced creative writing workshops. The result is the obscuring of race, identity, and social context that contributes to experiences such as the one described below:

> Situacíon: You are an artist. You create from la vida. Life is being Chican@, a poly-identity; you write to make sense of this & heal & heal others, hopefully. You cannot stop thinking in stories, meanwhile seeing the master story give praise to the white artists. You still ask yourself why these artists rally against diversity like you're taking away their favorite toy. You ask your mamá, why does history repeat itself? You don't want to forget.

My MFA says they can't wait until I write stories for non-Latinos. ("Our MFA Experiences")

Fraser emphasizes that "these pressures are amplified, rather than mitigated" (64) by a system which presumes to create a space of zero culture, which presumes that inequalities and even identity can be tidily bracketed away. We should be wary of an impulse to neutralize culture—for this Chican@ student who understands their writing as created from their own poly-identity, efforts to bracket inequalities become a "rally against diversity." As Noor Naga and Robert McGill put it, "when the cultural backgrounds of workshop participants are taken for granted, members of minority groups are liable to be further marginalized" (71).

From Public Sphere to Pedagogy

When we permit the complex identities of our students into our workshops, our pedagogies need to change. In "Negotiating Cultural Difference in Creative Writing Workshops," Noor and McGill, a creative writing student and workshop instructor, respectively, write about what that looked like in their class at the University of Toronto. They focus on several "axioms" of creative writing pedagogy that they believe should be reconsidered to better serve diverse writers. The adage "show don't tell" assumes a common cultural repertoire where a reader makes meaning from the "shown," while "find your voice" is advice that always comes "in relation to culturally dominant models of speaking." Through dialogue, Noor and McGill "consider how creative writing pedagogy might avoid replicating problematic social dynamics," especially where, "in the face of oppression and marginalization, the axioms of creative writing courses can be daunting for many writers" (70). I don't pretend that workshop is a monolithic method or that problems always manifest in the same way. But Naga and McGill show us one way of beginning the work of unravelling the writing workshop to reveal damaging effects of individual actions and pedagogical assumptions.

If we examine how the idealized public sphere is reflected in our workshops, we might reconsider how we conceive of "The Reader." In "'The Reader' vs. POC," Salesses notes that in workshop when we refer to "The Reader," we often mean "someone with a standard set of expectations." The result, Salesses argues, is "singular perspective." The singular perspective of "The Reader" may be every bit as flawed as the idealized conception of a singular public, in that both deny the multiplicity of identities and perspectives in a group of people. Salesses writes, "the way 'the reader' is discussed makes the reader white (and cis and straight and, often, male)" ("The Reader vs. POC"). It is under these circumstances that "deliberation can serve as a mask for domination" (Fraser 64). Or, as Salesses explains, "When the group critiques a piece of writing from the position of a single normative reader, when it claims that art speaks to 'universal' truths as if truth is not cultural, it demands that difference, individual difference, be erased or exaggerated." In my composition classes, I often find myself writing in the margins of a student draft—*who is we?* or *which people?* When I ask my composition students to consider their intended audience for an essay, they often begin with an assumption of universality: *people in general?* they might suggest. And yet, even in writing this essay, I have caught myself in the same patterns, writing "we" where I mean "I," assuming that you, my reader, have an experience of the world that mirrors my own. This singular, normative perspective of the reader is part of the problem of erasure embedded in the very assumptions workshops are constructed on. How then, as teachers, do we begin to deconstruct the whiteness of the writing workshop, and even reconstruct a more equitable model?

Mayers suggests we turn to other pedagogical options: "activities that, as a supplement to workshops, would allow for sustained reflection on the very enterprise of creative writing as it relates to larger social, political, and rhetorical trends" (148). While supplemental activities can bring identity and culture into the room and help students to position their writing in social and political contexts, this alone is likely insufficient to address the complexity of students responding to one another's work. Naga and McGill look for ways to reclaim the workshop, suggesting that "the inevitable multiplicity of backgrounds and cultural expertise among students and instructors alike is an impetus for authority sharing and dialogue about difference" (71). While they offer examples of what that dialogue might look like, the workshop they describe remains largely the same in its basic construction. And as Audre Lorde teaches us, when we use only the existing tools, tools that are racist and patriarchal in origin, then "only the most narrow perimeters of change are possible" (101).

Matthew Salesses aims to invert our existing tools, reversing the conventional workshop model which centers the workshoppers who speak and give feedback. He aims to "teach the workshop to resist the very rules it sets itself," and constructs a workshop where, instead of giving suggestions, the workshoppers ask questions of the writer, centering the writer's authority. While I can see the potential value in this approach, as someone teaching now in a predominantly white institution in the Midwest, I wonder what the consequences of Salesses' model might be when the writer being centered is white, cis, and male. Does this model leave room for BIPOC readers to voice concern over stereotypes in a text, or even racist content? Salesses' model resists centering "The Reader" by centering the writer instead, and if I conceive of a workshop in terms of "The Reader" and the writer, in terms of workshoppers and workshoppee, then Salesses' inversions seem like the only possible change. But what if I consider the identities that my students hold in a workshop as more fluid or complex—as being *always* both readers and writers whose cultured, gendered, raced, and classed experiences enter into the way that they interact with any text, whether their own or that of a peer?

By recalling that the workshop mirrors the problems Fraser and others have critiqued in the public sphere, I can see other avenues for reconstruction. Fraser suggests that while "participatory parity" may be an impossible ideal in settings (like a writing workshop) where power is unequally distributed, we may nonetheless move towards this goal if we model our interactions not on a single comprehensive public, but on a multiplicity of competing publics. Fraser's vision of multiple publics is overlapping and intersectional, much like the identities that assemble in a writing workshop. Can we change the single normative reader into a multiplicity of readers instead? How might our workshops change as a result? To imagine an answer to this question, I turn to Donna Haraway's theory of feminist objectivity often cited in critique of the Habermasian public sphere. Haraway's theory suggests that, rather than centering or decentering the writer and their readers, we should *situate* them. She argues that objectivity can only happen in specific embodied ways: "only partial perspective promises objective vision" (583). In other words, there is no "universal" or "neutral" or zero culture view that might give us an objective evaluation of a piece of writing. Rather, the way that we approach any question, any poem, or story, or essay draft, is from our own situated perspective. We can achieve a more conscious subjectivity by making the partial nature of our perspectives explicit.

The problem with "The Reader" is the claim of "standard" or "normative" views that a monolithic reader implies. As Haraway might describe it, "The Reader" is a "god trick," a means "of being nowhere while claiming to be everywhere equally" (583), thus absolving oneself of responsibility as a situated individual. Similarly, constructing workshops as zero culture spaces is an attempt to be nowhere, to efface the complex dynamics of culture and power. Guided by Haraway, we might conceive of the workshop instead as an assembly of readers, each with their own partial perspective. As Chavez describes it, "Your valuable insights spring not from immovable truth, but from biased perspective; your body, culture, class, and privilege influence your knowledge construction" (116). The goal of situating knowledge is not to limit our own views of a piece of writing or to make our perspectives unchangeable. Rather, Haraway suggests that a situated approach would "allow us to become answerable for what we learn how to see" (583), to "interrogate positionings and be accountable" (586). Applied to the workshop, Haraway's theory of situated knowledge prompts us not to construct our workshops as an idealized and ultimately hegemonic public sphere, but to map the situated perspectives of each individual in a workshop room—whether reader or writer (and in a workshop, are we not always both?). How might we workshop in a situated way with a "view from somewhere"?

Situating the Writing Workshop

Scholars in composition studies help me imagine what a situated critique, or a situated workshop, might be. Charles Lesh sees possibilities for workshops to be "permeable and potentially responsive to [students'] identities and rhetorical needs inside and outside of the classroom" (96). Deborah Britzman discusses the way in which reading practices can produce normativity, and proposes an alternative—thinking of reading practices (and I might add, workshopping practices) "as problems of opening identifications, of working the capacity to imagine oneself differently precisely with respect to how one encounters another, and in how one encounters the self" (297). When I think of what it might mean to workshop with a view from somewhere, I rifle back through my own workshop experiences, looking for moments which feel more (or less) situated to me. As Haraway teaches me, this partial view—this view from my own position—may still be valuable, if I can acknowledge its limitations.

I think of my small group of MFA classmates who gathered, for many years after graduation, in kitchens, in living rooms, often, for lack of furniture, sitting on the floor. The feedback that I got in that workshop was so valuable to me in part because it was, if not explicitly, certainly implicitly situated—it was situated by my knowledge of each person in the room, as writers, as friends. They weren't "the reader"—they were Michael, Tyler, and Alex. I knew their writing, where they grew up, what books they were reading, what beer they would order at the neighborhood bar. I knew, too, what their tendencies were in responding to a poem—I could count on Michael to help me unravel an image, on Tyler to probe for strangeness in syntax, on Alex to search a tightly crafted poem for its emotional, vulnerable core. And they knew enough about me, and my writing, to approach my work in a way that felt attuned to my needs.

In our classrooms, we don't have the benefit of that accrued knowledge to situate workshop critique—our students don't know each other's aesthetic priorities or feedback tendencies. They may not even know their own. Indeed, in a recent composition course, my students expressed trepidation around precisely this challenge. In that class, I assigned writing groups of three to four students who would work together for a full semester, hoping that this would help them build some of that valuable situatedness and rapport. Near the beginning of the semester, we read "The Thursday Night Writing Group," a multi-voiced essay describing the influence of a years-long writing workshop on its members (Beckstead et al.). I chose the piece because I heard in it echoes of my own workshop experiences—I wanted to give my students a glimpse of what a group of writers could do together. Reading the essay, my students admired the levels of accrued knowledge that the writers in that group had about each other—one of the members writes, "over time the group came to sense the type of responses I needed throughout the process" (192). But my students wondered how they would manage such familiarity themselves. One student reflected, "I am hoping that our small writing groups are going to be able to achieve this in the short time we have together. I am worried writing groups will only give positive feedback instead of constructive criticism at first for fear of hurting someone's feelings."

Here, it is worth noting that the only type of response this student can imagine is constructive criticism—a form of response that is inherently embedded in most workshop structures. Constructive criticism, though it may take different forms, carries the insinuation of objectivity: a nice way to correct a person, to set them on the right aesthetic path. But if our goal is not objectivity, but situatedness, then other forms of response might become valuable. Joy Castro, for example, uses Peter Elbow's technique of "pointing," asking every student in the workshop to read striking lines or phrases without any critique or commentary at all. Another of Elbow's techniques, "movies of a reader's mind," might be more situated—asking each workshop member to describe what happens inside their head as they read a draft (Elbow and Belanoff 44). And yet, given the pervasiveness of the idea of "the reader," this approach may need adaptation to emphasize the value of multiple readers, of multiple movies and minds. Although Salesses' models are mostly centered on some form of critique, he does probe more divergent possibilities too—using scissors and tape, drawing, or mapping the piece of writing (*Craft in the Real World* 137-138).

I return, though, to my student's other concern—"the short time we have together." In many of the early composition classes that I taught, I only found time for students to workshop or exchange peer feedback between one and three times in a semester—a short time indeed. Even in a creative writing class, where students often spend more time workshopping than in a composition course, a 15-week semester limits the accrual of situated knowledge that I experienced in my post-MFA workshop. Simply trusting that our students will "get to know each other" as a semester unfolds may not be enough. What might we do? To answer, I turn again to my own situated experiences.

Situating Writing with Author's Notes

In that post-MFA workshop, when we decided, after months of workshopping packets of poems, to turn our attention to our full-length manuscripts, we changed our method. We needed some way to signal to each other where we stood, where our manuscripts stood, so that we could offer useful critique on such substantial projects. Up until that point, we had given each other no context for our work—simply sending each other a file with a handful of poems. But when we sent our full manuscripts to each other, we included an extra page at the beginning, a letter addressed to the group.

Dearest Poets,

Here it is, my manuscript that I have been at times toiling over, and at times leaving fallow. I've been in a cycle for a while now of revisiting it roughly every four months, and at that juncture, making a few changes to order and sometimes cutting or adding a couple poems. This to say that there have been many changes, but small and slow ones spread over a long time. It's been a long while since I've had anyone else read this (besides contest judges), so I'm especially interested to hear how it reads as a collection, what the arcs or threads are that hold it together, and what the experience of reading it is in this form. What does the current order do to you as a reader? Are there places that feel less inevitable/that might need to be shifted?

As for the poems themselves, many of them will be familiar, though there are a few that I think have never seen workshop. I think the manuscript is about the size and length that I want it to be, but if there are poems that are clear weaklings and I should give up, please tell me. I don't have other poems on file that feel like they belong in this manuscript (much of what I've been writing lately feels separate from this project), but if there are gaps, or a style/type of poem that you think might help the balance – more of a particular color/texture/tone, I'd love to know that too so that I can think about writing to fill that gap.

Mostly, I'm grateful for your reading this, and helping me to find its form.

By this point, many of us were composition teachers, too, and so the move to include an author's note felt natural, even though it broke with workshop tradition in a number of ways. We understood that we wanted to be able to shape each other's responses to our work, that this in fact was part of what we gathered together in workshop to do.

Reading back over my author's note, I see a number of situating moves. I've told my peers where I am in my writing process, what other feedback I've gotten, and what questions I have for them as readers. Those questions are posed to suggest I expect a range of responses—they are even, perhaps, posed because they are the type of questions that wouldn't lead to consensus but rather to descriptive response. I've also made clear what type of prescriptive feedback I'm open to, and what type I'm unlikely to consider.

It's easy for me to imagine, looking back at this piece of writing, how this could become an assignment for my creative writing students. *When you send us your poems, include an author's note that tells us....*

While author's notes are a commonly used tool in composition classes, they are often positioned as a means of communication between the student and teacher, a sort of commentary on the draft that a teacher is about to grade. In fact, in one of the earliest publications referencing this strategy, it is called a "student-teacher memo" (Sommers). In the case of a workshop where the note is intended to situate the draft, then the note must be addressed not to the facilitator, but to the group of peers.

Any practiced participant in creative writing workshops will notice that an author's note works against one of the most commonly held tenets of a creative writing workshop: the silence of the writer. Not only is the writer traditionally asked not to speak during workshop discussion, they are asked not to preface their work or provide commentary in any way. Even in composition, Elbow echoes this common approach, urging writers to "bite your tongue" (101). One purported purpose of the writer's silence is to prevent them from somehow "spoiling" the reader's objective perspective on the work. If we accept, however, that the notion of a singular, objective reader's view is a "god trick," (Haraway 581), an impossibility that enforces inequality in our classrooms, then this argument for the writer's silence loses its footing. As Haraway suggests, there is no singular objective reading, only multiple partial perspectives that gain value by their situatedness. Indeed, I would argue that it is this assembly of multiple perspectives that gives workshops their enduring worth. The writer's silence not only presumes a singular objective reader, it also implies a sameness among a workshop's writers. Why would a writer need to speak if everyone in a workshop seeks the same sort of feedback, or has the same goals for their writing? If, though, we admit the diverse identities and situations of our students into the workshop space, then we need to account for the different priorities that our students have in their writing.

Instead of worrying about a writer's speech spoiling the readers' "objective" views, we might consider the ways a writer's direction can situate work for the diverse readers in a workshop, each with their own approach and positionality. An author's note is a way of giving the writer voice, of insisting that their own contexts for their work— racial, cultural, gendered, situated in intersecting ways—matter. Contextualizing and situating your own work is not automatic or easy; it is a learned skill. When I reread the author's note I wrote, I also see the things that I chose not to say. I didn't explain how I had decided to sequence the poems, because I wanted to know how someone else would describe that organization. I didn't ask the most burning question I had, *is this good enough?* because I knew it would only encourage my friends to reassure me instead of offering the critique that I desired. Over many years in workshops, I've learned to consider what I do and do not say, and how to ask for feedback that will be useful to me. If we ask our students to write an author's note to accompany their writing, we will need to help them consider the choices within it, and allow them opportunities to try situating their work in different ways.

Situating Feedback in Workshop Letters

When I moved away from New York, I left that post-MFA workshop behind, and I missed the feedback that had become so valuable to me. The first workshop that I took part in here in Nebraska felt like a big risk—suddenly, I was in a room full of people who knew nothing about my poems, and close to nothing about me. Would my poems still matter to them? Would their feedback still matter to me? This, I realize, is the position that our students are in every semester when they enter a new workshop.

When I brought my manuscript to this new group of peers, even though it wasn't asked for, I included an author's note in an attempt to offer some situating context to these new readers. The most valuable feedback I received in reply was feedback that was situated too. Feedback that told me something not only about their reaction to the work, but about where they were coming from as readers. Two of my peers opened their letters with a reference to their own grief, explaining how that impacted their reading of my work:

> "since I am so much in grief, it was difficult for me to read with a critical eye. Before I jump into the few critiques I do have to offer, I just want to say thank you, truly."

> "I am currently still deep in the throes of grief related to suicide, so while I found this manuscript hard to read on a personal level, I also found it beautiful and healing.... With all of that in mind, I tried to be as critical as possible while also taking care of myself."

Reading their notes, I was moved, not simply by the compliment, but by the way they made visible their personal point of connection to my poems. I realized that, for all of the many workshops these poems had seen, I'd never been told what it was like to read my manuscript—a manuscript about grief—from the position of someone grieving. It is little wonder, really, given that we were always taught that workshop was supposed to be impersonal, objective, focused on the writing instead of the writer. Feedback like this, as personal and partial a perspective as it offered, did something important for me, and for a manuscript I had been toiling over for years: it reminded me *why* I was writing it. I realized that, like my composition student, I hadn't known to ask for anything outside of constructive criticism. I hadn't known to ask for the subjectivity of my readers—I was so used to cultivating a distance from my work that I was missing something I needed just as much: closeness and vulnerability.

Other peers situated their responses to my manuscript by explaining how they approached it in the context of their own poetic expectations, making explicit those types of "implicit aesthetic norms" that Kearns describes:

> "I've read a lot of books about grief, but this book doesn't feel like it's so much about grief as it *is* grief."

> "Project books have felt trendy the last few years, perhaps because they're easy to say compelling things about on Twitter or to explicate in book reviews, and reading for contests you see a lot of books that seem like a good idea for a

short series of poems that has just been hammered into the ground. Yet [this manuscript] feels to me like it could only have emerged organically through the kind of patient labor so many of the poems describe, the daily contemplation, meditation, invention."

The simple act of making these expectations visible helped me in reading the rest of the feedback in each letter. I understood that the first reader was viewing my manuscript in conversation with other books they had read about grief, and that the second reader was viewing it in relation to other project books—this helped me situate their responses, and make use of them, regardless of whether I considered my manuscript to be a project book, a grief book, or something else.

Workshop letters are commonplace in creative writing workshops, so commonplace that sometimes we may forget to consider what work we want them to do. They are evidence of our students' preparation for a workshop, or a way for students to give individual feedback before the groupthink of workshop discussion kicks in. Reflecting on the workshop letters I've received, I wonder how we might better use those letters as a second point of opportunity to, as Haraway says, "interrogate positionings and be accountable" (586). If an author's note allows the writer to situate their draft and the way we approach it, then a workshop letter allows each reader to situate themselves in relation to the writing. It's an opportunity for us to "become answerable for what we learn how to see" (Haraway 583), to make explicit our partial perspective. These are difficult things to do, and especially difficult to do live, in a dynamic workshop discussion. Integrating these ideas into the workshop letter allows more time for reflection and practice, for students to consider what type of reader they are or want to be. But because the workshop letter is so commonplace, we may need to do more to guide the assignment to encourage students' reflection on their own perspectives, and situate their feedback as coming *from somewhere.*

When I think of the workshop letters I've written and received, almost all of them follow roughly the same expected formula. Begin with descriptive feedback, move to prescriptive suggestions. Or, begin with praise, move to critique. In assigning workshop letters to my students, unsurprisingly, I've carried forward this pattern. Indeed, I think there's a lot to value in it. But what would a workshop letter look like if the first direction was *begin with a view from somewhere*? I'd need to revise my assignment language to guide my students there:

> **Workshop Letter Assignment, 1st Revision***
>
> **italics* indicate new assignment language, ~~strikethroughs~~ indicate cuts to old assignment language
>
> ---
>
> Compose a letter to the writer. Begin with Dear _____, and then continue.
>
> In the first part of your letter, ~~describe the piece as you understand it.~~ *tell the writer where you're coming from as a reader. What perspectives, interests, or expectations are you bringing to their work?* You might talk about your experience reading the piece~~., and offer a summary. What is the piece about? What happens?~~ What words would you use to describe it? How does it make you feel?
>
> In the second part of your letter, offer some praise. Talk about ~~what is working well, or~~ what you enjoyed as a reader, and why. Be as specific as possible – you might include quotes or point to specific passages or features of the piece.
>
> Finally, finish your letter with a question or two that might help the writer continue working on this piece. As a reader, what do you remain curious about? Is there something that leaves you confused? Where are you left wondering? Is there something they might expand?

This revision is both imperfect and untested, but I want to pay attention to the language I needed to shift. First, I decided that I needed to ask explicitly about the expectations a reader was bringing to the work—I wanted to open space for the type of personally situated feedback that I received on my manuscript. Second, I decided to remove the ubiquitous workshop phrase: what is working well? I realized that it might invite students to pretend a sort of objective authority or knowledge of what "working" looks like. As Mary Ann Cain writes, "'what works' is defined by an unassumed, often unarticulated understanding of the social that tends to reproduce itself along dominant images of gender, race, class, and other underrepresented identities" (222). It's worth noting that these are small changes of language, and they may not be enough to encourage students—especially those with considerable workshop experience—to shift beyond the habit of pretending objectivity in their responses to each other's work.

I find myself dissatisfied, too, with my lack of revisions in the final paragraph, and especially to the direction to offer "a question or two that might help the writer continue working on this piece." Why should a student be guessing what might help their peer, when they could read an author's note that would guide them? Perhaps the most impactful revision, then, would be to frame this workshop letter not as a response to the writing, but as a response to the writer. If students write author's notes that situate their work and pose questions to open space for multiple perspectives, then the workshop letter need only be a thoughtful and thorough reply to the author's note. In my composition classes, this is already the approach I take, and so this second revision borrows some language from those assignments:

> **Workshop Letter Assignment, 2nd Revision**
>
> Compose a letter to the writer in response to their author's note. Begin with Dear _____, and then continue.
>
> In the first part of your letter, tell the writer where you're coming from as a reader. What perspectives, interests, or expectations are you bringing to their work? You might talk about your experience reading the piece. What words would you use to describe it? How does it make you feel?
>
> In the second part of your letter, respond to the questions and concerns that the writer outlined in their author's note. Be as specific as possible – you might include quotes or point to specific passages or features of the piece. Even if they didn't ask for it directly, you will likely want to offer some praise. Talk about what you enjoyed as a reader, and why.

Just as an author's note requires practice to become valuable, so too does a workshop letter—I've found it useful, early in a class, to give feedback not on student's creative work, but on the workshop letters they offer to each other. It may also be useful to frame a class discussion around the opening paragraphs of students' letters, allowing them to notice and appreciate differences among their situated views and to map how their partial perspectives contribute to the workshop, rather than looking for ways to arrive at consensus.

Practicing a Partial View

While I've discussed the value of authors' notes and workshop letters from the writer's position, I want to consider them from the position of a reader responding too. A few months after that first Nebraska workshop, I joined a small peer writing group. One member, another poet, asked me for feedback on some of his poems. Despite my years of workshopping experience, I felt hesitant. His work dealt with his personal experience as an adopted child, a trans person, a parent, and someone from the American south. If you mapped our situated perspectives, beyond the fact that we had both wound up in Lincoln, Nebraska for graduate school, we couldn't have been further apart. What could I have to offer to his work? When I opened his document, I was grateful to see that he had included small author's notes with each poem—questions, concerns, scraps of information to situate me. *I'm curious about the structure of this poem. What will make this poem stand out more? What is the relationship you see between the "she" and the "me"? Is the start dead weight? Can this poem be saved?* With these questions in hand, I felt much more confident in my own response, and what's more, I understood why he was bringing the poems to me, why he wanted an outside eye, a partial vision different from his own.

Our students are often in this spot—wondering if they have feedback worth offering, or fearful that they will stumble in responding to someone they've only just met. We can provide opportunities for them to approach that process more responsibly, by emphasizing their situated positions. When my composition student worried that writing groups would play it safe and stick to compliments, she was recognizing a common trend in creative writing workshops too. If instead we teach our students to ask for the kind of feedback they want, and to respond in a way that takes responsibility for their own partial view, then not only are we resisting that damaging assumption of a dominant reader, we are teaching them to be reflective about and ultimately accountable for the feedback that they give. But author's notes and workshop letters are both practices assigned outside of class that students write in preparation for entering the risky space of a workshop. Can notes and letters solve dynamic problems that happen live, in every conversation among students?

The honest answer is: no. But they can reconstruct our thinking as readers and writers (and indeed, as teachers) entering that workshop space. Both author's notes and workshop letters help writers and readers communicate. They give the writer a voice, and the writing a context, instead of presenting writing as race-neutral, in a zero-culture space. And they ask each person to respond to that writer and that context—not as a neutral or objective reader, but as another situated individual, someone writing from somewhere, who is responsible for their readings too. As such, I think they may be a valuable first step for my teaching.

These communications also serve a reflective purpose. Sandra Giles discusses the ways author's notes can help students reflect on and develop the intentions and aims of their writing. This type of thinking, according to Kathleen Yancey and Jane Smith, can also be a "method for assigning both responsibility and authority to a learner" (qtd. in Giles 198). In this way, an author's note gives the writer the authority and agency that both Salesses and Kearns advocate for. And it allows a writer the reflective space not always available in the quick dynamics of a workshop conversation. Workshop letters, which we may think of as simply a means of giving feedback, also encourage reflection. Writing a workshop letter where you are asked to describe your own perspectives, interests, or expectations in approaching a draft requires taking time to consider what those expectations are, and to take responsibility for them. To borrow Britzman's words, writing a workshop letter might be a moment "to imagine oneself differently precisely with respect to how one encounters another" (297). In a workshop tradition that imagines the reader and the writer—indeed, the public—as white, cis, straight, and male, these notes and letters might offer one way to rewrite how we imagine and encounter each other—and by extension, each other's writing.

Works Cited

"Our MFA Experiences." *The Acentos Review,* November 2016, https://www.acentosreview.com/November_2016/our-mfa-experiences.html

Alter, Alexandra, Jonah Engel Bromwich, and Damien Cave. "The Writer Zinzi Clemmons Accuses Junot Díaz of Forcibly Kissing Her." *New York Times,* 14 May 2018, https://www.nytimes.com/2018/05/04/books/junot-Díaz-accusations.html

Beckstead, Linda, Kate Brooke, Robert Brooke, Kathryn Christensen, Dale Jacobs, Heidi LM Jacobs, Carol McDaniels, and Joan Ratcliff. "The Thursday Night Writing Group: Crossing Institutional Lines." *Writing Groups Inside and Outside the Classroom,* edited by Beverly J. Moss, Nels P. Highberg, and Melissa Nicolas, IWCA Press, 2004, pp. 187-205.

Bennett, Eric. *Workshops of Empire: Stegner, Engle, and American Creative Writing During the Cold War.* University of Iowa Press, 2015.

Britzman, Deborah P. "Queer Pedagogy and Its Strange Techniques." *Counterpoints*, vol. 367, 2012, pp. 292–308.

Cain, Mary Ann. "'A Space of Radical Openness': Re-Visioning the Creative Writing Workshop." Donnelly, pp. 216-229.

Castro, Joy. "Racial and Ethnic Justice in the Creative Writing Course." *Gulf Coast*, Fall 2015. https://gulfcoastmag.org/online/fall-2015/racial-and-ethnic-justice-in-the-creative-writing-course/

Chavez, Felicia Rose. *The Anti-Racist Writing Workshop: How to Decolonize the Creative Classroom.* Haymarket Books, 2021.

Díaz, Junot. "MFA vs. POC." *The New Yorker*, 30 April 2014. https://www.newyorker.com/books/page-turner/mfa-vs-poc

Donnelly, Dianne, editor. *Does the Writing Workshop Still Work?*, Multilingual Matters, 2010.

Eberly, Rosa A. "From Writers, Audiences, and Communities to Publics: Writing Classrooms as Protopublic Spaces ." *Rhetoric Review*, vol. 18, no. 1, 1999, pp. 165–78.

Elbow, Peter. *Writing without Teachers.* Oxford University Press, 1973.

Elbow, Peter and Pat Belanoff. *Sharing and Responding.* Random House, 1989.

Fraser, Nancy. "Rethinking the Public Sphere: A Contribution to the Critique of Actually Existing Democracy." *Social Text*, vol. 26, no. 25/26, 1990, p. 56-80.

Gross, Philip. "Small Worlds: What Works in Workshops If and When They Do?" Donnelly, pp. 52-62.

Habermas, Jürgen. *The Structural Transformation of the Public Sphere : an Inquiry into a Category of Bourgeois Society.* 1st MIT Press pbk., MIT Press, 1991.

Haraway, Donna. "Situated Knowledges: The Science Question in Feminism and the Privilege of Partial Perspective." *Feminist Studies*, vol. 14, no. 3, 1988, pp. 575–99.

Harper, Graeme and Stephanie Vanderslice. "The Reason It Is; The Rhyme It Isn't." *Power and Identity in the Creative Writing Classroom*, edited by Anna Leahy, Multilingual Matters, 2005, pp. 205-214.

Kearns, Rosalie Morales. "Voice of Authority: Theorizing Creative Writing Pedagogy." *College Composition and Communication*, vol. 60, no. 4, 2009, pp. 790–807.

Lesh, Charles N. "Writing Workshops in the Public Turn." *Composition Studies*, vol. 2, no. 156, 2019, pp. 87–107.

Lorde, Audre. *Sister Outsider.* 1984. Penguin Books, 2020.

Martinez, Aja. *Counterstory: The Rhetoric and Writing of Critical Race Theory.* SWR, 2020.

Mayers, Tim. *(Re)Writing Craft: Composition, Creative Writing, and the Future of English Studies.* University of Pittsburgh Press, 2014.

Myers, David G. *The Elephants Teach: Creative Writing Since 1880.* Prentice Hall, 1996.

Naga, Noor, and Robert McGill. "Negotiating Cultural Difference in Creative Writing Workshops." *Pedagogy*, vol. 18, no. 1, 2018, pp. 69–86.

Pimental, Octavio, Charise Pimental, and John Dean. "The Myth of the Colorblind Writing Classroom: White Instructors Confront White Privilege in their Classrooms." *Performing Antiracist Pedagogy in Rhetoric, Writing, and Communication*, edited by

Frankie Condon and Vershawn Ashanti Young, University Press of Colorado, 2017, pp. 109-122.

Rivera, Alisa. "On Junot Díaz, From a Survivor." *The Rumpus,* 15 May 2018, https://therumpus.net/2018/05/enough-on-junot-Díaz-from-a-survivor/

Robillard, Amy. "From Isolated Stories to a Collective: Speaking Out About Misogyny in English Departments." *Peitho,* vol 23, no. 2, 2021.

Salesses, Matthew. *Craft in the Real World: Rethinking Fiction Writing and Workshopping.* Catapult, 2021.

---. "'The Reader' vs. POC: Time to Rethink the Creative Writing Workshop." *Gulf Coast,* Fall, 2015. https://gulfcoastmag.org/online/fall-2015/the-reader-vs-poc/

---. "Who's at the Center of Workshop and Who Should Be?" *Pleiades Literature in Context.* https://pleiadesmag.com/whos-at-the-center-of-workshop-and-who-should-be-part-1/

Sommers, Jeffrey. "Behind the Paper: Using the Student-Teacher Memo." *College Composition and Communication*, vol. 39, no. 1, 1988, pp. 77–80.

Vanderslice, Stephanie. "Once More to the Workshop: A Myth Caught in Time." Donnelly, pp 30-36.

Toward a Decolonial Creative Writing Workshop: *Mbari* as a Case Study in Examining Intercultural Models for Arts Education

James Ryan and Steve Westbrook

Abstract: *The creative writing workshop has been the subject of sustained critique for its tendency to reproduce dominant cultural norms, especially in spaces where admissions to the workshop do not reflect local ethnic and cultural diversity. In an effort to aid the search for alternate models/foundations for creative writing instructions, the authors turn to the history of mbari, a cultural practice among the Owerri Igbo of Nigeria, which was briefly adapted into the pedagogical foundation for a visual arts workshop conducted between the time of Nigeria's independence and the onset of its civil war. In its original form, mbari was a sacred, collective arts ritual through which practitioners cemented social bonds among diverse groups within the local community. In its later adaptation as pedagogy, mbari became an effort to produce "authentic" local art in a global marketplace. This essay examines the values and local social norms that made mbari so vital for the Owerri Igbo and then teases out cautionary lessons from the appropriation of mbari as a workshop pedagogy. The authors argue that, by examining the successes and failures of previous efforts to adopt "non-western" arts practices into workshop pedagogies, instructors and pedagogues can be more mindful about their efforts to reform the creative writing workshop.*

In recent decades, the rapid expansion of creative writing programs across the United States and the active recruiting of minority and international students by many universities have led to an influx into writing workshops of individuals with diverse backgrounds. Today, creative writing programs reveal more diversity than at any other time in the history of the discipline. The writers emerging from these programs have advanced a literary movement Mark McGurl calls "high cultural pluralism" and a body of literature that "joins the high literary values of modernism with a fascination with the experience of cultural difference" (32). This statement of praise—imbued with sincere reverence *and* potential danger—reflects an ideological paradox that continues to define much academic thinking on the subject. It recognizes the profound cultural worth this and related movements have added to contemporary literatures of the US in all of their expansive plurality. At the same time, lauding this "type" of writing (and, by extension, author) risks reinscribing a colonial history defined by the superficial or voyeuristic understanding of others—represented here by the term "fascination." At worst, depictions of these writers and their works may inadvertently echo the curiosities of Euro-colonial fantasy.

As teachers of creative writing studies in the US, we (James and Steve) find ourselves inhabiting subject positions that require us to continually reflect on our own roles in the perpetuation or cessation of this ideology. White males of European-American descent who work as critical educators within US universities, we inhabit a privileged and paradoxical space of our own. A recent graduate of the University of Wisconsin's PhD program in Composition and Rhetoric, James works as a teacher, scholar, freelance writer, and game designer; at Cal State Fullerton, Steve serves as an associate professor who specializes in creative writing studies and composition-rhetoric. Enfranchised within these structures, we value the intercultural communities of writers we collaborate with on a daily basis. But in order to adequately support the writers in our classrooms—to practice what Frank Martin and Fatima Pirbhai-Illich have called a "non-Othering pedagogy" (369)—we find ourselves increasingly working *against* the very model of education that (in part, at least) has provided us our privilege. Specifically, we refer to the legacy of the creative writing workshop.

To this end, we join an array of writer-scholars who have taken on two tasks: (1) to critically examine the ways in which the workshop—a mode of education with formalist and colonial roots—has failed to adequately address the complex pragmatic and theoretical challenges facing writers of varying cultural backgrounds, and (2) to create more socially just and inclusive strategies of reinvention from other traditions of knowledge-making. While this work does not fit in a neat timeline, it can be roughly characterized as follows. Early critiques of the workshop often arose from feminists seeking to disrupt patriarchal power dynamics (e.g., Domina, Haake, Miner, Shelnutt); their work was expanded by writers of color who often narrated their lived experience of alienation in MFA programs (e.g., Diaz, Kearns). More recently, a number of writer-scholars (e.g., Adsit, Chavez, Lee, Mura, Salesses) have built on these critiques to analyze the workshop as a historical site of intersectional oppression and to define pedagogies that intervene in this history. From their particular stances, they argue the writing workshop must learn to become inclusive not only of diverse bodies and identities, but also of diverse, even conflicting, aesthetic principles, modes of expression, artistic goals, and intended audiences with their varied tastes, expectations, and values. In sum, and to borrow from Felicia Rose Chavez's title, we join these writer-scholars in seeking to "Decolonize the Creative Classroom."

In order to expand this decolonizing work, we engage in a form of what Walter D. Mignolo calls "epistemic disobedience." Mignolo uses this term to describe practices that seek to disrupt "the coloniality of knowledge," an ideological inheritance that controls what kinds of knowledge-making are deemed legitimate by upholding situational and biased Eurocentric norms as somehow universal or superior to localized, indigenous ways of knowing (176). Rather than buttressing the traditional workshop—the controlling norm of our universities—we draw from a non-Eurocentric episteme to reimagine and improve our teaching practices. Specifically, we examine a model of arts education from southeastern Nigeria called *mbari*. Once a thriving communal and ritual arts practice of the Owerri Igbo, *mbari* was celebrated by novelist Chinua Achebe as a set of uniquely African aesthetic principles at the dawn of Nigeria's independence. In turn, Achebe's reinvention of *mbari* was further adapted for classroom use by Ulli Beier, a German-born phonetics instructor at the University of Ibadan, and his English spouse, Georgina Beier, a studio artist. In the discussion that follows, we treat the story of *mbari* as a case study in the nuances, potentialities, and pitfalls that accompany the use of a culture's indigenous artistic practices for the intended purpose of decolonizing arts education. While we explore the problem of cultural appropriation, we nonetheless attempt to articulate the potential value of a *mbari*-influenced approach to creative writing pedagogy. We begin this work by first outlining the historical development and expansion of the dominant US workshop model, revealing how its formalist biases reflect deeply rooted colonial prejudices that all too frequently continue to define contemporary educational contexts.

Unshared Silence: The Fiction of the Monoculture

The traditional workshop model we recognize today came into being at the University of Iowa in the 1930s. Transplanted from the university's existing PhD curriculum and placed into a new MFA program, creative writing classes quickly evolved into workshops based on the studio arts model, or European atelier, in which a master artist taught students the conventions of creative writing through a pedagogy of aesthetic formalism. The underlying theoretical influence was New Criticism, and the method was decidedly centered on the study of craft. Wilbur Schramm, who directed the Iowa Writer's Workshops from 1939 to 1942, touted the ability of this new model to enable students to approach one another's poems and stories "with the intelligent understanding of a fellow craftsman in order to see how others have met the common problems of the craft and to estimate the effectiveness of their solution" (165). While Schramm's statement clearly reveals the dominant practice of conceptualizing creative writing as a "craft," it also offers insight to the rather homogenous culture of the early workshop. It is an understatement to claim that in the pre-Civil Rights era of the late 1930s and early 1940s, the Iowa workshops were not rich in cultural or gender diversity. Schramm's "craftsman," indeed, inhabited an exclusionary Euro-American patriarchal space.

Given this reality, it is important to note not only the lack of diverse demographics but also the assumed singularity of aesthetic purpose that characterized the early workshop. When Schramm states that participants share the pursuit of "the common problems of the craft," he reveals a goal defined more by similarity than difference. The major assumption is, of course, that problems of craft are indeed "common," or universal: i.e., they do not particularly vary from writer to writer. This belief was supported by the reigning aesthetic theory of New Criticism, which suggested that the artistic quality of a piece of literature was to be determined by the sophistication or artistry of its deployment of internal poetic devices. In New Critical parlance, a mastery of craft was evident when these devices called attention to their own strangeness and beauty; in doing so, a successful literary work ultimately "embodied meaning" in the "vital unity" of its aesthetic form. It was to function as an *objet d'art*—to be appreciated for the way it revealed its artistic splendor without particular reference to the world outside (see Brooks and Warren 11-16). In fact, the New Critics regularly characterized writers who attempted to move beyond the boundaries of "the text itself" to address civic concerns, engage in community activism, or lobby for social change as inferior. For example, when discussing the work of W.H. Auden in *Modern Poetry and the Tradition*, Cleanth Brooks states the following: "In general, Auden's poetry weakens as he tries to rely upon an external framework—a doctrine or ideology" (126). Brooks goes so far as to label poets Langston Hughes and Genevieve Taggard, who attempted to use their work to intervene in social affairs, as "propagandists" (51). In fact, he criticizes and "convicts" them for being "preoccupied with the inculcation of a particular message" (49). Given the tenor of the time, we don't think it is entirely coincidental that the writers criticized by Brooks happen to be a gay man, a black man, and a socialist woman, respectively.

From a distance of history, it may not seem surprising that in the 1930s and 1940s writers of a similar background were brought together at Iowa to learn to produce a similarly defined version of literary art. We might say this problem was a product of its era, and it would be convenient to suggest that it was, indeed, *confined* to its era. However, this is not the case. While the demographics of creative writing classes have changed significantly, the dominance of the New Critical approach to craft has remained entrenched in their pedagogy, largely because of the way in which the Iowa model reproduced itself. As D.G. Myers suggests, the system started at Iowa became "a machine for producing more and more creative writing programs" (146). Eric Bennet similarly notes that "More than half of the second-wave programs, about 50 of which appeared by 1970, were founded by Iowa graduates." He goes on to state, "Third- and fourth- and fifth-wave programs, also Iowa scions, have kept coming ever since." In other words, the influence of the Iowa paradigm still runs deep. Surely, we don't mean to suggest that the workshop remains a monolithic entity entirely defined by its past; however, we can't deny Iowa's formative, expansive, and lingering effect on current articulations of creative writing pedagogy.

Today, our increasingly diverse student body brings with it issues of difference and inequality that are not always easy to address in a workshop model based on the Iowa paradigm. Students of various backgrounds and home discourses sometimes make use of language in radically different ways than what founders of the Iowa workshops might have envisioned. They also have divergent sensibilities about what good writing should look like and for whom it should be written. In workshops not prepared to accommodate these divergent sensibilities, minority students can feel ostracized by professors and classmates alike. For example, as Rosalie Morales Kearns suggests, the traditional workshop's "gag order"—the practice of *literally* silencing student authors by requiring them to refrain from speaking while their work is being critiqued—tends to marginalize some populations of students. For Kearns, the practice is strange and limiting, since it runs against the grain of her own cultural heritage: "The expectations about spoken interaction that I have internalized as a woman of Puerto Rican descent include the understanding that staying silent or imposing silence is unacceptably rude." As an MFA student, when Kearns saw how easily the other students in her workshops "acquiesced to the gag rule," she knew she was "in a profoundly foreign place" with values that did not match her own (794). As she was kept silent and required to witness the predominantly white writers of her program responding to her creative work, Kearns noticed that her classmates critiqued especially strongly those aspects of her writing that did not jibe with the values of the majority. From this experience, she concludes:

> the MFA curriculum assumes the existence of a particular type of student, a student firmly located in the Euro-American cultural tradition.... [T]here are many ways for students to be marginalized in relation to this "ideal" student: if our work alludes to authors and cultural practices about which he knows nothing; if we use narrative devices he dislikes or has never even seen; if we ignore his particular standards of coherence and intelligibility; if we write about

subjects he considers unimportant; if we do not valorize a lone individual; if we write about topics in a way that seems "ideological" to him because he holds different values. (800-801)

Within the context of the craft-based workshop, deviations from the "common" conventions by writers of color are sometimes too easily dismissed as instances of aesthetic immaturity—especially if workshop participants are unprepared to respond appropriately to creative work defined by profound inter- and intra-cultural disparities.

Jay Caspian Kang, author of *The Dead Do Not Improve* and *The Loneliest Americans,* recently shared a moment from his own MFA experience that echoes the problems described by Kearns. He discusses a workshop session in which his fiction was pigeonholed into an all-too-familiar genre of "immigrant narrative." Kang's professor offered the following feedback: "[W]hat we need to do is figure out a way to *elevate* it [the narrative] so that it's not just a telling of the way things are for a certain type of person." This advice prodded Kang to write his story for an audience that was decidedly *not* an eclectic group of Korean-Americans. It put him in the position of representing the immigrant experience and bearing the onus of "explaining all the nuances of the immigrant struggle to a presumed white, upper-middle class audience," an audience reflected most immediately in the demographics of the workshop, and more distantly as the presumed readership of an emerging US author. Privately, he began to question, first, why he should be writing for this audience at all and, second, if he were to do so, why he should be lumped into a broadly defined tradition of Asian-American literature including authors like Amy Tan, with whom he wanted no particular association. Ultimately, Kang suggests, this was one of many experiences that led him to fixate on the problem of his Korean-American authorial identity in relation to his potential audience in what he describes variously as a kind of "neurosis" or "anxiety": "Every capitulation to the 'white gaze' comes with shame; every stand you take for authenticity triggers its own questions about what constitutes authenticity." Kang admits he did not consider his professor's comments intentionally racist but given in a good-faith effort to improve the *quality* of his fiction. However, the limitations of this and similar "craft" conversations that assume universal aesthetics and a common audience failed to make room for larger, more nuanced questions about culture and identity. Kang says, at the time, he didn't bring up these questions with the professor because he was "too embarrassed." The culture of Kang's workshop may not have come with a literal gag order, but nor was it particularly accommodating to this author's need for more substantial inquiry about issues of diversity, representation, authorship, and audience.

As Kearns and Kang reveal, the devaluing of difference is not limited to the style of writing produced in the workshop but also concerns the style of *talking about* writing. In fact, we'd like to suggest that acts of marginalization too often occur because of an ideological inheritance that defines how writers are supposed to talk (or not talk) or more generally *behave* in workshop settings. Specifically, we mean that upholding the fiction of a universal quality of craft, above all other priorities, often creates a tacit code of etiquette that writers are expected to follow. In this sense it upholds what Mignolo defines as the two functions of colonial institutions: (1) the "training of new (epistemically obedient) members" and (2) the "control of…what knowledge making is allowed, disavowed, devalued, or celebrated" (176). In order to help improve each other's writing, workshop members are supposed to limit their conversations to discussing internal formal concerns *instead of* talking about larger more disruptive issues such as writers' attempts to claim different forms of power, texts' variant artistic *and* cultural functions, or profound variations in the discursive practices of different communities. As Kearns perhaps suggests, a rather ironic turn tends to occur when writers who represent minority positions find themselves confronting a radical difference in values. Instead of an author's difference being allowed to illuminate the very strangeness of the workshop system itself as hegemonic—the unnaturalness of craft-dominated approaches to study—this difference can be easily subsumed by the culture of the workshop; in its effort to create docile subjects or Mignolo's "epistemically obedient members," it writes the offending author off as naïve or unsophisticated. In this reinscribing of colonial ideology, instead of the writer being allowed to provide the group with a valuable moment of collective estrangement, in which workshop members may be inspired to see their own seemingly normative practices from an alternative perspective, the writer is faulted for their unfamiliarity with (or resistance to) the way the workshop is supposed to "naturally" work.

In other words, creative writing pedagogy too often replicates the limitations of what Martin and Pirbhai-Illich call the "object-based" intellectual tradition. This tradition, which is at once a product and enabler of colonialism, is defined by categorical thinking that produces "a separation of self and identity from language, and language from culture. Static and universal ideas about culture hold sway, and construct difference as 'Other' and as deficient when compared to the dominant group's standards" (360). Education in an object-based context consistently holds the colonized subject to the standard of the colonizer, without any acknowledgement of the interconnected nature of knowledge, language, identity, and culture. Martin and Pribhai-Illich contrast the object-based tradition with a "relational" one, grounded in the understanding of knowledge as a reciprocal phenomenon, one that comes into being through dialog and difference. A relational education is one in which "differences are revealed through relating to each other, and…this goes beyond superficial, visible differences (where culture is equated with race and ethnicity, for example, skin colour, first language) to differences that are not so evident (where culture is understood in the broadest sense to include religion, community, language, gender and so on)" (361). Rather than examining each student's work to see if it adheres to or strays from an inherited, "objective" aesthetic standard, relational-based creative writing pursues all students' work—collectively and holistically—as an effort to understand and value "not so evident" differences.

Although they do not necessarily apply Martin and Pribhai-Illichs's terminology, a number of programs have effectively redefined the workshop model as more relational. At Cal State Monterey Bay, Frances Payne Adler founded an innovative undergraduate minor in Creative Writing and Social Justice, which "brings together the study of creative expression, culture, communication, and community involvement" ("Creative")—an exploration of differences that radically departs from object-learning and craft-based pedagogy. Somewhat similarly, Hampshire College's Art and Social Action program and the University at Buffalo's Poetics Program have sought to break down barriers between creative writing classrooms, the politics of difference, and practices of cultural intervention. While we recognize and support these reform efforts, we'd like to explore the possibilities of moving even further away from inherited approaches to creative writing in US institutions and, as we've suggested, draw from a model well outside the parameters of Euro-American education: the Owerri Igbo practice of *mbari*.

Mum's Not the Word but *Mbari* Might Be?

We explore the possibility of *mbari* here precisely because it challenges the perceived disparity between issues of craft, representation, and culture that too often marginalizes writers of diverse backgrounds within the conventional creative writing workshop. Like the atelier tradition and the workshop model, *mbari* involves established artists teaching apprentices. However, the practice focuses not on the development of individual talent (as arts education is understood in the US) but on the enhancement of community life and the deepening of understanding across segments of society through artistic expression.

Historically, the term *mbari* made its way into U.S. educators' lexicon largely through the work of Chinua Achebe, who celebrated the Igbo tradition as an indigenous Nigerian aesthetic with relevance to the larger field of post-colonial literature. Perhaps his most comprehensive treatment of *mbari* appears in his essay "Africa and Her Writers," where he contrasts the term with two predominant, binary "streams" of European aesthetics: (1) the notion that art should always be created in the service of politics (a traditional Marxist stance), and (2) the idea that art should be "accountable to no one" and need "justify itself to nobody except itself" (the central tenant of aestheticism) (30). Achebe compares this polarized situation to a Yoruba story in which "Eshu, god of fate and lover of confusion" decides to play a trick on two farmers who work fields on opposite sides of the same road. Making himself half black and half white, Eshu walks along the road, causing an argument between the farmers over what color he is. Art, claims Achebe, is like this. It can neither be placed wholly in the service of politics nor can it exist entirely for its own sake. In this sense, the system Achebe describes does away with false bifurcations between propaganda and art, culture and craft, which have defined US creative writing pedagogy since its earliest manifestations (31). Achebe proposes that in Igbo society art has traditionally encompassed both the political and the transcendent, and that these two are not in conflict with one another. Rather, the political and transcendent are complementary and mutually dependent features, for art is simultaneously a sublime and communal experience. Achebe suggests that this relationship is perhaps most apparent in the tradition of *mbari*, which he describes as an artistic, cultural, and religious festival of "startling power and diversity" (33).

In this manner, Achebe uses the term variously to refer to an operational aesthetic and a specific cultural event. To better understand the complexity of *mbari*, we need to examine the latter in more detail (and move beyond the confines of Achebe's treatment). First and foremost, the term *mbari* describes the process and product of a religious ritual—the building of an artistically adorned house for a god, complete with what we might familiarly call a sculpture garden. The meaning of this term also includes the festival celebration of the house's completion. Thus, the making and celebrating of art are all enclosed within the same word. A unity is thereby expressed in *mbari*: an artistic artifact, in this context, cannot be meaningfully extracted from the community who invented the art, made it together, and gathered to celebrate its completion and beauty. To remove a statue from an *mbari* house and place it in a foreign museum, for example, would strip the statue of its meaning, which is to say its *purpose*. Behind glass in a foreign land, such a piece can only communicate the colonizer's object-based values: craftsmanship, artistry, and, above all, the "fascinating" foreignness of its shape and design. As we will see, *mbari* statues are not in any way made for the colonizing gaze. In fact, they are made specifically in response to emerging needs within a local community.

Although no longer practiced, *mbari* once thrived in the Owerri region of Igboland, home now to the modern city of Owerri, state capital of Imo, Nigeria. Henry Cole, the most frequently cited scholar on *mbari*, estimates the origin of the practice at least as far back as 1850.[1] It flourished in the 1920s and into the 1940s, and then, with the increasing influence of "European education and European missionaries," the practice of mbari began to decline and eventually disappear (3). As practiced by the Owerri Igbo, *mbari* was never intended as a system of arts education, nor was it meant as the proof or expression of an aesthetic theory. Instead, the construction and celebration of an *mbari* house was always the outgrowth of Igbo cultural and religious life. The decision to build an *mbari* was prompted by the will of an *agbara*, a god, frequently Ala, the Igbo earth goddess. When a deity "fears herself slipping in relative position," she "troubles her priest, asking for more attention, more wealth, more servants, a new house (mbari), all in an effort to regain her proud place in the conference of gods" (Cole 59). The deity does this by sending signs and omens. A surge in infant mortality, drought, or unexplained deaths of livestock might indicate that local life is out of proper relationship with the divine. States Cole: "In such major, pervasive crises when nature and the gods have tipped the scales against a community, no ordinary sacrifice can redress the balance… An *agbara* is calling for the greatest offering it can demand: *mbari*" (71).

Building an *mbari*, then, is meant to restore the community to right relations with its gods, and to boost a particular deity's standing among her peers. But *mbari* is a cultural as well as a religious endeavor, and as such, it has social consequences. From the villages that agree to participate in an *mbari*, a priest and a diviner select family groups who must send participants to a compound where they will live and work together for one or more years. This is no small sacrifice, and it binds all the villages and families who contribute. Because groups, and then individual participants from those groups, are chosen by divination, rather than being chosen on the basis of interest or talent, they "vary

---

1. While a significant body of scholarship covers artifacts that emerged from the mbari tradition, exceedingly few available resources discuss *mbari* as an extant cultural practice. Sylvester Okwunodu Ogbechie summarizes the problem of the "extinct tradition" this way: "The demise of Mbari among the Owerri Igbo…means that there are few ways to engage this practice except through focus on the archival record," which is largely based on the work of Cole, an art historian whose field observations remain "the most significant research on *Mbari*" (64). For this reason, we find ourselves joining the likes of Ogbechie and others in relying heavily on Cole's scholarship for our reconstruction of mbari as a cultural practice.

widely in age, occupation, temperament, and sex" (80). In short, a diverse cross-section of society is selected this way.

Once selected, participants leave their lives and families and move to the priest's home for three eight-day weeks, during which time they are initiated into *mbari* with ritual scarification, the adoption of new names, and the assignment of new spousal couplings, which may or may not be platonic. Following their initiation, the participants move to the *mbari* site, where they are to live as spirits in a parallel world, in which they will be born, married, labor and (symbolically) die in the service of their god. These "spirit-workers live a life…as sacred actors in the cosmic drama" (Cole 217).

Overseeing the labor of *mbari* participants is an artist, who learned his[2] trade through an apprenticeship lasting six to ten years. As Cole suggests, the artist serves as "architect, sculptor, painter, building supervisor, and priest" (77). However, though the ritual and his role in it are both religious, "little mystical aura appears to surround the artist; he is appreciated simply as one who does well the job he knows. Both his attitude toward himself and that of others toward him suggest that 'craftsman' may be a more appropriate description of his function" (77). At the same time, the craft of each *mbari* artist produces work of distinctive quality and style. Quoting from several respondents, Cole offers the following statement on craft: "Skilled workers always do what comes out of their minds; they each do their own work and their handwork is varied. Their work cannot be the same" (169). It seems that, for the Owerri Igbo, the unique talents of individual artists are not shrouded by the "mystical aura" often attributed to artists in Europe and the US. Artistic craft is respected, even in a religious context, without attributing undue powers or status to its practitioners. The entire concept of craft is not an issue of pedagogy. Participants working under the main artist are not necessarily aiming to acquire the skills of *mbari* building; they are here to perform their religious duties as a service to their community. It is this service, rather than the unique skills of the artist, that is seen as bearing the greatest relevance. As Cole puts it, "Here ideology obscures personality; an mbari is made by and for a specific community, and this, rather than the handiwork of [any specific artist], is the sociological reality" (169).

After one or two years of isolated labor to construct the house, populate it with statues, and paint the whole project, the *mbari* is complete. In a review process of sorts, patrons are invited to view the work and give critical feedback, which the artist and participants address before the approaching festival. Then, people gather from all around to celebrate the completion of the work, the appeasement of their god, and the return of their loved ones from this long ordeal. Now that their work is complete, the participants undergo a ritual death before returning to their lives and families. They leave behind their assumed names and never mention themselves in relationship to the *mbari* house again. There is a strong taboo against claiming any ownership over the completed artwork, for to do so would anger the deity and defeat the overall purpose of promoting the betterment and longevity of society as a whole. Now that their work is done and those identities discarded, the spirit-workers who built the *mbari* are considered to be deceased.

---

2. According to Cole, mbari artists were always male.

Reanimating the Social Function of Craft in Festivals of Power and Diversity

In addition to the obvious disparities in religious and secular contexts, radical contrasts are apparent between traditional *mbari* practice and creative writing pedagogy in US institutions. The multiple ways in which art and community life intersect and inform one another set *mbari* apart from the workshop tradition that would have specialized aesthetes writing for specialized aesthetes. For example, Schramm's "craftsman" ideal for writers is quite different from the Igbo concept of the "master artist." The Iowa model suggests that the craftsman's job is to create finely made objects of art and place these on display; the public's job is then to admire and celebrate the craftsman's talent. Only a few people are talented and well-trained enough to qualify as craftsmen, and only these few have any business making art. The Igbo master artist, like the craftsman, devotes his life to perfecting artistic craft, but does so in the context and service of his community. The master artist's job is to create a *festival*, rather than individual objects of art, and this requires the participation of diverse community members. The role of the master artist is that of an expert mentor, someone entrusted to provide "discipline, instruction, and guidance" to *mbari* participants (34). As Achebe puts it, "Mbari does not deny the place or importance of the master with unusual talent and professional experience. Indeed, it highlights such gift and competence by bringing them into play on the seminal potentialities of the community" (35). In other words, the festival these artists produce is not meant to celebrate their own talent, innovation, or genius but rather the whole of Igbo life.

Further, *mbari's* unification of artists and their community sets it apart from the workshop tradition, which, as we have seen, sets a rigid barrier between makers and consumers of culture, one that defines what qualifies as creative writing and who is permitted to inhabit the role of creative writer. Advantages have traditionally been given to cisgender males of European descent, and now, even in more diverse settings, privilege goes to those writers who are most comfortable working in the Euro-American literary tradition. As we have suggested, students outside of that tradition who point out its limitations are too often silenced or sidelined. This phenomenon might be found in any number of artifacts within creative writing culture. Perhaps the most glaring example occurs in Robert DeMaria's *College Handbook of Creative Writing*. Here, DeMaria claims his book "takes the writer's approach," which is concerned exclusively with "the practical aspects of craft." In contrast, he states he simply will not address the needs of a group he defines as "*special interest readers,* who have politicized the study of literature and are preoccupied with such things as race, ethnicity, and gender" (1). From page one, students who write outside the white, patriarchal tradition of aestheticism are asked to leave the conversation (before it even begins). They can be consumers, or critics, or "readers" of culture, but not its producers, not its writers. In contrast, *mbari* participants are selected precisely for their differences, which are valued as essential to art. The process of *mbari* "crafts" the culture as much as the works of art, but not in some didactic way. *Mbari* is not agitprop; instead, the inclusive practices of the master artists allow them to shape culture by inviting many to participate. Or, as Achebe has famously stated, "*there is no* rigid barrier between the makers of culture and its consumers. Art belongs to all and is a 'function of society'" (34).

Finally, it is worth considering the power and effect of *mbari's* participant selection procedure. Through divination, Igbo religious leaders arrive at a pool of participants that represents a cross section of society. It is due to the differences among this set of participants that *mbari* is able to both represent Igbo society and bind it together. In other words, *mbari's* primary artistic value and effect arise not from the skill of the master artist but from the selection of diverse participants who are not artists and do not even aim to be. Achebe tells us that not even the combination of divine appointment and expert instruction "would insure infallibly the emergence of a new, exciting sculptor or painter. *But mbari was not looking for that*" (34, emphasis added). Instead, *mbari* was looking to make *good art*, "good" in the sense that art was good for the Igbo ancestors, who "created their myths and legends and told their stories for a human purpose.... Their artists lived and moved and had their being in society and created their works for the good of that society.... *Good* in that sense does not mean pretty" (29-30). Rather than objects of exquisite beauty whose primary purpose is to be admired, these artists produced objects that were aesthetically rich *and* produced social value in an effort to bring their communities together. In other words, *mbari* primarily produced *relations* rather than *objects*, for the objects it did produce were created for the purpose of redefining and/or reinforcing social bonds among participating groups and their dieties.

We would like you to imagine, for a moment, how a creative writing workshop would work if it were to take these values and procedures seriously. What would a workshop look like if it placed social good and community unification over (or at least on par with) "beautiful" or "talented" writing and therefore selected its participants primarily on the basis of their representative and relational diversity. Imagine that the goal of writing workshops was not to produce *publishable* and *literary* writers working for an audience of strangers, but to produce *good writing* (under Achebe's definition of this term) that is unifying for subgroups of an immediate or localized culture. How would our approach to teaching creative writing change if it were developed with these values in mind?

From Practice to Pedagogy: *Mbari* Clubs and their Visual Arts Workshops

As much as we perceive *mbari* as a valuable model for arts education, we don't mean to idealize it as some sort of overlooked or exotic panacea for addressing the inherited problems of the creative writing workshop. Like any systematic production of culture and art, it may have contained its own exclusionary practices or been subject to prejudices within the strata of Igbo society, of which we—from our distant positions in history and location—are completely unaware. More importantly, as we consider the potential influence of *mbari* for creative writing classes in the US, we don't want to engage in harmful acts of cultural appropriation: i.e., we don't want to serve as the curators taking the *mbari* sculpture out of its cultural context for display behind glass on a museum wall. Rather than discussing strategies for creating a "*mbari*-style workshop," we turn instead to a complicated, somewhat cautionary tale from Nigeria's post-colonial history, which speaks to the possibilities and problems of understanding *mbari's* relevance to global education, writing, and arts initiatives.

For our purposes, this part of the story begins with an unlikely character: Ulli Beier, a Jewish refugee who fled with his family to Palestine during WWII. In 1950 he secured a position as a professor of phonetics at the University of Ibadan, later transferring to the Extra-Mural Studies department where he had greater freedom in his research and service. In the late 1950s, Beier became interested in supporting Nigerian artists and writers, in hopes of cultivating a cultural scene that would put Nigerian art and literature on a global stage. In 1957, he co-founded *Black Orpheus*, a literary magazine "conceived of as a laboratory of new ideas, practices, and activities spanning theater, fine arts, and literature by an emergent postcolonial generation" (Okeke-Agulu 156). Four years later, he brought together a community of writers (including Wole Soyinka, John Pepper Clark, Christopher Okigbo and Ezekiel Mphahlel), and co-founded a club with them. This new club ran a publishing house and an art gallery with a courtyard where plays were performed. When trying to come up with a name for the group, Beier recalls receiving a phone call from Chinua Achebe, who suggested "*Mbari* Club." Beier's reaction reveals his enthusiasm for what he considered the indigenous aesthetic: "Immediately I knew that this was it. *Mbari* suggests creativity in its purest, most vital form. Creativity as a ritual act, rather than a commercial activity for the production of marketable objects. Creativity as a communal act, as a revitalizing force" (Ezenwa-Ohaeto 84). Even though Achebe had little to do with the Mbari Club after suggesting its name, the club soon became a center for Igbo artists and luminaries, especially those associated with Ibadan University. However, the flourishing arts and literary scene that emerged from this center was not to Beier's taste. In spite of his enthusiasm for *mbari* in name, Beier quickly lost interest in the Mbari Club at Ibadan, which he saw as a mere "rendezvous for intellectuals" from the university rather than an expression of creativity on par with *mbari* as formerly practiced in Owerritown (Beier, "When we see" 102).

Beier became interested in seeing if he could produce artists from among untrained Nigerians who had not been exposed to European traditions and who therefore would produce their art from the perspective of, Beier thought, a more authentic local aesthetic. At the same time, Duro Ladipo, a Yoruban musician and primary school teacher, became inspired by Ibadan's Mbari Club and decided to start one of his own in Osogbo. Ladipo converted his father's bar into an art gallery and built a stage in the back. He began writing and performing plays and hosting exhibitions for local artists. Ulli Beier hosted several visual arts workshops at Ladipo's club, named Mbari Mbayo (translated from Yoruba: "When we see it, we will be happy"). These workshops reached their peak effectiveness in Beier's estimation (i.e., they produced the most unique and famous artists) under the leadership of afforementioned artist Georgina Beier. Out of Georgiana Beier's workshops came artists who won acclaim in European art circles: Adebisi Fabunmi, Jimoh Buraimoh, Rufus Ogundele, Muraina Oyelami and Twins Seven Seven.

Ulli Beier described the Mbari Mbayo workshops as successful for two primary reasons. First, they kept participants grounded in a local aesthetic. The location of Osogbo, in contrast to Ibadan, was well positioned to keep workshop participants from the distractions of European tourists and artistic sensibilities. Back in Ibadan, "the intellectual, university-trained Nigerian artist is chiefly concerned with establishing a new identity.... His problem is that he has to proclaim it to the European audience.... He establishes his newly gained identity in the art galleries of Europe more often than in the villages of Nigeria" (Beier, "When we see it" 109). For the participants in the Beiers' workshops in Osogbo, on the other hand,

> the problem was how to retain the inspiration they could draw from their own environment and how to develop their talent within the framework of their own society.... In the end it was this local participation that made it possible to obtain local commissions: murals in palaces of Yoruba kings, decoration of an Esso petrol station opposite the Mbari Mbayo Club, church doors and theatre sets. Firmly rooted in such local activity, the artists could sell to European collectors and could work for exhibitions abroad without losing their bearings. (109-110)

It was the central location of Ladipo's club, visited regularly by Yoruba market women and government officials alike, that gave workshop artists a grounding in the tastes and values of their local audience. Ulli Beier saw this locatedness, rather than any specific pedagogical intervention, as the primary value of the Mbari Mbayo workshops.

Accordingly, the second reason for the Mbari Mbayo workshops' success was their very lack of pedagogical intention. In fact, the Beiers both suggest that Georgina Beier's skill as an "instructor" was, essentially, her lack of instruction. Instead of a teacher, Georgina reports acting as a peer of her students, learning alongside them and, in Ulli's words, "aiming at...a working community in which artists stimulate and criticise each other" (Beier, "When we see it" 110). Her pedagogy "was unpremeditated...and one had no time even to conceive theories or formulas that could have been imposed on the artists" (111).

In Georgiana Beier's reflections on the Mbari Mbayo workshops, she describes starting with a set of untrained, local painters and gently guiding their individual development without forcing them in any particular direction. At the same time, Beier required multiple paintings per day from students, and she picked out their best work for display each evening. In this way, Beier says, the developing artists were guided to see what was unique about their individual styles. Beier also moved from paint to linocut in hopes of exaggerating the differences among participants: "It was through this medium that Rufus and Afolabi matured in different directions: Rufus's work became more and more angular and energetic, while Afolabi's shapes acquired an undulating flow" (68). After some days of working this way, Beier believed she had gained "an instinct for discovering the visual element that is unique to a person. Running a workshop is not simply a matter of providing materials and 'encouragement' and letting anything happen. It is like hunting for the original element, trapping it and making it safe, before it gets confused with so many other, alien elements" (68). In short, according to the Beiers, the location of Mbari Mbayo along with Georgina's "teacherless" teaching style were sufficient to produce several accomplished visual artists with an international audience.

Careful readers will, of course, recognize the bias of European primitivism shaping the Beier's perception of Nigerian artists. Here, the "instinctual," "native," or "primal" creative act is valorized as uniquely authentic, superior to supposedly more adulterized versions of Nigerian art. Indeed, critics of the "Osogbo school," as it became known, suggest that this particular bias played a far more active role in shaping the art and artistic careers of the workshop participants than the Beiers would be willing to admit. In délé jégédé's view, for example, the Osogbo art school was established specifically "to demonstrate Beier's academic art degeneracy theory…Osogbo art attempts to validate anti-formalism…a concept in which Beier strongly believes: less sophistication equals more imagination" (78). In other words, the Beiers—far from uncommitted bystanders who watched passively as their workshop participants made art—created conditions at Mbari Mbayo that were meant to prove a preexisting theory of artistic production, namely that formal education in art and literature was bad for artists, who would naturally produce better, more distinct and personal work from a state of artistic naivety. We can see this theory at work in Ulli Beier's interest in Osogbo for its lack of university connections and its involvement of untrained participants. We can also see Georgina Beier's hand on the scales of the Osogbo experiment in her selection each day of each student's "best" art for display, guiding each participant to a "personal" style that was, in fact, largely shaped by this feedback. Finally, the "success" of the Osogbo school artists, due to Ulli Beier's promotion of their work, is measured in conflicting terms by Beier. He suggests that Mbari Mbayo successfully kept its participants grounded in a "local" aesthetic while simultaneously pointing to their international acclaim as proof of the workshop's effectiveness.

In sum, the Beiers' workshops were, at best, a distant cousin to the practice of *mbari* from which they drew their name. Ironically, in their quest for "authentic" art, the Beiers helped facilitate a pedagogical experiment that did not actually resemble the cultural practice of *mbari*. The goal of Mbari Mbayo workshops did not arise from the community but from outsiders looking to prove a theoretical premise. Rather than working to produce a cultural *festival* created by and for the community, the workshops aimed at the production of individual artists, whose paintings and linocuts would prove themselves "authentic" largely through assessment by foreign-born art instructors and their appeal to an international, mostly European, audience. In a sense, this conundrum presents a kind of loose precursor to the more diasporic, post-colonial workshop problem faced by contemporary U.S. writers like Jay Caspian Kang and Rosalie Morales Kearns, which we discuss earlier in this essay: despite the locality, the artist is positioned within a Euro-American market defined by the values of a white upper-middle class audience.

At the same time, we would be remiss not to point out that the Beiers' workshops were successful on their own terms. They produced artists with unique personal styles, who gained a local and international following for their work. Even though this "success" had little if anything in common with the "success" of an *mbari* house, it still had real value for a newly post-colonial nation seeking to establish itself politically and culturally in relation to other countries, including its former colonizers. Chika Okeke-Agulu sums up this complex predicament:

> As it happened, most of the Mbari Mbayo artists, in coming to terms with their postcolonial condition, simultaneously drew from indigenous notions of being and creativity, and a modernistic imaginary of the artist persona as an individual creator and mythmaker. In this sense, Mbari Mbayo presents a complex scenario of collapsed boundaries, a nonlinear flow of artistic influences,

and a compelling manifestation of an aspect of modernist experience in which émigré Europeans, black diaspora, and postcolonial Nigerian artists created a laboratory where local and appropriated forms from diverse artistic genres and disciplines coalesced to produce a thriving, contemporary visual culture. (157)

Mbari and not *Mbari*: Coming to Terms with Community

What can we learn from this story about an indigenous Nigerian cultural practice and a German-born educator's attempt to reproduce this practice within the format of the fine arts workshop? The Beiers, like us, were outsiders to the *mbari* tradition. They were not Owerri Igbo; they never took part in an *mbari*; and they held values and perspectives different from those of the *mbari*-makers. In spite of (or perhaps *because of*) their outsider status, the Beiers were inspired by the tradition of *mbari*: it seemed to hold the answer to a pressing question for them, as it seems to hold a promising possibility for us. And so they charged ahead with perhaps more passion than reflection and attempted to create an arts workshop they thought would represent the essentialized "spirit" of *mbari*. In doing so, they dropped the religious aspects of the tradition (which, of course, were not "aspects" to the Igbo, but rather the entire point), and in doing so, they dropped *mbari's* process of selection. Instead of gathering local stakeholders and discovering who would and who would not participate in an *mbari* and then divining which families from these groups would contribute laborers, the Beiers selected their participants more or less by hand, focusing on a particular type of individual. In fact, they moved from Ibadan (in Igboland, where *mbari* was invented) to Osogbo (in Yorubaland, which had no tradition of *mbari*) in order to avoid participants with university training. In place of the social and religious purposes of *mbari*, the Beiers substituted an educational one: although grounded in a specific locality, the function of their workshop was to produce talented artists who would be recognized as such on a global stage. In their "instructionless instruction," the Beiers at once erased and inhabited the role of "master artist," the experienced craftsperson who was responsible for training apprentices and constructing *mbari*. By suggesting that there were no teachers in their workshop, the Beiers devalued the role of a trained artist in *mbari*, and by actually performing instruction (unacknowledged and under another name), they took on the role of a guiding force—based largely on their primitivist ideology—in the artistic development of their students.

As we imagine what an *mbari*-inspired creative writing workshop might look like now, we find ourselves moving well beyond the precedent set by the Beiers and trying to avoid the pitfalls of cultural appropriation. We see potential in *mbari* not for any kind of "authentic" representation of African art, but for its cultural value as a system of community-driven creative activity that blurs the lines between artistic producers and consumers, or in our case creative writers and conscientious citizens. In this regard, the representative cross-section of participant selection—ignored or undermined by the Beiers—is of paramount importance to us. We want to imagine how a creative writing workshop could change if it involved collaborating with community stakeholders: churches, mosques, temples, unions, hospitals, treatment centers, non-profits, community organizers, activists, government offices, K-12 schools and districts, community colleges, and so on. Securing support and participation from as broad a selection of stakeholders as possible, we imagine a workshop that represents a diverse set of perspectives in terms of age, gender, orientation, race, class, occupation, religion, political affiliation, and life experience. Ideally, participants would learn the art of writing precisely by understanding and valuing each other's differences. In fact, this process of mutual understanding through creative action would serve as the primary purpose of this kind of workshop. Rather than serve to produce literary authors, advance American literature, realize a particular theoretical notion of beauty, or pursue other object-oriented goals, this relational workshop would serve the primary function of bringing a local community together.

What we describe above may sound like familiar variations in service learning or project-based pedagogy. Why, then, turn specifically to *mbari* as a model for this kind of learning—especially given its postcolonial entanglements and appropriative history? We do so largely for two reasons. First, we see a need for US institutions of higher education to offer more diverse models of arts education from different areas of the world. With the diversification of student demographics should come a diversification of approaches to learning. Second, it offers a key difference from many entrenched models of service learning through its emphasis on the festival, in which community members produce art in a celebration of their own image and for their own betterment. Here, creative writers would work not, per se, in service of other communities (in acquiescence to the university's inherited and problematical *noblesse oblige* model); rather, community members—working alongside creative writing mentors—would use their work to fulfill the needs expressed by the very communities to which they belong. In other words, the festival would enable participants to share their work in an effort to unify, stabilize, and celebrate their own social cohesion.

Although rare in the world of creative writing, examples of this kind of festival-influenced practice certainly exist. For instance, several years ago, U.C. Berkeley's Center for Race and Gender and Department of Theater, Dance, and Performance Studies collaborated with community organizations, master artist Favianna Rodriguez, and *CultureStr/ke*, a literary/activist magazine focused on issues of immigration, to produce UndocuNation!, a cultural event created by and for Americans of undocumented status. Undocumented students, artists, writers, and allies developed a series of performances aimed at "spotlighting the consequences of violence against immigrant communities and liberatory visions for interventions based on creativity and art practice" ("UndocuNation!") The student and faculty organizers of the event sought very consciously to strengthen the festival through the inclusion of as diverse an assortment of voices as possible, perhaps in an effort to represent "the total life of the community." In their promotional materials, they state:

> Artists from different racial and sexual backgrounds, immigration history and documentation statuses will be sharing artwork and cultural interventions about the current immigration crisis through performances, film excerpts, installations, music and readings. The collaboration of these creative artists attempts to use images and stories to facilitate dialogue that can inspire. ("UndocuNation!)

The creation of this temporary, public performance echoes some of the central tenets of *mbari* we have outlined.

Another example of a related approach to arts education comes from the organization Herstory, which promotes a style of memoir workshop developed by novelist Erika Duncan (Burke and O'Neal). Working in a community setting with untrained writers, Duncan bases her workshop on what she calls "the dare to care." In essence, the memoir writer must dare a stranger to invest their time and attention in the writer's story while also daring themselves to trust that someone will hear their story and care about their wellbeing. Since its early development in the 1990s, this empathy-driven approach has proven powerful not only in helping new writers to grapple with complex issues of narrative craft but also in creating a communal bond among the participants, thus uniting the pursuits of artistic and community development.

Through the years, as the Herstory network of empathy-based workshops spread into college classrooms and women's prisons, stories surfaced of survival from trauma, war, immigration, and criminal abuse. Some of these stories garnered large readerships and effectively intervened in social and legal policy. Denise Irby, for example, participated in a Herstory workshop in a women's correctional facility where she wrote about giving birth while incarcerated. In the detailed scene of her traumatic birth experience, Irby described being shackled during labor. Because her state was considering legislation to outlaw the practice of shackling prisoners as they give birth, Irby was able to read her story first to fellow workshop participants and then to state lawmakers, who were moved by her story and subsequently passed the bill. In this way, the Herstory workshop created a broader circle of relationality and empathy. As we see it, Herstory loosely approximates *mbari*'s underlying ambition: through communal artmaking, it unifies diverse community members who work for their own individual and collective wellbeing and, in turn, enable broader societal interventions.

So where does the history of *mbari*—coupled with these examples of community artmaking—leave us? We want to recover *mbari* as a valuable model of artistic production, one that has the potential to dethrone an entrenched colonialist model through Mignolo's vision of "epistemic disobedience"; i.e., we believe it can supplant an inheritance of object-based, colonial education with a localized, indigenous Nigerian artform and relational way of knowing. At the same time, however, in our survey of loosely related models within the contexts of public, secular universities and US nonprofit arts organizations, we have moved further and further away from its actual history and practice. In doing so, we are by no means presenting a faithful approximation of a ritual that was never intended to serve a pedagogical purpose. Further, if we seek to design a specifically *mbari*-style workshop, we risk replicating the kinds of appropriative practices and unconscious biases that defined the legacy of the Beiers. In this context, we want to echo Aimée Knight's observation that writing instructors involved in community-engaged pedagogy must attend to the many emerging "opportunities for continuous reflection and improvement, for humility, for recognizing where we may cause harm and where we made the wrong choices." Without serious and ongoing self-assessment of this kind, "we risk the danger of contributing to the reproduction of systemic oppression" (93). For these reasons, we would like to conclude our work less with any sort of prescription about how to engage in *mbari*-style education and, instead invite readers to examine the potential value of the "festival" models we have briefly surveyed while reflecting on how they might engage in their own decolonizing work.

With this thought in mind, we *would* like to advocate for disrupting the creative writing workshop in two practical ways. First, we suspect that many instructors still conduct workshops based on colonial, object-based notions of "talent." In such cases, we recommend that careful interrogation of the structures that produced these conditions be followed by relationship-building efforts with local community groups and aggressive restructuring of workshop admission policies. If there is one principle we would borrow directly from *mbari*, it is to treat the workshop as a liminal space where communal relations are first negotiated and then strengthened. Second, we would ask readers inspired by *mbari* to take Martin and Pribhai-Illich's call seriously and cultivate relational understandings of language, art, identity, and knowledge. The learning that takes place in a creative writing classroom is never merely about craft, for all craft conversations come wrapped in cultural assumptions that, if left unexamined, reproduce the logics of colonialism. We feel it is our responsibility as instructors to explore models of education that allow us to more expressly value difference over talent, identity over aesthetics, and dialog over critique.

Works Cited

Achebe, Chinua. "Africa and Her Writers." *Morning Yet on Creation Day: Essays*, Heinemann, 1975, pp. 29-46.

—. "African Literature as a Restoration of Celebration." *Kunapipi*, vol. 12, no. 2, 1990. pp. 1-10.

Adsit, Janelle. *Toward an Inclusive Creative Writing: Threshold Concepts to Guide the Literary Writing Curriculum*. Bloomsbury, 2019.

Beier, Georgina. "To Organize is to Destroy." *Thirty Years of Oshogbo Art*, edited by Ulli Beier, Iwalewa House, 1991, pp. 67-70.

Beier, Ulli. "When We See It, We Shall Be Happy…" *Contemporary Art in Africa*, edited by Ulli Beier, Praeger, 1968, pp. 101-112.

Bennett, Eric. "How Iowa Flattened Literature." *The Chronicle of Higher Education*, 10 Feb. 2014. www.chronicle.com/article/How-Iowa-Flattened-Literature/144531

Brooks, Cleanth. *Modern Poetry and the Tradition*. Chapel Hill: University of North Carolina Press, 1939.

Brooks, Cleanth, and Robert Penn Warren. *Understanding Poetry*. 4th edition, Holt, Rinehart, and Winston, 1976.

Burke, Jennifer and Merle O'Neal. "Herstory Writers Workshop: Where Activists & Storytellers Meet." vimeo. https://vimeo.com/82032794. video.

Chavez, Felecia Rose. *The Anti-Racist Writing Workshop: How To Decolonize the Creative Classroom*. Haymarket Books, 2021.

Cole, Herbert M. *Mbari: Art and Life among the Owerri Igbo*. Indiana University Press, 1982.

"Creative Writing Minor." *Cal State Monterey Bay Humanities and Communication*. California State University, Monterey Bay. 22 Oct. 2010. http://hcom.csumb.edu/creative-writing-minor

DeMaria, Robert. *The College Handbook of Creative Writing*. 4th edition, Wadsworth, 2014.

Diaz, Junot. "MFA vs POC." *The New Yorker*, April 30, 2014. www.newyorker.com/books/page-turner/mfa-vs-poc

Domina, Lynn. "The Body of My Work Is Not Just a Metaphor." *Colors of a Different Horse: Rethinking Creative Writing Theory and Pedagogy*, edited by Wendy Bishop and Hans Ostrom. NCTE, 1994, pp. 27-34.

Ezenwa-Ohaeto. *Chinua Achebe: A Biography*. Indiana University Press, 1997.

Haake, Katharine. *What Our Speech Disrupts: Feminism and Creative Writing Studies*. NCTE, 2000.

Herstory Writers Workshop. herstorywriters.org. 2016.

jégédé, délé. *Trends in Contemporary Nigerian Art: A Historical Analysis*, dissertation, Indiana University, 1983.

Kang, Jay Caspian. "The Many Lives of Steven Yeun." *New York Times Magazine*, 3 February 2021. https://www.nytimes.com/2021/02/03/magazine/steven-yeun.html.

Kearns, Rosalie Morales. "Voice of Authority: Theorizing Creative Writing Pedagogy." *College Composition and Communication* vol. 60, no. 4, 2009, pp. 790-807.

Knight, Aimée. *Community is the Way: Engaged Writing and Designing for Transformative Change*. The WAC Clearinghouse; University Press of Colorado, 2022. https://wac.colostate.edu/books/practice/community/

Lee, Sherry Quan. *How Dare We! Write: A Multicultural Creative Writing Discourse*. Modern History Press, 2017.

Martin, Fran and Fatima Pirbhai-Illich. "Towards Decolonising Teacher Education: riticality, Relationality and Intercultural Understanding." *Journal of Intercultural Studies* vol. 37 no. 4, 2016, pp. 355-372.

Mayers, Tim. *(Re)Writing Craft: Composition, Creative Writing, and the Future of English Studies*. University of Pittsburgh Press, 2005.

McGurl, Mark. *The Program Era: Postwar Fiction and the Rise of Creative Writing*. Harvard University Press, 2009.

Mignolo, Walter D. "Epistemic Disobedience, Independent Thought and Decolonial Freedom." *Theory, Culture & Society* vol. 26, no. 7-8, 2009, pp. 159–181.

Miner, Valerie. "The Book in the World." *Creative Writing in America: Theory and Pedagogy*, edited by Joseph M. Moxley, NCTE, 1989, pp. 227-236.

Mura, David. *A Stranger's Journey: Race, Identity, and Narrative Craft in Writing*. University of Georgia Press, 2018.

Myers, D.G. *The Elephants Teach: Creative Writing Since 1880*. Prentice Hall, 1996.

Ogbechie, Sylvester Okwunodu. "The Historical Life of Objects: African Art History and the Problem of Discursive Obsolescence." *African Arts* vol 38 no. 4, 2005, pp. 62–95.

Okeke-Agulu, Chika. "Rethinking Mbari Mbayo: Osogbo Workshops in the 1960s, Nigeria." *African Art and Agency in the Workshop*, edited by Sidney Littlefield Kasfir and Till Förster, Indiana University Press, 2013, pp. 154-187.

Salesses, Matthew. "Pure Craft Is a Lie." *Pleiades*, www.pleiadesmag.com/pure-craft-is-a-lie-part-1.

Schramm, Wilbur. "Imaginative Writing." *Literary Scholarship: Its Aims and Methods*, University of North Carolina Press, 1941, pp. 175-213.

Shelnutt, Eve. "Notes from a Cell: Creative Writing Programs in Isolation." *Creative Writing in America: Theory and Pedagogy*, edited by Joseph M. Moxley, NCTE, 1989, pp. 3-22.

"UndocuNation!—U.C. Berkeley" University of California, Berkeley Center for Race & Gender. UC Berkeley, n.d. Web. 10 Oct. 2021. http://crg.berkeley.edu/content/undocunation

ESSAY

Spring Break in Chernobyl: Urbex, Apocalypse, and Materiality in Writing Classrooms

K. Shannon Howard

Abstract: *The practice of urban exploration, or urbex—an activity in which we confront and document landscapes of ruin and make meaning from them—acts as a focal point through which students may investigate and write about the world surrounding them by gaining new perspectives of physical spaces and objects that often go ignored in daily living. More importantly, urbex inspires writing that responds to existing problems in our world (resource scarcity, lack of sustainability, and environmental trauma) while also helping students to conceptualize a better one.*

Introduction: Lingering as Awareness

Many in the field of writing studies share a perspective that "economic disruption, endless violence, and, perhaps most important, environmental collapse should force us to reexamine what it means to work in the field" of composition (Lynch 458). This reexamination leads us to wonder how writing tasks in a composition classroom might become more reflective of and responsive to negative trends without pressing the doom button, so to speak, in our pedagogy. To that end, I argue that the practice of urban exploration, or urbex—an activity in which we confront and document landscapes of ruin and make meaning from them—may inspire writing that both responds to existing problems in our world and helps us conceptualize a better one. In doing so, students find new ways to "be" in the world, where, as Robert Yagelski says, we "begin to erase the boundary between writer as subject and world as object" (65).

Urbex, when approached with humility and awareness of privilege, encourages us to slow down and to linger in places where we once passed quickly—"to go where *everyone* has gone before, but where few have bothered to linger" (Bogost 34). Although Ian Bogost was not speaking about urbex when he encouraged this practice, the work of lingering leads us to more thoughtful reactions to the world's ruin and abandonment, which seem to encroach upon all public spaces now due to the earlier Great Recession and the current Covid-19 pandemic, both of which forced many businesses to close and homes to be foreclosed. Engaging in urbex, or urban exploration, both inside and outside the classroom makes our student writers and ourselves better stewards of the environment, and I believe, like Paul Lynch, that such stewardship is, most certainly, part of the writer's work at this particular time.

Fig 1: Author photograph of an abandoned motel in Eufaula, Alabama

Urban Exploration and Narratives of Ruin

James Nestor explained years ago that urban explorers are known for "closely examining and understanding the inner workings of our constructed world, of seeing civic society in its real, raw, unpainted, unplastered and unprettied state. It's internal city touring, but without guides, double-decker buses, maps or directions." Jeff Chapman, a zine writer who published about urbex and referred to himself as Ninjalicious in the underground exploring community, explains that those who engage in urbex avoid "passively consuming entertainment" because they "participate in the secret workings of cities and structures" and "appreciate fantastic, obscure spaces that might otherwise go completely neglected" (3). More specifically, participation in and appreciation for urban exploration cannot help but address what photographer Matthew Christopher calls "an age of consequences." By this phrase, Christopher explains how his work as a photographer of abandoned places has revealed that such places are not "anomalies" but ubiquitous reminders of "our current culture and the losses and failures that we are now sustaining" (4). In a nutshell, the work of exploring underground or abandoned places suggests what dystopia might bring and how it is already a part of many cities and towns in the developed world. Consequently, writing classrooms can incorporate this exploration to respond to and immerse participants in physical surroundings that might otherwise go unstudied by students regularly tied to screened worlds and digital platforms.

Pop culture narratives also point toward a new preoccupation with decay and ruin. Structures like former indoor malls, vacant downtown shops, and foreclosed homes form a new landscape that reveals the nature of a precarious and uncertain time; moreover, such settings are located not too far from college campuses and town squares, making debris and rubble common to those living and navigating even the most affluent sections of town. These texts in all media forms—novels, films, photography, streaming tv, and video games—inspire and inform a pedagogy based in the material world. Depictions of ruined landscapes and rubble did not begin in the 2010s; such images have always been present on screen, particularly during the twentieth century Cold War with Russia (think abandoned bomb shelters and hidden spy camps) and the horror genre post-Columbine in the early 2000s (abandoned schools and backpacks left behind). Ellen Jones, who has referred to the 2010s trend of urbex as "ruin porn," notes that cinema in particular has always believed that abandoned buildings "look great on film." However, these depictions are particularly common in our students' lifetimes—the late 2000s, 2010s, and today.

To begin, it may be no surprise that HBO's series *Chernobyl* (2019), the recent dramatization of the 1986 nuclear accident in Russia, garnered nineteen Emmy nominations. Although scenes from Chernobyl appear in other popular culture artifacts like the horror film *Chernobyl Diaries* (2012), which features young adults becoming prey to radioactive zombies, the HBO series treats the nuclear accident with a gravitas that belies our insecurities about current national governments and their failures to accept responsibility for planetary destruction. Referencing the proliferation of nuclear plants, authoritarian governments, and environmental problems the world has experienced recently, reviewer David Fear at *Rolling Stone* quips, "It doesn't take a nuclear physicist to see why it makes a lot of sense to look back on this moment right now." Urban explorer and photographer Rebecca Litchfield, in her collection *Soviet Ghosts*, describes how visiting the Chernobyl disaster site "opened [her] mind to the fragility of humanity and how what humans create can cause so much damage to the world" (1).

Video games commonly reveal landscapes where practicing urbex is common. A student alerted me years ago that characters must escape a landscape of rubble and destruction in the first-person shooter game *S.T.A.L.K.E.R.* (2007-2009). Additionally, the more recent *Chernobylite* (2021), also features "a lowly stalker trying to survive in a radioactive hell." The game's company, Farm 51, even creates an authentic landscape out of scanned images of 1986 Pripyat. HBO is also adapting the post-apocalyptic video game *The Last of Us* (2013-present) for the television screen due to the game's popularity and its compelling narrative. Like *The Walking Dead* (2010-present), which is based on a series of graphic novels, *The Last of Us* is an example of how apocalyptic narrative will soon be adapted for more than one medium, even if its characters fight to live in an abandoned American setting rather than in the midst of Chernobyl disaster imagery.

Fig 2: Author photo of an abandoned structure in rural Georgia that was repurposed for filming *The Walking Dead*. The words "away with you" and this wall were featured in the opening credits during the early years of the show's run.

Still, 3-D models of Chernobyl are not needed to imagine such a world among us today. A scene of a search through what appears to be apocalyptic rubble occurs inside a best-selling novel and film of the early 2010s, which could easily be imagined as a video game where a man must hunt for his missing wife. An abandoned indoor mall in Gillian Flynn's *Gone Girl* (2012) includes the narrator Nick's description of a once bustling shopping center turned wasteland in small town Missouri, a common site after businesses and malls closed due to the Great Recession. This description from the novel, strangely enough, sounds more like an account from Chernobyl or a horror film than from America itself:

> I'd expected the mall smell as we entered: that temperature controlled hollowness. Instead, I smelled old grass and dirt, the scent of the outdoors inside, where it had no place being. The building was heavy-hot, almost fuzzy, like the inside of a mattress.... It was surburbia, post-comet, post-zombie, post-humanity. A set of muddy shopping-cart tracks looped crazily along the white flooring. A raccoon chewed on a dog treat in the entry to a women's bathroom, his eyes flashing like dimes. (154)

More focus on ruins and less on apocalyptic hellscapes occur in blockbuster movie franchises like *Jurassic World* (2015), where the characters of this dinosaur sequel find refuge in the 1990s abandoned park. The old visitor's center, now in ruins, becomes a temporary haven where children engage in a form of urban exploration as they locate an old Jeep and repair it (a scene that also appeals to multiple generations in families watching this new trilogy of films). Adhering to genre expectations and debuting the same year as *World*, the opening scene from the spinoff series *Fear the Walking Dead* (2015-present) features the protagonist running, in order to escape a zombie, through an abandoned church covered in graffiti. In this series Los Angeles becomes a ruined landscape that contrasts sharply with the original show *The Walking Dead*, which is filmed in rural Georgia. As noted earlier, urbex as a term extends from the words "urban" and "exploration," where ruined buildings and deserted cities are common.[1]

In contrast to *Jurassic* blockbusters, Sean Baker's acclaimed independent film *The Florida Project* (2017) features an urban Orlando beyond Disney World's gates, the one that includes strip malls and defunct motels. A turning point in its narrative occurs when a group of abandoned buildings, affectionately labeled "the Abandids" by its six-year-old protagonist Moonie, become a playground for children who eventually destroy the place by lighting an old pillow on fire. The children's actions in the Abandids set off a chain of events that lead to Moonie's separation from her mother by Child Protective Services; nevertheless, the residents of the nearby hotels cheer on the destruction of these derelict buildings, gossiping that they were just a haven for drug users and prostitution. In most of these narratives, abandoned structures often symbolize and reinforce economic precarity and societal unrest, which speak to a twenty-first century fixation with apocalyptic scenarios and environmental dangers.

New Materialism: "Is" not "About"

The examples mentioned above often point toward some anxiety about entropy and destruction on a more global scale, not just in fiction but in our actual surroundings. Environmental philosopher Timothy Morton, in his description of ecological thought, explains that changing perspective through attention to the physical world is vital to understanding how to live responsibly: "It isn't *like* thinking about where your toilet waste goes. It *is* thinking about where your toilet waste goes" (127). Scholars focusing on materiality, or materialism, see the things of our world and the humans in it as participants in the same ontological space. This kind of perspective then prevents writers from writing *about* something as if it were separate or sublimated to human experience. Such divisions between the subject and object, as Yagelski suggested earlier, are counterproductive. He advocates for moving beyond the dualism of Cartesian knowledge—a philosophy where our senses and physical experiences are largely divorced from our minds at work. Instead, the world that contains issues and controversies *is* the world of

---

1. Rural exploration (or rurex, to some), while not discussed here, offers a similar canvas for thinking and writing. In truth, some of my students living in the country are more likely to pass abandoned farm equipment in a field rather than a deserted building downtown.

the writer, as both are caught up in what Morton describes throughout his work as a "mesh" of existence. (51). In her award-winning text *Still Life with Rhetoric,* Laurie Gries also explains that those who study writing are called to think about their physical existence, digital encounters, and their composing as intertwined, circulatory, and hard to separate. She, among others, has been a leader in addressing the use of what she refers to as "new" materialism to transform the fields of writing studies and rhetoric. Jane Bennett, although not a writing scholar, also prompts us to see the physical matter around us as "ad hoc groupings of diverse elements, of vibrant materials of all sorts" (23). Once we do so, she argues, cause and effect no longer matter; instead, we all, humans and nonhumans alike, "rebound" on one another (33).

Still, scholarship addressing the material world has a reputation for being obtuse and jargon heavy. Most humanists and posthumanists dealing in arguments of object-oriented ontology and materialism find refuge in a dense prose that alienates most instructors who might learn from it. Therefore, it is helpful to pause and reflect on scholarship older than the texts mentioned above. Derek Owens's 2001 text *Composition and Sustainability* actually calls for a check on inaccessible and specialized theory in favor of having "generalists and experts" work together to solve problems related to the physical world, particularly a world in jeopardy (133). Over twenty years ago Owens imagined a pedagogy where students "think critically about past, present, and future of their communities," and where teachers introduce new ways of thinking about a troubled environment close to home (76). Likewise, Charles Bergman, a Renaissance literature scholar in the Pacific Northwest, explains that studying the way his university manages water as a resource opened his eyes to how much the academy might offer us as a "silent syllabus" in teaching us the "meaning of place" and the value of sustainability (66). Richard Miller's *Writing at the End of the World* also provides essential questions and personal testimonials for framing an apocalyptic pedagogy in the face of disaster. Miller argues, with a photograph of Chernobyl on his book cover, that "hope can only be generated by confronting our desolate world and its urgent, threatening realities. The only way out is through" (27). Written for a more public audience, Andrew Blackwell's *Visit Sunny Chernobyl* also details the writer's own adventures through the world's most polluted locales with a bit more levity and accessible language, although its ethical center remains focused on the societal ills that create dispossessed peoples across the globe. Although such texts are illuminating, the use of urbex in a writing classroom need not include championing one specific cause or grounding a student in a specific political view. Instead, a focus on urbex often leads to a more organic change in the explorer/writer's treatment of a threatened environment. Such a change in perspective results from witnessing the aging and neglected places of the world that no one pauses to consider. Confronting abandoned structures naturally reminds us of our "human frailty" (Gates 104) and leads us to reconsider our place in the ruins.

My approach to English Composition II, a second semester writing course required of all freshmen, was the idea of "Apocalypse." When students arrive, I explain that this writing class is, in short, a new perspective on how places and objects make arguments in our daily lives and how such objects and places may determine their ability to survive in an apocalyptic scenario. Throughout the semester, I use activities to teach students how "joining the conversation" of academic research is based on images and ideas associated with abandonment and urban decay. Their ultimate goal, by the semester's end, is to create a research document in which they propose the recycling or upcycling of a specific tool or building to help people survive a large-scale disaster in our city. In doing so, they imagine what a thing or building might *be* or *become* when humans in their local area cope with disaster.

During the brainstorming and inquiry phase of their research, I start by challenging students to find rhetorical meaning in the structures around them. On Day One, much like Marilyn Cooper who prompts her students to address "a startlingly general topic" like the water supply (237), I challenge students to find an answer to the question, "Where does our water come from?" Cooper's pedagogy, grounded in ideas of what she refers to as "enchantment ontology," focuses on having students "engag[e] with others to make changes in the world and, in turn, themselves" (8). To accomplish a similar goal, I balance local and more global examples of the physical world in action and how students might become enmeshed in it more fully. After viewing a slide show about Disney World's physical layout and learning how Walt Disney himself chose to locate trash bins every thirty feet (he observed that guests tend to toss their candy wrappers at that distance), I ask students to walk outside the classroom and document how frequently trash cans and recycle bins are located around the building. Days later, I also request that they find a professor door that intrigues them and analyze the door's decorations and flyers in order to speculate what kind of person works inside the office. These early writing prompts help ease students into a different way of viewing their environment. In a sense, they teach them to "linger" (Bogost) rather than pass by the mundane structures that surround them. Once their perspective begins to shift and their comfort level with the theme is established, I offer a scholarly model to showcase ways that the material world may be more formally studied.

One model I offer in the early weeks is Thomas Rickert's study of Windows startup noises in *Ambient Rhetoric*, where "thinking about something as transparently given as an operating system's startup music, then, opens us to deeper reflections on the stretched and stretching nature of rhetoric.... More pointedly, it concretely demonstrates the limitations we set for ourselves in focusing on the salient, the visual, the semiotic, and the utilitarian. The world of our involvements is much richer than this" (133). The sentiment here prompts a reconsideration of sound, while most of the course I teach is dedicated toward a reconsideration of the ruin we see. Nevertheless, the challenge to focus and reflect on previously ignored parts of our daily lives is the same: the world of physical and sensory data is rich, persuasive, and underappreciated, but we may improve our ability to become attuned to it.

Examples like Rickert's research work because they call attention to the mundane and prompt a reconsideration of its importance. I also incorporate sections of Bergman's piece on the campus plumber to illustrate how a close study of our campus's hidden rooms and spaces reveals the university's priorities and goals in ways that most casual walks through a grassy quad might ignore. At this time, I explain that an underground tunnel exists on campus for maintenance purposes and that a cabin in the woods behind our classroom includes the ruins of an abandoned home from the 1960s. After a short walk to this location, I ask students to think of ways to repurpose this cabin so that future generations at the university might benefit from it. Urbex, therefore, is closer to home than students might initially surmise. In order to find these locations, however, campus residents have to go out of their way to study the world around them. No pictures or GPS can reveal what these places look like.

Finally, during the inquiry phase of this research, I ask students to recall memories in order to link prior student knowledge and personal narrative to larger issues of materiality during an apocalyptic event. One writing prompt that has gone viral is the task of writing about objects and places from one's childhood home, a writing assignment called "Where I'm From" that is used on both the high school and college level. In the "Where I'm From" poem by Kentucky poet George Ella Lyon, the poet describes her childhood not in terms of her fears or dreams but in terms of concrete objects surrounding her. The poem begins, "I am from clothespins, / from Clorox and carbon-tetrachloride. / I am from the dirt under the back porch. /(Black, glistening, / it tasted like beets.)." After listening to Lyon's impressions of childhood, made powerful by sharp sensory impressions of the physical world, students then write their own "Where I'm From" poem, describing the past in terms of their physical surroundings. These activities provide opportunities for students to look outward rather than inward, yet such writings often frame and illustrate more of a student's world view as well as a literacy narrative would. In other words, the students who often feel awkward describing a past experience with writing or reading are often more willing to describe physical settings that allow the "I" to act as an observer of reality rather than a champion of inner reality.[2] A description of a town or house often allows students to maintain some distance from self-obsessed thinking that may result from well-meaning questions such as "explain one interesting thing about yourself that we do not know." The defeatist response—"There is nothing interesting about me"—is harder to maintain when describing a place rather than one's own personality. The focus on physical reality also bridges the differences among student majors. Sherry Turkle explains that objects "bring philosophy down to earth. When we focus on objects, physicians and philosophers, psychologists and designers, artists and engineers are able to find common ground in everyday experience" (7-8). The embodied work of field observation on one's own campus, whether it leads to counting trash cans or describing doors, makes the work of learning and writing a visceral task rather than an abstract one. When students complete these activities, they must photograph and document where they have been and upload the results to their class blogs on Weebly or Wordpress. The inquiry phase of research ideally ends in a collection of notes and pictures from both class activities and homework assignments, all hosted digitally so that other students and I may explore alongside them.

Potential in Apocalypse

To visit abandoned places means confronting apocalypse now but also seeing potential for the future. As we move closer to the final research project due date, students are given

---

2. For example, past experience with more general writing prompts that ask students to talk about a memory that shaped their early life often led me to confront two problems: either I learned too much too soon about a student's traumatic history, or I learned nothing at all due to the personal nature of the questions.

time in class to investigate artists and urban planners who renovate spaces and find new uses for them. One is Anna Schuleit Haber, who created an installation called "Bloom" in the Massachusetts Mental Health Center that featured the planting of 28,000 flowers in a once deserted asylum (Vonnegut). Another repurposing movement has grown up around empty phone booths. Lara Georgieff explains how these "depressing husks" become free wifi kiosks for people in all five boroughs in New York. Margaret Ronda characterizes such objects as things that "have become unfastened from the productive circuits of capitalism, while remaining irreducible to the cyclical temporalities of biotic life" (83). In other words, many inventions and devices become outmoded quickly and then cannot decompose, even with some attempt to salvage or recycle parts. To upcycle or repurpose a thing is an attempt to stop the process of what is often planned obsolescence, which is characterized by Ronda as a "strategic evacuation of value" (78, 84). While obsolescing can hardly be stopped with one or two restructured phone booths, the option to redesign and fashion something new out of the old is evidence of problem solving abilities and creative visions needed to make the future sustainable. This is why students must find a solution to an apocalyptic scenario by refashioning or inventing something that will help others survive after the destruction.

The discovery of artists and planners who repurpose abandoned structures means finding potential in the midst of decay and ruin. Making something from nothing, or rather, from abandoned structures, involves thinking that is typical of what Claude Lévi-Strauss called bricolage. Lévi-Strauss explains that the bricoleur's approach centers on using existing resources rather than planning beyond them:

> Further, the "bricoleur" also, and indeed principally, derives his poetry from the fact that he does not confine himself to accomplishment and execution: he "speaks" not only *with* things, as we have already seen, but also through the medium of things: giving an account of his personality and life by the choices he makes between his limited possibilities. (21)

Studying the repurposing efforts of artists and city planners brings students back to the realm of possibility. While the work of the bricoleur does help the individual find power in a place where they formerly felt none, it does not detract from the power of things or structures to humble us, as some critics of composition's new materialism fear. This idea of bricolage seems most closely related to the recent trend of the "maker movement" in education. Kristin Arola has explained in multiple presentations and talks why the maker movement sometimes reveals troubling assumptions about a human's relationship to materiality. Arola stresses the need to cultivate "slow composition"—one that requires more "mindfulness" and "consideration" when dealing with materials that become our partners in creation. The idea of a "maker" controlling her surroundings is ultimately counterproductive if it doesn't aid us in respecting the physical world around us. In other words, through bricolage and attention to the physical we see that things operate partially due to human intervention but also partially through combinations and juxtapositions of moving parts outside our own control, parts that transform the "mesh" inside which we exist. The work of bricolage need not detract from a thing's power; rather, it amplifies it and makes it more agentive.

Fig. 3: Author photograph of an abandoned structure located behind campus. Alongside the anthropology department, students visit this location during a class meeting and take notes.

As students narrow their focus and begin to advance their own arguments, they submit written drafts in which they propose new use for abandoned malls in our current city (similar to the one featured in *Gone Girl*) or abandoned fertilizer plants that left many unemployed in their childhood towns during the recession. Students also focus on ways in which abandoned cars on private property affect neighborhoods and how such vehicles can be used in an emergency. Most interestingly, a few students, moving just a few meters beyond the property line of their own family residences, discovered old structures or corner stores in ruin and then considered how to transform them. Such work led them to interview and engage with neighbors in ways they had not done previously. Through peer review and workshopping these drafts, students told animated stories of how they explored various places and learned unexpected things about their communities.

Fig. 4: Author photograph of a drainage tunnel beneath a neighborhood road.

(Re)discovery: Knowledge Hidden

In Moses Gates's memoir *Hidden Cities*, the author explains that by taking part in urban exploration, we gain a needed perspective on the cities we travel through day by day (25). After a trip down into the Paris catacombs, Gates also describes walking the Parisian streets and not needing a map; his sense of direction had been honed. Time underground gave him "an almost instinctual sense of navigation and understanding" (72). Steven Johnson's concluding pages of *The Ghost Map* also productively hint at the invisible wonders that determine our health and quality of life: "The construction of the new sewers [after a cholera outbreak in London] was every bit as epic and enduring as the building of the Brooklyn Bridge or the Eiffel Tower. Its grandeur lies belowground, out of sight, and so it is not invoked as regularly as other, more iconic, achievements of the age." He goes on to say, "Tourists may marvel at Big Ben or the London Tower, but beneath their feet lies the most impressive engineering wonder of all" (207-08). The same may be said about confronting urbex in the writing class: new relationships to the physical world where material hierarchies are reevaluated and dismantled make for more observant, concerned, and flexible citizen-writers whose studies have immediate impact on how they view their own campus and city. Likewise, exploration of infrastructure in cities leads to curiosity about the history of hidden systems beneath our feet. Such knowledge prepares future citizens to imagine how abandoned and hidden structures might be protected, updated, or repurposed.

In the course I approach these topics without continually invoking the term apocalypse, even as students look at the recent movement of extreme tourism that brings people to visit the still radioactive site of Chernobyl. As a practice project leading up to the final one, students must write an argumentative letter to a future first-year student who, when planning their Spring Break vacation, is considering engaging in extreme tourism, a trend in traveling to some of the most deserted and dangerous places on the planet. In this situation the hypothetical student has been given an opportunity to travel to Pripyat, where the 1986 nuclear disaster occurred. The letter incorporates research from credible sources that support or disagree with the choice to travel there. Surprisingly, some composition students do agree that the trip is worth it, citing the need to accept such waste and destruction as part of our history that bears no repeating. For those arguing otherwise, their opposition is often a matter of expense: trips to Russia include flight costs, hotels, and arrangement of tours with companies that might take advantage of naïve Americans interested in exploring. They also mention that confronting a place like Chernobyl causes stress rather than relaxation and, consequently, would make a terrible vacation for any student overwhelmed by classes, jobs, and family. Yet it is always surprising how many people see the importance of such a journey. During this process, students also begin to recognize why Chernobyl's abandoned site might provoke strong feelings about environmental stewardship and the need to protect future generations from devastation.

Explorer and writer Robert MacFarlane explains that Stephen Graham, who wrote the *Gentle Art of Tramping*, was "one of a line of pedestrians who saw that wandering and wondering had long gone together." In the act of tramping, Graham was able, MacFarlane notes, to "make a stale world seem fresh, surprising and wondrous again, to discover astonishment on the terrain of the familiar" (230). This same experience is what urban exploration brings to the classroom: the opportunity to "resee" the ordinary and consider how things and places persuade us without using language. It also involves the entire body, since walking is a requirement for the exploration that occurs. Rather than educate the head in isolation, this form of study involves physical and tactile encounters, the kind that aid us in shaping knowledge and memory. Such physical and mental activity demonstrate how, as J. Michael Rifenburg has argued, "the body and the mind are inextricably linked during the composing process, how our skin and bones impact our writing, how our breathing and heartbeat impact how and what we write." Yagelski's desire to break the Cartesian habit of dividing body and mind seems fulfilled here in the work of urban exploration and the kinesthetic opportunities it offers.

Nevertheless, the romantic idea of the solo traveler traipsing across the countryside also raises an important concern. To return to an example mentioned earlier, the horror film *Chernobyl Diaries* follows genre expectations by featuring naïve young travelers who unwittingly become trapped in a deadly place due to a lack of humility. In this film two college students, romantically involved, kiss and pose for a selfie in front of a view of the Chernobyl nuclear reactor that caused so much damage in the 80s. The group of students takes photographs everywhere at the abandoned site, but the one they stage together in this scene occurs in someone's former apartment. Inside this same room are abandoned family photos, books, and furniture. One of the students even starts to pick something up when Uri, their guide, stops him and warns him of the radiation. This clip, along with giving students a sense of what the nuclear accident did to the Russian landscape, raises important questions for them and me about the colonizing nature of urbex. Although practitioners of urbex are typically not known for stealing from the places they visit (Jeff Chapman cautions people not even to leave traces of footprints in construction sand) (26-27), collections of lost items and personal photographs remind us how quickly exploration becomes colonial and exploitive in nature.

When students do consider exploring as part of their projects, I urge them to stay far away from the former private residences of others and to focus on the city's infrastructure and design as it has aged over time in order to avoid appropriative voyeurism. In looking more at the city's physicality and avoiding abandoned homes, students are led to find solutions to local problems rather than being led to gawk at someone else's foreclosed property. Likewise, I urge students to remember how race and class play a role in how someone might navigate off the beaten path in such a city. As a white woman, I have often peeked inside old buildings or climbed old fences without suffering any consequences. The most disturbing moment I encountered was not that threatening at all: my cousin and I sought a view of the riverfront from the vantage point of a dirt road and what I had assumed was an abandoned property at the end of it. The owner approached our vehicle angrily, asking what our business was in coming so far off the main road. Once he saw two white women inside the vehicle and understood we were trying to catch a glimpse of the river, he relented and even pointed out the best locations to capture photos. My whiteness allows me to explore such areas in ways that my Black students may never feel comfortable doing due to possible confrontations with law enforcement or other individuals who use firearms to protect their residences. Learning respect for the physical world does not mean we depoliticize it for our own purposes and ignore the privilege inherent in straying from the pavement.

The respect my freshmen have shown both the environment and the research tasks during the course is refreshing. Students have been overwhelmingly positive about the experience of focusing on the material world and learning about a place on the opposite side of the world that confronted this destruction. Throughout the various classes I have taught, class members have stressed the value of learning to see the world differently and being prompted to change their perspectives about the environment. The experience of moving, at least moderately, from a solely anthropocentric view of the world to a view that takes "things" into account is evident in their attitudes about the curriculum. Such a change in perspective occurs through researching, thinking, and even moving differently in our surroundings as well as writing about them. Rather than lead us away from human concerns, the material investigations we conduct as part of urbex often lead us back to essential questions about what kinds of humans we are now and hope to be in the future.

Works Cited

Arola, Kristin. "Slow Composition: An Indigenous Approach to Making." Skype Presentation. *Conference on College Composition and Communication.* Tampa, FL. March 18-21 2015.

Bennett, Jane. *Vibrant Matter: A Political Ecology of Things.* Duke University Press, 2010.

Bergman, Charles. "What I Learned from the Campus Plumber." *Placing the Academy: Essays on Landscape, Work, and Identity,* edited by Jennifer Sinor and Rona Kaufman, Utah State University Press, 2007, pp 65-82.

Blackwell, Andrew. *Visit Sunny Chernobyl and Other Adventures in the World's Most Polluted Places.* Rodale, 2013.

Bogost, Ian. *Alien Phenomenology or What It's Like to Be a Thing.* University of Minnesota Press, 2009.

Chapman, Jeff (Ninjalicious). *Access All Areas: A User's Guide to the Art of Urban Exploration.* Infiltration, 2005.

Chernobyl, directed by Craig Mazin, performances by Jared Harris, Stellan Skarsgard, and Emily Harris. HBO, 2019, www.hbo.com/chernobyl.

Chernobyl Diaries. directed by Bradley Parker, performances by Jesse McCartney, Jonathan Sadowski, and Olivia Taylor Dudley. Warner Bros, 2012, *Amazon,* www.amazon.com/Chernobyl-Diaries-Devin-Kelley/dp/B009KS5SJ6/ref=sr_1_1?dchild=1&keywords=chernobyl+diaries&qid=1615082832&sr=8-1.

Chernobylite. All in! Games SA, 2021.

Christopher, Matthew. *Abandoned America*: *The Age of Consequences.* JonGlez, 2014.

Cooper, Marilyn. *The Animal Who Writes: A Posthumanist Composition.* University of Pittsburgh Press, 2019.

Fear, David. "'Chernobyl Review': Revisiting Russia's Nuclear Disaster as a Season in Hell." *Rolling Stone,* 6 May 2019, www.rollingstone.com/tv/tv-reviews/chernobyl-tv-review-hbo-830621/.

The Florida Project, directed by Sean Baker, performances by Willem Defoe, Bria Vinaite, and Brooklynn Prince, A24, 2017.

Flynn, Gillian. *Gone Girl.* Random House, 2012.

Gates, Moses. *Hidden Cities.* Penguin, 2013.

Graham, Stephen. *The Gentle Art of Tramping.* Budge Press, 2007.

Georgieff, Lara. "NYC Phone Booths Will Become Free Wifi Kiosks in All Five Boroughs." *AdWeek,* 20 Nov. 2014, www.adweek.com/brand-marketing/nyc-phone-booths-will-become-free-wifi-kiosks-161569/.

Gries, Laurie E. *Still Life with Rhetoric: A New Materialist Approach to Visual Rhetorics.* Utah State University Press, 2015.

Johnson, Steven. *The Ghost Map.* Penguin, 2006.

Jones, Ellen E. "'Ruin Porn' and Cinema's Obsession with Disused Buildings." *The Guardian*, 14 Aug 2017, https://www.theguardian.com/film/2017/aug/14/ruin-porn-cinemas-obsession-with-disused-buildings-grey-gardens-la-soledad.

Jurassic World, directed by Colin Trevorrow, performances by Chris Pratt and Bryce Dallas Howard, Universal, 2015.

The Last of Us. Sony Computer Entertainment, 2013.

Lévi-Strauss, Claude. *The Savage Mind*. University of Chicago Press, 1966.

Litchfield, Rebecca. *Soviet Ghosts*. Carpet Bombing Culture, 2014.

Lynch, Paul. "Composition's New Thing: Bruno Latour and the Apocalyptic Turn." *College English*, vol. 74, no. 5, 2012, pp 458-76.

MacFarlane, Robert. *The Wild Places*. Penguin, 2008.

Miller, Richard E. *Writing at the End of the World*. University of Pittsburgh Press, 2005.

Nestor, James. "The Art of Urban Exploration." *SFGate*, Aug 16, 2007, www.sfgate.com/travel/article/The-Art-of-Urban-Exploration-2546675.php.

Owens, Derek. *Composition and Sustainability: Teaching for a Threated Generation*. NCTE, 2001.

"Pilot." *Fear the Walking Dead*, directed by Adam Davidson, performances by Kim Dickens and Cliff Curtis, AMC, 23 Aug. 2015, www.amc.com/shows/fear-the-walking-dead/episodes/season-1-episode-01-episode-1--1235.

Rickert, Thomas. *Ambient Rhetoric: The Attunements of Rhetorical Being*. University of Pittsburg Press, 2013.

Rifenburg, J. Michael. "Writing as Embodied, College Football Plays as Embodied: Extracurricular Multimodal Composing." *Composition Forum*, vol. 29, 2014, https://compositionforum.com/issue/29/writing-as-embodied.php.

Ronda, Margaret. "Obsolesce." *Veer Ecology: A Companion for Environmental Thinking*, edited by Jeffrey Jerome Cohen and Lowell Duckert, University of Minnesota Press, 2017, pp.76-89.

S.T.A.L.K.E.R. GSC Game World Publishing, 2007.

Turkle, Sherry. "Introduction." *Evocative Objects: Things We Think With*, edited by Sherry Turkle, MIT Press, 2007, pp 3-11.

Vonnegut, Nanette. "Transcendent and Tenacious." *The Take Magazine*, 1 Oct 2015, thetakemagazine.com/transcendent-and-tenacious/.

Yagelski, Robert P. *Writing as a Way of Being*. Hampton Press, 2011.

CONNECTING

Can We Flourish?

Christy I. Wenger

Teachers and students alike can agree on one shared truth of this past academic year: it was tough. Even though many of us found our way back into classrooms, sometimes masked and sometimes not, Covid continued to present new hurdles to our tried-and-true active teaching methods. Students struggled to keep up with the social and emotional demands of the face-to-face classroom after so many pandemic interruptions over the past two years, and teachers struggled to foster engagement and make meaningful learning gains in their classes. I met weekly with the instructors in my writing program to talk through classroom engagement and to brainstorm new ways to keep our students participating, learning, and simply just showing up for class. Just about every campus-wide workshop I held through my Center for Teaching and Learning focused in some way on getting students engaged in class and involved in their learning. Inevitably, these pedagogical discussions of our classrooms gave way to connected conversations about the emotional state of those in attendance, faculty and staff who were not only carrying the burden of increased emotional labor through the pandemic as teachers but also as sisters, brothers, spouses, and more. The consensus was clear: no one on campus was flourishing.

The widespread burnout and low morale that has transformed higher education culture has been dubbed the "great disengagement" by many who have attempted to account for the somewhat lower percentage of job turnover in higher education but the overwhelming fracture in belonging and community on university campuses across the nation (Lubell; Fea). Faculty may be remaining in their jobs (in part because of the abysmal academic job market) but they are discontent and distant. Unlike in other sectors, "faculty members are not walking away in droves, but they are waving goodbye to norms and systems that prevailed in the past," says Kevin McClure and Alyssa Hicklin Fryar in a recent *Chronicle of Higher Education* article. We could view McClure and Fryar's statement with caution and wonder how higher education could possibly perform its mission without the boundless passion of its professoriate to tend to the needs of our increasingly academically malnourished students. Faculty may well be examples of the phenomenon of "quiet quitting" which has been much-discussed of late. According to NPR, "Quiet quitters do only the work assigned and nothing more" (Kilpatrick). Quiet quitters aren't flourishing, and they do not see the value in going above and beyond the letter of their positions.

We could use these stories as a sign that the sky is indeed falling. Or we might use these observations as an opportunity to question the norms that have prevailed in higher education that are simply no longer tenable; we might use it to create new systems that work better for more of us. Quiet quitting and the great disengagement may be signs that we need to examine ways to create healthier work-life boundaries and a larger indication that the norms and systems that prevailed in higher education prior to Covid will not suffice as we move into a world marked by endemic Covid. We might see them as a call to create a culture better committed to flourishing and wellbeing.

We know that some of those norms and systems that prevailed in higher education were not serving our teachers, our staff, or our students. Covid itself exposed long-held distrust against distance learning. My residential, regional university, which prides itself on small class sizes and intimate instructor-student relationships, is an illustrative case. During the worst of Covid, we transitioned to emergency remote teaching like everyone else and celebrated our success. But as emergency remote teaching gave way to more thoughtful and prepared discussions of distance learning, as we were called upon to create a measured response instead of a knee-jerk reaction to Covid, the celebrations gave way to entrenchments. Face-to-face teaching is such a deeply rooted norm at my institution that higher administration assumed it should and could return to its pre-Covid level of offering less than ten percent of courses online this past academic year even while Covid still raged our campus and community outbreaks were common. Our students rebelled, and some faculty who discovered immeasurable benefits of teaching online dug in. In the end, we ran closer to thirty percent of courses online. As a campus leader of online education efforts at my university, the rapid growth of remote leaning options and infrastructure is one of the most exciting of Covid outcomes for me though my excitement is certainly not shared by all.

Covid didn't create all of our problems in higher education, but it did certainly help to make visible where our systems needed changing and norms needed addressing. In my career as an academic, I've been committed to considering how higher education has promoted *eudaimonia*, Aristotle's term for flourishing, a happiness based in long-lasting well-being and not a fleeting emotion. Too many institutions have neglected to create an environment where individuals can flourish, a place where a commitment to well-being remains a feature. My academic research and labor has centered on encouraging well-being in the academic workplace by intervening in the status quo and by inventing different creative environments in which flourishing can take place. Sometimes sustaining well-being is about enabling better work/life boundaries for our faculty and staff, and sometimes it is about embracing an online teaching environment that enables accessibility to more students, especially non-traditional and rural.

I read this edition of "Connecting" through the lens of well-being and encourage others to as well. To figure out how we claim a culture of flourishing, we need not only to address the phenonmenon of disengagement but to also look more deeply at our existing successes as well as the failed norms and systems that need revising to promote well-being. Maybe it is time to take another look at passion, as Joonna Smitherman Trapp does in her opening piece. Smitherman Trapp finds hope in her discovery that passion may well indeed be the catalyst for career engagement, even in our current cultural climate that is hostile to the profession. Passion for teaching is a norm Smitherman Trapp finds worth redeeming. Jamey Gallagher too investigates the stakes of passion for teachers. He urges readers to rediscover passion by upending norms and by embracing the nontraditional: non-traditional ways of teaching; non-traditional students; and non-traditional deadlines. Gallagher reminds us that if we are looking for passion in our classes and from our students and teachers and cannot find it, perhaps we are defining it too narrowly or looking in the wrong places; it is our norms that need addressing not the emotional investments of our students and teachers. Naomi Gades rounds out our section with two poems that reconsider the process and value of two of our profession's most emotionally laborious tasks: grading and applying for positions. We may not know where Covid will take us this academic year, but one valuable practice we can continue together is investigating and advocating for what will make us flourish together.

Works Cited

McClure, Kevin R. and Alisa Hicklin Fryar. "The Great Faculty Disengagement: Faculty Members Aren't Leaving in Droves, But They Are Increasingly Pulling Away." *Chronicle of Higher Education*, 19 January 2022, https://www.chronicle.com/article/the-great-faculty-disengagement?cid2=gen_login_refresh&cid=gen_sign_in.

Fea, John. "College and university faculty members are disengaging." 21 January 2022, https://currentpub.com/2022/01/21/college-and-university-faculty-members-are-disengaging/.

Kilpatrick, Amina. "What Is 'Quiet Quitting' and How It May Be a Misnomer for Setting Boundaries at Work." 19 August 2022, https://www.npr.org/2022/08/19/1117753535/quiet-quitting-work-tiktok.

Lubell, Mark. "The Great Disengagement: Has COVID Changed the Culture of Higher Education? *CEPB*, 18 May 2022. https://environmentalpolicy.ucdavis.edu/news/great-disengagement-has-covid-tranformed-culture-higher-education.

A Meditation: Why Teach?

Joonna Smitherman Trapp

What makes teaching a vocation that continues to draw smart and talented people even though the pay can be less-than-great, the workload damaging, and the rewards from societal and political opinion currently nonexistent? Frederick Buechner, a presbyterian minister, talks about the notion of vocation in his well-known book, *Wishful Thinking*. Our English word "vocation" comes from *vocare*, a Latin word meaning "to call," and Buechner further defines the word as signifying "the work" we are "called to do" (118). I'm always amazed at my university that teachers haven't heard about this idea. To them, vocation smacks of career-mindedness and doesn't fit very well with a liberal arts impulse.

But Buechner rehabilitates the word, making it soar above the mundane meaning of modern usage. And you don't have to be a person of faith to understand this at all. Consider these further comments he makes. The kind of work we ought to do (we are called to do, in his words) is the "kind of work (*a*) that you need most to do and (*b*) that the world most needs to have done." To Buechner, how we choose to work and live is two-pronged and best expressed by his most famous statement: "The place God calls you to is the place where your deep gladness and the world's deep hunger meet" (119).

In my experience, the younger generation of teachers entering the academy are quite exceptional in their ability to communicate ideas, in their desire to serve the institution, and in their passion for research. The academic job, however, is not without its complications. Researchers report that negative attitudes in a competitive job climate often speak to job dissatisfaction, loss of job security, and the unkind and or harsh working environments that many teachers in our fields experience. Yet, I meet teachers who demonstrate a genuine love of what they do all the time. How is it possible that a profession so full of troubling trends can still claim people who are committed teachers? Some of this answer might lie in Buechner's idea of vocation.

We notice other illustrations of *vocare* around us in other fields. Teaching isn't the only profession peopled by passionate practitioners. My son is an artist. He works two other jobs to have money to live so that he can spend his free time doing his art. After a day of working in elementary education, he goes to his tiny, cluttered artist studio in downtown Fort Collins, Colorado, and sketches and colors. He attends conventions and other artsy-fartsy events to sell prints and promote his work. He works on weekends at an artist supply store, probably spending much of his money from that job on supplies. His Christmas wish list for the family always includes expensive markers and art boards.

In him, I see joy and excitement, love and passion. The kinds of values that only a true doer of the art could manifest. He has a real *vocare* for art. I get that because (most of the time) I feel the same way. Even when I'm exhausted because I stayed up until three in the morning responding to student writing, even when my paycheck doesn't make it to the end of the month, even when I get so upset with a class that I want to yell at them, even then—I still know that I have a joyous vocation.

Of course, I have met teachers who cannot live in the same heart-space. And for reasons that make good sense in this current environment. Perhaps for them, teaching goes hand-in-hand with something else they love to do—research or engaging in public debate or dialog, for example. Around my college, those of us who geek out about teaching find each other. We are the ones who show up for pedagogy workshops or teaching tools demonstrations. We're the ones in the halls after class who have to find someone to share "what just happened in my class" stories. You can't shut us up. We babble on about something we tried that was cool. We incessantly chatter away about our funny and brilliant students. And we diligently seek help for our student in trouble, worrying into the night about how to make a difference for that individual.

Yes, we are an annoying lot. We are like my son who can't wait to show a new caricature he has done, looking eagerly into your face to see what you think, hoping to catch a light in your eyes of recognition or appreciation. We may find satisfaction in college service or in our research, but at heart, we recognize that we are teachers, and that is our *vocare*.

That is not mere career-mindedness! Buechner gives us a heuristic about how to make some sense of the joy we experience in our art of teaching. That passion is not self-serving. Yes, we can take pride in our work and feel confidence that we know our field and our students, but more importantly, it is satisfying because it serves the great hunger we feel exists in this world. We are teachers. And nothing that is said or done in the political world can diminish the deep gladness we experience in the midst of such doing.

And for those of us who are called to be teachers and are finding the current situation challenging or are experiencing a sense of defeat or loss, we also realize that teaching doesn't just happen in the academy. Teachers who communicate well and care about the world and its hunger are needed in all professions everywhere. The best leaders and shapers of community in this world are people who can talk to others and help them learn.

I'm so grateful for everyone with a call for teaching, whether you are in the academy or finding other ways and venues to make a difference. The world needs you.

Work Cited

Buechner, Frederick. *Wishful Thinking*. HarperOne, 1993.

An Encomium for Community College Students in Five Scenes

Jamey Gallagher

Scene 1: The Committee

Books start arriving at my apartment by the boxful. As part of the committee judging the CCCC Outstanding Book Contest, I am inundated with books, and I am excited to get down to reading them. I feel like a graduate student all over again, reading things I would never read if I weren't "made" to (New Materialisms, anyone?). Most of the books excite me and make me think about how I can move forward as a teacher of first year writing. Some of them hurt my brain. Some of them annoy me.

But what I'm most struck by is the fact that almost all of the books, monographs and collections, feature writing that situates students as traditional— just coming out of high school. Almost all of this writing is coming from folks in four-year universities. Writing students are depicted as young, embarking on adult life but not quite there yet. The books have some relevance to what I'm doing at the community college, but I am struck, again and again, by how much these folks are missing.

What happens when we define our students as young, as young adults, as nascent, as inexperienced? We lose the good that adult students bring to the classroom with them.

Scene 2: The Online Literature Class

I have taken over an online Brit Lit II class for a colleague on leave. I change things in the course minimally— replacing *Hard Times* with *Mrs. Dalloway*— knowing there is only so much I can do, given the constraints of "Quality Matters" and...time. (I teach 5/5.) I have taught two literature classes since arriving at my institution ten years ago, but those classes were very small and comprised almost exclusively students that had been in my classes previously and knew what to expect from me.

This is a whole new ballgame.

I notice a difference right away, even before the class has officially started, when one student starts his introduction with the word: "Salutations!" Again, before the class has even started, students are emailing me about the broken links to a Wordsworth documentary. Are they actually going to *watch* that, I wonder?

Ah, I think, *so this is what some of my colleagues want*. They want students who, like them, are serious and delight in language. A certain kind of challenge.

I prefer my students turning shit in late and questioning why we're doing what we're doing. I prefer the question "*Why* are we doing this again?" (a question I got last night) to a full embrace of the academic venture. I prefer a different kind of challenge.

I teach the Brit Lit II class to the best of my ability, but I have no desire to repeat the experience.

Scene 3: Placement

I read thousands of responses that were written for our self-directed placement tool, as I'm working on an article about the reading practices of incoming "returning" students. "Returning" students are defined in this case as over 30. Is there a good term for these students? "Adult learners?" "Returning students?" Nothing quite captures it.

People.

I am amazed and impressed by what I read. Some of these in-coming students write about their love for urban fiction and religious literature. They talk about reading to improve their lives and their communities. They write about who they want to come back to school for: themselves, their children, their communities.

I learn more about these students through their responses than some of my colleagues learn in their classes. I am convinced of that. The personal histories of these students are kept hidden in many classes, like in my own Brit Lit class. We don't allow our students to bring their lives into the classroom with them— not often enough, at least. In turn, we don't make it possible to get the best, most engaged work from these students.

Scene 4: The Faculty Meeting

There is trouble in the English Department (is there ever *not* trouble in the English Department?). We meet in a large room to hammer out a "mission statement." There are more than forty of us in the room (pre-Covid, of course). We get into groups to discuss. The "reporting back" gets contentious.

A colleague claims that our students don't have any passion anymore. Where is their passion? I respond by talking about the self-directed writing projects my students do and how much passion I see every semester.

But what about the humanities, he replies, what about English majors?

Another colleague tells a story about a young man who didn't like *Jane Eyre*. I keep waiting for the story to shift, to change, for some character development, but that's the whole story: she is surprised that this student didn't like *Jane Eyre*.

And I realize: maybe some of my colleagues can only see passion on their own terms.

Scene 5: The Classroom

Let me tell you, things are not always easy in my classroom. Sometimes it is a place of great tension. I yelled for the first time in eighteen years in class last fall semester. There is sometimes a whole lot of tension in classes, especially wildly diverse classrooms with students of all ages.

But, damn, people are bringing themselves to the classroom. Once you open them up, things can happen.

In the community college, we are serving all kinds of people. I considered having a list here of some of the students I have this semester, but I don't want to minimize them, shrink them down to ages, ethnicities, races, jobs, responsibilities. Suffice it to say: they have all kinds of identities. They are working just as hard or harder than most of us who have become PhDs and teachers.

There is one thing that I know for sure: these are not the students that scholars in my discipline are writing about, and they are not the students that some of my colleagues recognize as passionate. But these students are driving forward what we're doing in interesting ways, by asking those questions about why our courses and their writing matter. They know what matters. They bring reading histories we too often ignore. They are in the "real world," however we want to define it.

They can tell us a lot. If we listen.

grading

i, too, dislike it: there are things that are enjoyable beyond all this shuffling.
  doing it, however, with a perfect contempt for it, one discovers in
  it after all, a place for the splendid
    paragraphs that can cohere, theses
     that can control, conclusions that can persuade
      if they must, these things are important not because a

letter grade can be assigned to them but because they are
  useful. when they become so unintelligible as to become unreadable,
  the same thing may be said by all of us, that we
    cannot admire what
    we cannot understand: the phrase
      dangling at the beginning of a sentence or in search of something to
modify, fragments languishing, a naked quote dropped in, a cliched introduction
  to start off, the misreading student twitching with glee like an eager cross-
examiner, the passive-
  voice fan, the late turn-in—
    nor should we exclude
      the "throughout histories" and
"debated topic todays"; all these phenomena we mark.
  one must make a distinction
  however: when dragged into an essay by half effort, the result is not an a
    nor till the students we teach can be
     ciceronians of
     the current day---beyond
      five paragraphs and can present
for inspection, convincing essays with real thought in them, shall we enjoy
  it. in the meantime, if you look for on the one hand
  the raw thinking of freshmen in
    all its rawness and
    that which on the other hand is
      genuine, you are interested in grading.

—Naomi Gades

dear search applicant committee:

i would like to
regret to inform you
that i am a highly qualified candidate
for this position.
due to an overwhelming number
of courses presentations papers articles
book chapters evals letters
service commitments
applications received
we are not able to offer
the health insurance i need
though a paycheck would be nice, too.

i actually enjoy teaching students
and i am desperately ready to
keep your application on file
and develop four entirely new preps
if that's what you need
for subsequent searches.
we wish you the best of nameless luck
or blessings as may be appropriate
in your future endeavors
like scholarly publishing cover letters
filling out human resources forms
and producing beautiful spreadsheets
the color of despair (red).

we enjoyed our electronic and/or physical interaction and
given your excellent achievements we are sure
you will find success
in again mustering your small army
of sample syllabi and teaching philosophies.
i promise if you hire me
i will do a good job and profess
publish and serve with top marks
and also win the peace prize
and compose questionable poetry.

best,
best wishes,
sincerely,
and again with regrets,
and absurdly undying hope,

email auto signature.

—**Naomi Gades**

BOOK REVIEWS

The Pandemic Forces Us Back to Our Roots

Irene Papoulis

This year's wonderful group of reviews begins with a book that predates the pandemic and assumes that students fully exist as bodies in the room (Wenger, reviewed by Overstreet). How much has changed since Wenger's thoughtful reflections about yoga practices in teaching writing!

By now, of course, we have all learned to work on screens, sometimes with our students present only in their little squares. However, that new reality points us as well to how *little* has changed. The Expanded Perspectives that AEPL is founded on are more necessary now than ever. As we exist in our current era of technology, we have even more of an imperative to continue to honor our students' bodies and their lived experiences in our classrooms. Our students, most of whom "live in a world where they never had a paper-centric sense of privacy," (Knudsen, reviewing Miller) have a profound need for guidance on how to navigate productive relationships with their inner selves, with each other, and with the world.

These books offer a range of ways to help students do that, even while online (Borgman and McArdle, reviewed by Crozier). They offer new ways to cultivate creativity (Dively, reviewed by Williams), and to delve deeper into the knowledge of self and others that is fostered by autoethnography (Jackson and McKinney, reviewed by A. Scott). They also invite us to move forward by looking backward, to the lessons that await as we contemplate the history of progressive education (Suhor, reviewed by S. Scott).

It is heartening to know that the work of AEPL persists, and *will* persist, through struggles of all kinds. We all live in our bodies, and the more we can encourage our students to remember and manage that fact by approaching their own, and others', mysteries with compassion and ideally a clear philosophical foundation (Smith, reviewing Nelson), the more we will all be able to continue to thrive.

✦

Book Reviews

Wenger, Christy. *Yoga Minds, Writing Bodies: Contemplative Writing Pedagogy.* WAC Clearinghouse and Parlor Press, 2015. 199 pp.

Matthew Overstreet
Khalifa University

When given the chance to review a book for *JAEPL*, I immediately suggested Christy Wenger's *Yoga Minds, Writing Bodies*. Not only is this a book I highly respect, but one of its themes is perhaps more relevant than ever today, some six years after its publication. As we struggle through a seemingly interminable pandemic, frustration and frayed nerves abound. Now is an apt time to slow down, to consider our embodied reality and the automated, habituated responses that often alienate us from ourselves and the world. Wenger's book, apart from being philosophically insightful and artfully written, provides practical guidance as to how we might do such work with our students.

Wenger is an advocate of contemplative pedagogy, an oft-discussed topic in *JAEPL*, to which, you might have noticed, she has been a contributor as well as the editor of "Connecting." *Yoga Minds* details her efforts to integrate her preferred contemplative practice—yoga—with college writing instruction. Admittedly, I'm an odd choice to review a book about yoga. I'm a fairly staid 40-year-old man who has never done yoga and who tried meditation once only to be profoundly bored. I also, I'm ashamed to admit, have not yet incorporated into my pedagogy the contemplative practices for which Wenger advocates. That said, even if they are not my own, I can see the value of Wenger's teaching methods. I can also see the value of her theoretical insights, particularly as they relate to the role of embodiment in the writing and thinking process. All told, I believe that the ideas in *Yoga Minds* can be of broad relevance.

Structure-wise, *Yoga Minds* consists of an introduction, then three theory-centric chapters along with three extensive interchapters in which teaching practices are discussed. The theory portion centers on explicating and showing the value of mindfulness, defined as "embodied self-reflectivity" (40). Mindfulness, achieved through non-judgmental focus, Wenger argues, "creates a critical distance, a space between perception and response, that allows for . . . intentional response as opposed to automatic, unthinking and habitual reaction" (11). This more intentional orientation towards self and world, she argues, can greatly benefit writers and thinkers. It can help us notice and adjust habitual practices or default reactions that might interfere with knowledge-making. Through attention to our bodies and the affective energy they generate and channel, Wenger argues, we can move beyond the limits of self-consciousness or self-centeredness, become more attuned to others and the world, and ultimately become more generous and effective meaning-makers.

In pressing her case, Wenger draws on contemplative pedagogy scholarship, the teachings of yoga master B.K.S. Iyengar, and feminist theory, particularly that of Donna Haraway. The concepts of the "writing yogi" and the "embodied imagination" are at the core of her analysis. The writing yogi is the type of student subjectivity Wenger hopes to cultivate. Such beings are "situated, connected knowers," capable of weaving together personal and community knowledge, as well as reason and emotion (105). They recognize the partial and interested nature of their own perspective and can use "the insertion of the self in knowledge production as a way to generate reflection and analysis" (105). The embodied imagination, in turn, is the faculty by which body, heart, and mind are combined within the writing yogi's practice. When writing is informed by this faculty, knowers "experience the self in relational webs" (30). Wenger sees deep ethical implications in such positioning. Via deployment of the embodied imagination, writing yogis become more open to the world and its varied inhabitants. Integrally, for Wenger, this is all a very material process. It is only through attention to the individual, thinking-feeling body, paradoxically, that openness to the world can be achieved.

In the pedagogy-focused interchapters Wenger illustrates how the above ideas might inform work in the writing classroom. She presents a writing class centered around the investigation of embodiment. In addition to the standard practice of reading and writing about the topic, though, Wenger makes the very brave move of integrating yoga into the daily workings of the class. The result is a fascinating example of theory and practice informing one another.

Wenger believes that her students can use yoga as a site to generate knowledge about the writing process. Writing assignments in the class are designed to facilitate linkage. Students write "body blogs," for instance, in which they consider how their physicality is implicated in writing and learning. Wenger believes that embodiment is key to how we make sense of the world, but that the connection between mind and body has been obscured by conventional education. When writing is "rematerialized" students come to see how bodily needs, actions, and positioning can and do impact writing and thinking. This insight is key to developing the ethically informed "embodied imagination" discussed earlier. It also allows students to use knowledge from physical activities (e.g., sports, yoga) to inform intellectual work. To prove such transfer is possible the interchapters are filled with examples of students drawing generative connections between their work "on the mat" and their work "on the page."

Overall, I think Wenger makes a strong case for the pedagogy proposed. Ideally, I would like to see some extended samples of student writing to illustrate the gains in openness, audience-awareness, and general writing ability Wenger claims to achieve (the book mainly draws on textual snippets in which students profess change). It would also be interesting to check back with students, say a year or two later, to see if any of the lessons learned stuck after the class ended. These are minor quibbles, though. *Yoga Minds, Writing Bodies* is a valuable piece of scholarship. It can obviously be of great use to those who wish to incorporate contemplative practices into their teaching. Perhaps less obvious, though, it can also serve as a model for what rhet/comp scholarship can be. First off, though informed by her personal interests, Wenger's project remains deeply rooted in the practical work of writing instruction. The danger with pursuing your passions as a writing teacher, I've found, is that those passions can decenter writing. You end up teaching something else, in other words. I don't think that happens here. Also, *Yoga Minds* is, simply put, a well-written book. Wenger combines rigorous scholarly argument with detailed description of teaching practices and does so in an artful and, honestly, quite entertaining manner. This formal elegance is why I wanted to review *Yoga Minds* despite having little interest in yoga.

I would like to close by pointing out one area in which I believe Wenger's work may have unexplored implications. As you may know, in the past ten years there's been much talk of a "material turn" in rhetoric and composition. The general idea is that writing studies scholars should do more to account for the role of material forces in the writing and thinking process. Wenger's work is exemplary in this regard. Throughout *Yoga Minds* she foregrounds the active role of individual human bodies in the construction of knowledge. In doing so, she forcefully rejects the postmodern notion that bodies are simply vehicles via which cultural scripts are performed. Integrally, *contra* much so-called new materialism, she also insists on the reality and importance of the embodied self. As Wenger puts it, she refuses to allow the "I" to be dissolved either in discourse or "a vortex of intertextual materialities" (55). This is a quietly radical orientation. It posits a self that can stand in ethical relation with other selves yet maintain its fundamental integrity. I would suggest that this conception of social space has much to recommend it. It respects empirical reality as well as the phenomenological reality of everyday experience. To my knowledge, the consequences of Wenger's body-centric individualism—and how it connects with and pushes against other work in feminist theory, materialist-oriented writing studies, and embodied rhetorics—has yet to be explored. I urge scholars to take up the challenge.

✦

Borgman, Jessie, and Casey McArdle, editors. *PARS in Practice: More Resources and Strategies for Online Writing Instructors*. WAC Clearinghouse, University Press of Colorado, 2021. 384 pp.

Madeline Crozier
University of Tennessee, Knoxville

The charge that "we are all online writing instructors" should resonate with any composition instructor who has taught during the Covid-19 pandemic (Borgman and McArdle 3). This exigent universal truth gives rise to the compilation of this volume. The well-timed collection builds on Borgman and McArdle's co-authored book *Personal, Accessible, Responsive, Strategic: Resources and Strategies for Online Writing Instructors*, which earned the 2020 Computers and Composition Distinguished Book Award and introduced the PARS approach to online writing instruction—Personal, Accessible, Responsive, Strategic. (Yes, it's a golf metaphor for achieving the goal of shooting a *par* score.) The unique PARS framework provides a generative, systematic approach to creating and sustaining more effective and equitable online writing courses, and *PARS in Practice* builds on this landmark contribution with an even greater range of practical approaches that instructors, administrators, and scholars can use to develop their theories and practices of online writing instruction (OWI). As a graduate student who began a PhD program and became a first-year composition (FYC) instructor during the pandemic, the collection guided me to develop sound online teaching practices, and it reminded me to do well by my students in a time of crisis.

As Borgman and McArdle explain in their introduction, "PARS spans three layers: design, instruction, and administration," and "when these layers are combined, they equal the user/student experience" (5). Much like the components of the PARS approach, these layers intersect and overlap productively throughout the 20 core chapters of the book. This open-access resource functions as a handbook for online writing instructors: each section begins with a brief overview from the editors, and each chapter includes an abstract and list of relevant keywords. The book is an accessible addition to the OWI scholarship because the practice-oriented chapters share a "citation lite" writing style (8). While the chapters are theoretically sound and well-grounded in composition pedagogy scholarship, the authors forego lengthy literature reviews to center on their own contributions to the field, making for a personal reading experience. Each chapter forges a robust connection between OWI and PARS, demonstrating how well this heuristic works in practice.

The collection begins with Section I, "Design," a compilation of five chapters that address the challenges of course design for administrators and instructors who make decisions about the content and layout of online writing courses. Although I began my teaching career by following a standardized FYC curriculum, I still had copious decisions to make about how to effectively design the layout and trajectory of the course. In other words, while the learning outcomes and major projects of my FYC courses had already been set, I had the responsibility to plan the day-to-day steps we would take to achieve those goals. Two of the most readily useful chapters in this section demonstrate how to choose appropriate online tools and organize meaningful group discussions. "Online Writing Instructors as Strategic Caddies: Reading Digital Landscapes and Selecting Online Learning Tools" by Kristy Liles Crawley models strategic course design by integrating the PARS approach with Jody Shipka's statement of goals and choices (SOGC) as a framework for OWI (20). The adapted SOGC questions guide instructors to determine any online resource, platform, or "tool's capabilities, audience, and contexts" and "weaknesses and strengths compared to others" to make strategic decisions about online learning resources (Crawley 20). Along with the keen use of digital tools, productive group discussions reflect a cornerstone of many effective online writing courses. In "The Literacy Load is Too Damn High! A PARS Approach to Cohort-Based Discussion," Alex Sibo promotes a PARS approach to online discussions that emphasizes quality over quantity. This persuasive chapter makes a strong argument for the effectiveness of "cohort-based discussions"—small-group discussions that occur regularly throughout a term—while leaving room for instructors to personalize the strategy to their own institutional and classroom contexts. During the pandemic, as I moved modalities from asynchronous online to hybrid synchronous to masked in-person classrooms, I continuously appreciated cohort-based discussions for generating productive conversations and meaningful relationships among students.

Section II, "Instruction," covers perhaps the most important aspect of writing instruction—that our pedagogy itself should always aim to be personal, accessible, responsive, and strategic. Never has this rung truer than during the Covid-19 pandemic. Writing instructors who teach courses in any modality or environment can turn to these chapters for pedagogical strategies and instructional approaches. In "Finding the Sweet Spot: Strategic Course Design Using Videos," Christine McClure and Cat Mahaffey further the argument that videos and video conferences make OWI more personal and effective. The authors develop specific strategies and best practices for creating videos for online courses with several detailed, visual step-by-step guides. This chapter offers a far more pedagogically sound resource for creating and adding videos to online courses than the results from random Internet searches for tutorials that instructors might have relied on through sudden shifts to online instruction (as I did).

Another significant addition to the collection is "Designing a More Equitable Scorecard: Grading Contracts and Online Writing Instruction." Angela Laflen and Mikenna Sims demonstrate a PARS approach to labor-based grading contracts and antiracist assessment practices. They astutely identify challenges with implementing labor-based grading contracts, such as student perceptions and LMS barriers, while suggesting ways to develop responsive grading contracts in online writing classrooms (122). Their chapter includes references to many additional grading resources and strategically presents a road map for how instructors can use labor-based grading contracts in their writing courses (133-139).

Section III: "Administration" includes five chapters that, most relevant to writing program administrators, focus on the larger pictures, goals, and outcomes of OWI. One of the most interesting chapters, "Create, Support, and Facilitate Personal Online Writing Courses in Online Writing Programs," draws on focus group research to explore how instructors and administrators can forge strong personal connection in online spaces (Thomas et al.). Based on their research, the authors offer practical tips for building rapport, strengthening personal connections with students, and developing community in online courses. Four appendices provide practical tips and anecdotal experiences from the authors (203-207). Jason Snart's contribution, "Online Writing Instructors as Web Designers: Tapping into Existing Expertise," explores the professional development challenge of guiding online writing instructors to think of themselves as instructional designers.

The final section on "User Experience (UX)" faces the daunting task of integrating the three layers of design, instruction, and administration in the PARS approach, and delivers on this goal. A highlight, "The Bottom End; Transposing Online Bass Lessons to Online Writing Instruction" by Dylan "Too Fresh" Retzinger, promotes a UX-driven PARS approach to the instruction, design, and administration of online writing courses. Retzinger emphasizes that UX "means being critically and culturally aware of the experiences that shape us as instructors and researchers" (278). Consistent with the approach to perceiving students as users, Joseph Bartolotta develops a framework instructors can use to test their courses' usability, or "the extent to which your students are able to complete the goals you have created for your online writing courses" (305). He suggests that instructors should first model his task-based usability testing approach and then subsequently develop their own usability practices for their classrooms. Both chapters speak toward the future—toward a "new" normal in which instructors adapt their online teaching practices to meet the needs of a face-to-face classroom (instead of the other way around). The guidance to follow the strategies but then personalize and expand them also reflects the goal of many chapters in this collection.

PARS in Practice is one of the most practical recent additions to writing pedagogy scholarship, and online writing instructors will find it immediately useful. As Borgman and McArdle conclude, this book can serve as a personal impetus for action and inspiration. For me, becoming an instructor during the Covid-19 pandemic meant becoming an *online* instructor—a role I only stepped into with the help of close colleagues and the guidance of foundational pedagogical texts, like this one. By the time I finished reading the book, I had already started to follow some of the advice and suggestions in my hybrid first-year composition course, with even more ideas for designing my course next semester. I realized how to enact my teaching philosophy in practice, transforming my commitment to equitable assessment into implementing grading contracts, and aligning my empathetic approach to online instruction through a focus on the student-user experience. *PARS in Practice* promises to meet you where you are in your OWI journey and help you grow and learn, for the benefit of yourself and your students. The only thing this book needs is you.

✣

Miller, Richard E. *On the End of Privacy: Dissolving Boundaries in a Screen-Centric World.* University of Pittsburgh Press, 2019. 256 pp.

Kandace Knudson
Sacramento City College

Although I no longer grade student papers, I work closely with students and my faculty colleagues in support of the online learning environment. Need some advice about how to design your online course to increase student engagement? Need to know what the institution's rules are as they relate to online teaching? Yes, I'm that person: accessibility laws, copyright laws, college policy, how to get this photocopied article into the learning management system, where to click to do this or that. As faculty coordinator of distance education, I aim to make the online learning experience not only legal for the institution but an actual learning experience that's worthy of our students. I work with students to understand and improve their digital experience and with faculty to help them understand and employ 21st-century tools in the online environment. My job is as much strategic as it is practical, counselor as much as it is coach.

Colleagues lately have flooded me with complaints about students not "engaging" with the learning materials that have been placed so painstakingly and thoroughly in the learning management system (in our case, Canvas). Students, on the other hand, vent their frustration at how hard it is to find their assignments and relevant information. And sitting squarely in the middle, I see both sides: the faculty compulsion to add more and more content and expectations to their online courses, yet the student overload with the layered, confusing, and multiplicitous digital learning environment. Even best practices in online education, however, may not be enough for students who are overwhelmed with life or only one broken screen or one lost wifi service away from dropping out...or worse. And although Miller's *End of Privacy* seemed at first glance to be about something else entirely, I found it to be a helpful prism through which this challenge of student engagement in the online learning environment can be examined.

In 2010, Miller launched himself into a 7-year journey down the rabbit hole and into an exclusively digitally mediated world, a paper celibacy, in order to "take a break from academic writing" (xi). But what begins as a seemingly innocuous pattern interrupt— like a refreshing afternoon walk in a day of committee work drudgery—ends up as an exercise in human curiosity and academic work resulting in this book. It is an insightful meditation on the galaxy-sized gap between print culture oriented college professors and their digitally inclined students, between those of us seeing and living life through the lens of a paper-centric world and those young people who are living lives mediated through a screen-centric one.

Miller asserts that the cornerstone of the paper-centric world has been and remains the provision of narratives that interpret raw data, practically meaningless on its own merit and dependent on the storytelling of the paper-centric era to provide meaning to audiences. That's successfully contrasted by what happens to raw data in today's Internet-centric and screen-centric world where snippets of private moments are thrust into the public sphere of social media without the benefit of such interpretation, context, and meaning-making. This is our new world where privacy is practically nonexistent, thanks to ever-on video cameras and digital breadcrumbs that live on beyond their moments of relevance when we least expect it.

In so many ways, this book is also about failure: the failure of a top-notch institution such as Rutgers to be able to save one of its students—symbolic of all our students—from himself. Tyler Clementi, a freshman at Rutgers in 2010, jumped off the George Washington Bridge to his death following what was an insensitive and illegal invasion of his privacy by his roommate who blasted to social media that his gay roommate was having a date night in their shared dorm room, using technology to open a web cam channel into the private affairs of an adolescent who was expecting to keep his affairs private.

This book is also about the failure of us as keepers of The Institution to be able to see and understand the lives of our charges and how their lives—and ours—have been transformed by what Miller refers to as a "screen-centric world," juxtaposed dramatically with what we know and are grounded in as a "paper-centric world."

And in smaller ways, this book is about the failure of the military, the failure of our justice system, and the failure of our political system to understand and deliver justice in a new world where what was once mediated by carefully crafted narrative is now raw and often graphic data transmitted directly to the eyeballs of the world via the ubiquitous internet and the devices and platforms that tantalize and titillate. It's the medium as sensational tabloid. And we are—as humans drawn to the supercharged intimacy of nakedness and spectacle—practically helpless against it and escorted through Miller's own presentation of these sensational, sex-charged examples.

Miller's imperative, of course, is for us to be able to see the world our students inhabit. The imperative, of course, is to replace any of our blame about students' lack of [follow-up, reading, attentiveness, or whatever] with compassion, with empathy, and with understanding. The imperative we arrive at in the end—somewhat surprisingly—is to pull our students back and away from the quantification of education, away from the "bean countery" and "testocracy" of the neoliberal educational enterprise of the last couple decades. Replace it, he asserts, with efforts at meaning-making, reflection, and explorations into the ethics of this modern life.

In many ways, Miller's leap to this message about the vacuousness and impact of the No Child Left Behind era is less jarring than his narrative trajectory—the non-linear mosaic of interesting and often titillating vignettes and anecdotes such as Weinergate, Bill Clinton's Cigargate, and rape accusations leveled against Julian Assange and other powerful men. Much like a momentary internet search for a quick bit of data morphs into an afternoon spent inside the Oz of an internet browser, ping-ponging between the click-bait distractions of endless relevant tidbits, Miller's narrative bounces from Clementi to Hillary's email to Bill's cigar to Anthony Weiner's sexting to Chris Christie's Bridgegate and back and forth and all around between seemingly endless examples of private-messages-gone-public. It's jarring, and I believe that is one of the most important messages we take from Miller: the screen-centric world our students live in is as jarring as it is abusive to our sense of personal boundaries.

Perhaps Miller's message is that *because* of the shift to screen-centric universe where privacy has dissolved, we are compelled via the compassion we have for our students to see and understand their world and what compels them to act in the ways they act. Because they live in a world where they never had a paper-centric sense of privacy the way we had, they cannot be expected to behave in the ways we expect. Why, for instance, do young people seem so indifferent to ethical and moral lapses in exposing others' private lives? In a world where sex tapes and hard-core porn are easily visible on any internet browser via an ever-increasing number of virtually uncountable websites and platforms, we begin to see how indifference replaces a paper-centric sense of privacy and thus how it replaces outrage when that privacy is transgressed.

If we are to help them—truly help them and not just provide pieces of info that is interesting just to us—we must see from their perspective. Miller helps us do that by showing us how the internet-mediated world has disabused us of our paper-centric and old-fashioned expectation of privacy. Ultimately, Miller's exhortation on the perils of screen-centric indifference upends the notion that our students are to blame for not being able to thrive in the paper-centric worlds we may have created for them in those layered and multiplicitous Canvas course shells. We must meet them there in Internet Oz, understanding the landscape between us and the dissolution of boundaries between indifference and compassion.

✦

Nelson, Steven T. *Teaching the Way: Using the Principles of* **The Art of War** *to Teach Composition,* **Ten 16 Press, 2022. 198 pp.**

Christian Smith
Coastal Carolina University

First, an admission, or perhaps a confession: my enthusiasm for teaching composition has been waning in the last year or two. I don't know if it was the pandemic coupled with the resulting year on Zoom or the cumulative effect of teaching writing for the last decade and a half, but somewhere along the way it became a different experience. All too often after grading or having a lesson plan fall flat, I would repeat the first two lines from Geoffrey Sirc's underappreciated review article, "Resisting Entropy," when he says "Teaching writing is impossible. You have ten to fifteen weeks to do … what?" Despite countless hours prepping, grading, investing in student progress, I am too often left wondering what was accomplished and what the students will take away from the course. Indeed, as Sirc observes a little later in the same essay, "one's faith in the enterprise is always tested, and hope is hard to sustain" (508). Such sentiments have become especially pertinent in the last couple of years, but thankfully in a moment of kairos, *Teaching the Way* crossed my desk just to remind me why this teaching endeavor is still worth all the effort.

Using Sun Tzu's *The Art of War* as a framing device, Nelson's book conveys the hard-won wisdom of someone that has been running thoughtful composition classes for a quarter of a century and does so in lively conversational prose. As a result, Steven's book never runs the risk—as far too many books concerning writing pedagogy do—of getting unnecessarily bogged down in theoretical jargon or the latest trend. No, *Teaching the Way* is a solid work of practical advice for anyone interested in what kind of teacher you should strive to be, how to best plan out a semester's worth of instruction, and, most importantly, how to view our students. It is not, however, overly prescriptive, or heavy-handed in any way. As such, I think the ideal audiences for Nelson's book is two-fold: first, new writing instructors who are looking for concrete examples and guidance. For instance, I plan to assign this book to our university's second-year MA students who are enrolled in a practicum for instructing first-year writing students. Second, there are those, like me, who are experienced teachers but could use a bit of revitalizing from time to time.

It is worth noting here that potential readers do not have to be familiar with *The Art of War* or Sun Tzu at all in order to get the value of Nelson's work; and, in fact, Nelson rightfully dispels any possibility of misinterpretation: this is not a book that uses the metaphor of war to define the relationship between students and teachers, rather, as the book clarifies early on, Sun Tzu's philosophy is "not so much a book about warfare, destruction, or violence as it is about strategy and human nature, leadership and morality, and directing the energy of the universe to where it needs to go" (17)—all things that, as teachers, we are *de facto* invested in as well. The only war Nelson is interested in waging is one against the forces of Bad Writing and, in that war, the teacher and students are on the same side. It takes a wise instructor, however, to persuade students that they are in on this struggle as well and "by making them active participants in the process, by making them *want* to write" (17) we are simply and competently doing our job. Nelson convincingly argues that Sun Tzu can help us accomplish this.

For instance, the second chapter, "How to Present Yourself," uses Sun Tzu's definition of a good leaders as someone that uses the twin notions of *deception* and *formlessness* to enable students to become invested in their own writing. Anyone that has been teaching long enough knows that students often try to "figure out" the teacher—their values, their world views—in order to write towards those things as a shortcut to the hard work of thinking and writing. In other words, students strategize for grades rather than Good Writing. Here Joan Didion's guidance towards what inspires Good Writing is crucial as she notes, "I write entirely to find out what I'm thinking, what I'm looking at, what I see and what it means" (qtd. in Nelson 36). This is impossible to do if writing is to conform solely to a teacher's ideals. To thwart this motivation, Nelson draws from Sun Tzu and advises that teachers aim for a kind of deception in that we stand back, "putting them in positions to figure things out on their own and do the work they need to do to grow as writers" (29). As Nelson observes, "it might seem easier to simply *tell* them what to do, but they won't learn that way" (30). In many ways this kind of deception is where the real work of writing gets done and the outward façade of the course—the syllabus, the weekly schedule, the Student Learning Outcomes—provides the opportunity for this deeper level of personal engagement with writing and the resulting growth that can occur for us as writers and as people.

Similarly, *formlessness* here means to not explicitly reveal why students are doing certain writing tasks, but to design the course in such a way so that students stop asking for the reasons or consulting the SLO's on the syllabus, but rather learn by doing instead. As Nelson says, "I always ask myself if I would get bored completing the assignment. Would I have to think critically and creatively to complete it? If the answer is no, I come up with something better" (44). Throughout the book, Nelson not only tells us *that* he comes up with something better, but he *shows* us just what those things are and invites us to adapt them to our classes.

This kind of demonstration is, for me, the strength of *Teaching the Way* and while there are other examples that exist—Thomas Newkirk's wonderful *Nuts and Bolts* comes to mind—this is a welcome addition that also delivers, in Nelson's use of Sun Tzu, a philosophical foundation in a unique way that goes beyond being merely instructional resource material. It is also worth noting here that, in addition to the audience mentioned above, teachers and scholars interested in Barry Kroll's influential *The Open Hand: Arguing as an Art of Peace* might also find this volume a useful companion.

Work Cited

Sirc, Geoffrey. "Resisting Entropy." *College Composition and Communication*, vol. 63, no. 3, 2012, pp. 507–19.

✦

Dively, Rhonda Leathers. *Creativity and The Paris Review Interviews: A Discourse Analysis of Famous Writers' Composing Practices.* **Anthem Press, 2022. 204 pp.**

Heidi M. Williams
Tennessee State University

Only by fate and fortune would an apprentice receive the opportunity to review the work of a master. Nearly 14 years after sitting as a doctoral student in her Creativity Theory course, I am pleased to review Dr. Ronda Leathers Dively's text, *Creativity and The Paris Review Interviews: A Discourse Analysis of Famous Writers' Composing Practices*. Dively has written and published on the topic of Creativity Theory since the late 90s and is notably one of the pioneers for applying Creativity Theory in the composition and expository writing classrooms.

As a former student in her theory class, I recall Dr. Dively saturating the chalkboard with her expertise, while providing her students with plenty of readings, visuals, creative projects, and reflection assignments. *Creativity and The Paris Review Interviews* echoes her voice that I vividly recall, offering extensive qualitative research through in-depth discourse analyses of interviews featured in *The Paris Review* that "work to illustrate and complicate understanding of the creative process elements as experienced by the featured writers," while "establishing expository composition as a creative process" (33). Extending an interdisciplinary and cross-disciplinary approach, and nodding to neurobiology and cognitive science, this text is designed for creators, writers, and educators.

I identify as a creator, writer, and educator and find the organization of the text a creative move in and of itself. After outlining the "Impetus, Contexts and Methods" in chapter one, and "Composition through the Lens of Creativity Theory" in chapter two, the next six chapters guide readers through the model of creativity that has become prevalent (see Rob Pope's *Creativity: Theory, History, and Practice* for various definitions of "creativity" through a more historical lens). As such, Dively defines the paradigmatic creative process model through these stages: first insight, preparation, incubation, insight, and verification. Dively then organizes and analyzes portraits of famous composers' processes from interviews published in the *Paris Review* from the "2006-9 four-volume anthology" (13). Specifically, some of the noted poets and fiction-writers in the study are: Maya Angelou, James Baldwin, T.S. Eliot, William Faulkner, Earnest Hemingway, Ted Hughes, Stephen King, Philip Larkin, Toni Morrison, Philip Roth, Salman Rushdie, Kurt Vonnegut, Eudora Welty, and William Carlos Williams, just to name a few of the 64 total interviews discussed in the text.

The chapter that follows outlines the "Emergent Patterns" from "651 passages" that "ultimately disperse across six subcategories: reasons for writing; role of art, including writing; difficulty of writing; confidence, or lack thereof; conditions for writing; and attitudes toward creative writing courses" (123). These emergent themes not only validate the theoretical framework of the creative process and its intersections with the composing process (invention, drafting, revision, editing), they also substantiate a sense of authentication for creators at any level: even renowned authors labor and struggle while creating a masterpiece. Furthermore, Dively's text provides plenty of evidence that the creating and writing process is complex enough not to be reductive, and thus the book in no way presumes a one-size-fits-all approach insofar as no two people fit succinctly into one process.

Congruent with Dively's previous work, *Creativity and The Paris Review Interviews* includes contextualized implications for the research study by offering practical suggestions for composition instructors. The final chapter of the text is a call to action for instructors to assist students in becoming "aware of how incubation, insight, and all other components of the creative process model function and how they can be productively managed" (158). As in the previous chapters, Dively's analysis spans each step in the creative process model offering recommendations and pedagogical strategies for guiding students through their own writing processes. Chapter nine, in particular, left me thinking about my students and where I position myself within their writing processes. I wondered if I am stifling their creativity by the writing assignments I design, and how I might revise my pedagogical approaches to "include not only teacher-led activities and exercises that compel students to become aware of how incubation, insight, and all other components of the creative process model function" by designing more "scaffolding aimed at helping [students] enact these creative subprocesses on their own" (158).

By implementing the creative process model juxtaposed with the composing process model, instructors will inspire knowledge transfer and creative problem solving, thereby encouraging students to gain "some measure of control over their individual writing processes" in order to "master finer points of rhetoric, genre analysis, style, etc." (152). I am excited to implement these concepts in my expository writing classes, as I already view my students as incredibly creative, highly intuitive, and inventive. I am also excited to engage in some metacognitive reflection about my own writing and creating processes, and this text is designed for anyone who wishes to do the same.

Work Cited

Pope, Rob. *Creativity: Theory, History, Practice.* Routledge, 2005.

✦

Jackson, Rebecca and Jackie Grutsch McKinney, editors. *Self+Culture+Writing: Autoethnography for/as Writing Studies.* Utah State UP, 2021. 238 pp.

Amanda E. Scott
Western Michigan University

This volume brings together a compendium of works that explore autoethnography and its emerging applications. A qualitative approach that first appeared in the social sciences, autoethnography has recently gained traction within other disciplines over the last two decades, including rhetoric and composition studies. However, due to its theoretically and methodologically amorphous qualities, over the years researchers have struggled to firmly define autoethnography, especially as the field continues to evolve. Still, many within writing studies have championed the method and now understand it as a recursive tool for studying "the relationship between self and other and all of its dimensions" (Kafar and Ellis 134). As more work has been published in the autoethnographic tradition, so too has the need for a deeper understanding of its current function and future possibilities, a task the editors and contributors take up in this timely collection—the first of its kind in the field.

Writing in their introduction, Jackson and Grutsch McKinney explain the project's origins and their interest in reframing this method, noting the glaring absence of codified literature in the broader discipline: "We'd both looked unsuccessfully for years for books on autoethnography we could use in our undergraduate and graduate writing studies courses...but there was no robust or sustained discussion of autoethnography in the field of writing studies" (3). Accordingly, the book is separated into three parts, with topics ranging from autoethnographic explorations of the self to autoethnography and multimodal compositions to autoethnography as a method for historical recovery.

As a method historically invested in disrupting conventional narratives focused on dominant social groups, namely white and middle-class, autoethnography is particularly valuable when applied to experiences underrepresented in the mainstream, for it encourages individuals "to engage in various forms of systematic reflection on experiences and memories to craft richly reflexive personal accounts that map onto or interrogate cultural attitudes, ideologies, practices, and times" (8). Thus, when situated within the larger critical theory movement, autoethnography becomes a crucial lens for continued shifts toward more socially conscious and just practices within writing studies.

As a Latinx scholar and adjunct college instructor having taught a variety of composition and rhetoric courses—ranging from first-year writing to computers and writing to editing—I embrace inclusive pedagogical practices that platform students' lived experiences and language as significant rhetorical artifacts worth examination. With experience teaching primarily at HSI-designated institutions with large first-gen populations, I find this mission to be particularly essential in reaching students of color, nonbinary and queer-identified students, and students from working and middle-class backgrounds. Genres like personal narratives are indispensable as they invite students to contemplate the intimate, metacognitive qualities of their research and writing processes. Likewise, autoethnography thoughtfully builds on this principle as a broader, systems-oriented mechanism for reflection and, within rhetoric and writing studies, becomes a vital method through which to probe institutional power and influence over language, identity, and culture. Thus, upon scanning the collection's table of contents, I was encouraged to see the editors' consideration of these issues and purposeful curation at play that gradually builds over three major sections, moving from methodological concerns to the teaching of writing and finally to practical applications.

Fittingly, the collection's first section opens with Tiffany Rainey's "Her Own Words: Coming Out in Academia with Bipolar Disorder," a compelling meditation both on the triumphs and trials of living with a disorder that is often stigmatized, including within academia, and on how we might use rhetoric to refute harmful ideas about mental health. Following the evocative autoethnographic form, Rainey uses plain, vulnerable language to capture its pathos-driven style and lift the veil on mental illness in hopes that "readers are able to see themselves in us [and] us in themselves" (43); in other words, to establish a channel through which both audience and subject can engage in meaningful discourse about and establish a shared understanding of bipolar disorder. This introductory piece sets the tone for the remaining works in the first section, which explore a variety of autoethnographic forms and styles: evocative, analytic, and collaborative, among others.

Responding to calls for greater equity and inclusion in academic learning spaces, the chapters in the book's second section explore disruptive, critical strategies for shaping a new pedagogic paradigm. Situating the writing classroom as a contact zone (see Pratt), Amanda Sladek's "'Say What You Want to Say!': Teaching Literacy Autoethnography to Resist Linguistic Prejudice" unpacks the complexities surrounding multilingualism within the canon of Western discourse and first-year writing. As with other pertinent discussions within the discipline—namely regarding linguistic expression, code-meshing, and the role of writing-centered discourse communities—knowledge-creation through personal narrative can serve as a powerful tool for multilingual and international students. Refashioning and recasting the well-known literacy narrative assignment as a literacy *autoethnography*, Sladek claims the distinguishing factor between the two is that the autoethnographic form, generally, has a vested interest in engaging with culture in a way that "puts the author's representation of their literacy acquisition into dialogue with the ways their literacy is represented by the dominant culture" (127). As a result, this technique equips student writers with greater autonomy to parse out their often-contentious relationship with the English language. Other chapters in this section extend this mission, including Sue Doe et al.'s "What the Students Taught the Teacher in a Graduate Autoethnography Class," which takes a Freirean approach to responsive, collaborative student-teacher research, and William Duffy's "Agentic Discord in Writing Studies: Toward Autoethnographic Accounts of Disciplinary Lore," a fascinating reckoning with the cognitive dissonance between one's own lived experience and interpretation of disciplinary norms—in this case, composition studies and professional writing.

As the collection comes to a close, the editors make way for future-oriented contemplations of autoethnography's potential for theoretical, pedagogical, and practical use. Specifically, these final chapters challenge the construction of traditional autoethnographic work, envisioning a narrative landscape that embraces embodied experience, especially by those who have been historically marginalized. Visceral and unapologetic in its criticism, Louis M. Maraj's "You Can't Do That Here: Black/Feminist Autoethnography and Histories of Intellectual Exclusion" confronts the reality that autoethnography and other reflection-based approaches have, in part, emerged from earlier storytelling modes—namely those found in the Black polyphonic narrative tradition. Ironically, as a method meant to allow for greater metacognitive awareness of one's identity, culture, and language, current interpretations of the form unfortunately foster experiential erasure and bias, especially against people of color, womxn and queer-identified people, and people with disabilities. Consequently, Maraj argues, these groups "create knowledge that should not be dismissed as lesser than, untrue, or stereotypical based on white heteropatriarchal conceptions of what it means to consciously be" (184).

As the collection demonstrates in both scope and eclecticism, autoethnography may fulfill a few important roles: as a powerful tactic for "making meaning, as a method of inquiry, [and] as a teachable genre" (20). Gradually, what was once thought to be an exclusive method has emerged as a transformative practice many seem willing to take up in their own writing, research, and pedagogy, an evolution I've seen first-hand as my own department prepares to implement the genre in its first-year writing curriculum. Thus, when examined from different vantage points, one can forecast the potential for future autoethnographies that expand on current forms to deepen our understanding of language and culture—and that cultivate respectful and representative writing practices that honor our shared collective. While some scholars may contest autoethnography's legitimacy as a method, those who side with Jackson and Grutsch McKinney will clearly see its significance to the field, paving a path forward for researchers and practitioners alike interested in joining this promising disciplinary movement.

Work Cited

Kafar, Marcin, and Carolyn Ellis. "Autoethnography, Storytelling, and Life as Lived: A Conversation Between Marcin Kafar and Carolyn Ellis." *Przeglad Socjologii Jakosciowej*, vol. 10, no. 3, Aug. 2014, pp. 124-143.

✦

Book Reviews

Suhor, Charles. *Creativity and Chaos: Reflections on a Decade of Progressive Change in Public Schools, 1967-1977.* NewSouth Books, 2020. 304 pp.

Stan Scott
University of Maine, Portland

In the title of Charles Suhor's engaging memoir, the words *progressive, change,* and *creativity*—even *chaos*—will I suspect light fires of the imagination for many progressively inclined teachers and other readers. That goes all the more for those of us who lived through the upheavals and exciting breakthroughs of the late '60s and '70s, who may also have fought battles, like the ones recounted by Suhor, on behalf of our own students and children, to bring progressive changes to schools and colleges. As a former professor of English and philosophy and co-chair (with my friend and colleague Irene Papoulis) of the Assembly for Expanded Perspectives on Learning, I have a special admiration for Charlie Suhor's work as an educational reformer and his vision as one of the founders of this Assembly of creative teachers and scholars.

As suggested by its Latin original *educere,* to lead out, the word *education* names—for reformers like Suhor and progressive philosophers of education like myself—an arena of opportunity to lead students out from "the numbing effects of...inherited traditional programs" (54), from the deadening effects of mass culture, peer pressure, and the threatened social construction of an anti-democratic political reality, etc. In one of his zinging judgments, Suhor writes: "In the progressive years, the enemy of exciting learning was the weight of tradition. The past, as Hawthorne said, 'lies on the present like the body of a dead giant.'" And in the book's final chapter "Update: The (Non)Persistence of Innovation" he says, "The hazard today might well be both the persistence of conservative goals and an overabundance of electronic means in a 'cybernetic ecology,' like Richard Brautigan's dystopia where we are 'all watched over by machines of loving grace'" (217).

Today, in tune with the positive thrust of Suhor's vision, we might argue that education still has a great imperative to give students tools to navigate the cybernetic ecology, to decode the flood of electronic messages, advertising, social-media, etc., and learn either to dismiss them or to interpret them constructively. The tools offered by progressives—e.g., critical and creative thinking, genuine dialogue (with emphasis on *genuine*), and writing to discover--- if taught well may enable students to see the difference between the minefields of disinformation found on the internet and daily conversation, and authentic knowledge, found only by experiment and genuine discovery. They can also point to the possibility of escape from conventional but unproductive teaching and learning, cutting loose from toxic political clichés and from structural prejudices like racism, sexism, and classism. Suhor describes himself early in his career as a "young Catholic idealist" and many readers, including myself, will identify with the underlying idealism in his conception of school. For people like us, school is or can become a place for nurturing our own and our students' capacities for creative imagination and intuition—largely neglected in traditional schooling that emphasizes rote learning, overly prescriptive writing instruction, etc.

Such idealism, stemming in part from John Dewey's monumental *Democracy and Education* (1917), expresses itself in contemporary theory and practices that treat language as a dynamic medium of the creative process leading to discovery, rather than just a means of transmitting static information. Among other things Suhor's book is a breath-taking series of personal narratives and historical facts about what he calls "the progressive decade" (1967-77), including an account of the conservative reaction that dismantled, and today still threatens to dismantle, the gains of progressivism. Without sturdy leadership like that of Suhor and his co-workers, the elements of progressive education—like student-centered learning environments, treating subject matter from multiple perspectives, expressive writing, small group discussion, and respect for reason and truth—can be replaced by curricular trends like back to basics, skill-and-drill phonics instruction, and rote memorization that may discourage individual creativity and sometimes undermine reason itself.

In *Creativity and Chaos*, Suhor opens a window into this vibrant period of progressive change, and its eventual decline. He presents a granular chronicle including the names and much detail about colleagues, events, and policies in the institutions in which he worked—New Orleans public schools as a teacher and English supervisor and the National Council of Teachers of English. For readers with no connection to New Orleans politics, social climate, or educational institutions, the sheer number of names, titles, and actions taken by members of this large cast of characters may seem like oversharing. For those from the local area, especially those who recognize the names and faces in the photos, the book will be an unalloyed pleasure. But for any sympathetic reader, Suhor's first-person narrative voice, peppered with persuasive documentary evidence, will bring battleground issues of the progressive era to life, potentially bringing inspiration and stirring the imagination to see new possibilities for future reforms.

In moments when he takes a step back from the details of personalities and events, Suhor paints a big picture of the dialectic gripping American society and its educational systems in that era, when an entrenched traditional foundation built on conservative premises and standards is followed by a dynamic progressive upheaval. Supporting the latter became the main purpose of Suhor's life work. But the dynamism and success of the progressive decade is eventually overturned by a "backlash" from opponents of change and reversion to traditional ideology and teaching methods. Suhor's skill in accounting for the turmoil and changes in American society and education offers a perceptive history of the nation at that time. Though focused on changes in schools in his native New Orleans, Suhor portrays his home-town district as a microcosm of struggles and changes in the nation as a whole. This enables him to give first-hand testimony to the controversies between progressive and conservative forces that rocked educational systems from coast to coast. "The developments in New Orleans schools were variations on themes of the national progressive movement" (xiii), he explains. These developments included curricular innovations such as emphasis on "reasoned interaction" (79) in small group discussion and moving away from mainstream writing instruction that is "rule governed" toward "real-world writing," treated as "a communication event" (91). It also included efforts on Suhor's part to validate the grammar of non-standard forms of English (NSE) like Black English, in a very public dispute with (among others) TV personality Edwin Newman, who strove to argue that there is only one "correct" system of grammar and usage, Standard English (or SE).

Though he deals mainly with public high school issues, there is enough pointed emphasis on post-secondary English to make it of interest to college and university educators of a progressive bent as well. After teaching for nine years in New Orleans public schools, Suhor moved "from the classroom to district curriculum work [as a K-12 English supervisor], to further graduate study, a doctorate, and textbook writing" (15), to employment with the National Council of Teachers of English, where he eventually became deputy executive director. In the large project of educational reform, "progressive leaders needed to be research-savvy teacher educators," he says. "They had to be both aggressive and humble in selling new programs and methods. They needed to select and train teachers in the new concepts, then observe how they were incarnated in the classroom." The research Suhor speaks of often involves the gathering and skillful interpretation of data about such things as standardized test scores and other quantifiable outcomes of teaching and learning to be used as evidence for the effectiveness of a progressive agenda. At times he uses research of a more conceptual nature, as in making a case against memorization of grammatical rules. He writes:

> With the dissemination of knowledge about Piagetian psychology it became clear that definitions and rule-centered instruction had failed because few adolescents have reached the stage of mental development needed to learn, interiorize, and readily apply the highly abstract rules of grammar. Even when understood, the concepts are easily forgotten.... Independent reviews of research on the teaching of grammar in the 1960s and beyond confirmed, to the embarrassment of the profession, that knowing about the structural elements of SE [Standard English] grammar had no effect on changing most students' oral and written *language behavior.* (72)

Though clearly an inspired teacher-researcher and activist, Suhor explains little about the sources of his own inspiration to pursue a path based on progressive principles. But from time to time he mentions Dewey, Moffett, and other pioneers in contexts where their ideas were influential or relevant. He writes that "the profusion of research and practice materials for teachers on classroom interaction in the progressive decade was astonishing. It rekindled the Deweyan idea that social interaction skills are part of intellectual growth and an absolute necessity in a democratic society. The emphasis was shifting slowly from recitation of memorized responses to the elaboration of thoughts in large and small group discussion" (212). But in his 2020 update, he tells us, "Belief in rich, open, tolerant classroom talk still runs strong among enlightened educators—and it is still honored more in the breach than in observance." However, in light of research near the time of this update, Suhor claims "the dominant pattern was [again] teachers doing most of the talking as they presented materials elaborated by handouts designed to facilitate the recall of information" (213). Further he writes, "vigorous progressive protests against mass testing and the promise of healthy innovations from the National Assessment of Educational Progress (NAEP) were no match for the popular hunger for 'objective' data on student performance, the pressure for teacher accountability and the politicization of testing in the years that followed" (217).

In an endnote to chapter five, "Grammar, Usage and Oral Language," Suhor writes that James Moffett was "a true visionary, a philosopher/practitioner of immense knowledge, range, imagination and compassion. At his most radical—e.g., *The Universal Schoolhouse* [1994]—I wasn't with him, but I was usually just a few steps back, gathering insights that informed my view of the profession. Moffett was the chief inspiration for NCTE's Assembly for Expanded Perspectives on Learning [AEPL], which I co-founded with Richard Graves and Alice Brand in 1993." This and a slim thread of personal comments in other parts of the book hint a little about Suhor's personal beliefs and reasons behind his interest in moving educational leaders beyond "objective" data to the inner or spiritual life of individuals. Is this inner dimension important in the framework of a progressive agenda that emphasizes creativity and personal motivation above following external authority and memorization of objective facts? Like other reformers, Suhor does not typically express himself in the language of spiritual ideas. Spirituality may have been of little interest to him during the progressive decade, and from this book it seems likely he found little value in incorporating it into his language and activities either in the schools or at NCTE.

Why wasn't Suhor "with him" in '94 when Moffett took a stand for "spiritual awakening through education" as he puts it in the subtitle of this most radical of his books (*The Universal Schoolhouse*)? As Suhor argues the case for establishing progressive schools and programs, having to clear many hurdles along the way in the administrative and political arenas, he uses the tools he had mastered in his doctoral program at Florida State and found effective in his work as an English supervisor in New Orleans schools. These clearly involve quantitative research to gather objective data, and the calculative reasoning to interpret it, to the advantage of the programs he believed in. There is an odd paradox in Suhor's use of the very "'objective' data on student performance," which he considers reactionary in the passage above, in order to promote his progressive principles. These, as he well knew, emphasize personal, subjective engagement with subject matter, and such intangibles as student creativity, originality, and interpersonal skills, while de-emphasizing memorization of objective facts. The paradox is a partial answer to my question about why Suhor couldn't take a stand with Moffett in the early '90s about education as spiritual awakening. Whether or not Suhor believed (or believes) personally in such a thing as spiritual awakening is not clear from his book. But he was a soldier in multiple battles for elements of the progressive agendas at the local and national level. For his part, Moffett was a warrior in a big battle in Kanawha County, West Virginia, over censorship of textbooks he'd written. But when he taught secondary school, it was at the elite Phillips Exeter Academy, not public schools. And after he became a faculty member at Harvard's Graduate School of Education, he was able to write (among others) his great theoretical works, *Teaching the Universe of Discourse*, *Harmonic Learning*, and *The Universal Schoolhouse*, relating to spirituality in education. He was perhaps more like a general overseeing a war and less like a field captain. On the field, Suhor needed to use the weapons he had—objectively valid data and reasoned interpretation—to win his gritty battles for progressive principles, many of which he shared with Moffett.

The list of great practitioner-theorists of progressive education with roots in spirituality besides Moffett includes (among others) Parker Palmer with his vision of "education as a spiritual journey" and others. But Moffett stands out for his "immense knowledge, range, imagination and compassion" (in Suhor's words) which made him an inspiration for the founding of the Assembly for Expanded Perspectives on Learning, and a kind of prophet of the expansive learning possibilities that organization promotes. In a culture of secular humanism like ours, dominated by scientific materialism, the word "spiritual" in its most enlightened sense signifies a core element in experience that is non-material (*consciousness* itself, the power that drives imagination, and other intangibles like compassion, integrity, etc.). It names something beyond whatever is objectively known (like the very idea of *potential*). It refers to "the more" in William James's usage, the phenomenological intuition that there is always "more" to present and potential experience than meets the eye. In this perspective spirituality might be a first principle of progressive education. In a progressive context, "the spiritual" suggests that our "job" as teachers and students is primarily to exercise creative imagination and intuition to make discovery of new ideas, new perspectives, and new articulations of the "more" that is present though hidden in the shadows of experience. In an enlightened vision of education like Moffett's, *spirituality* is the universal human capacity for growth and change in a person's outlook and personality. It is not a reference to sectarian belief. So, to treat it in a public-school setting as a matter to be adjudicated by appeal to the constitutional separation of church and state, as in Moffett's dispute with Kanawha County (recounted in his *Harmonic Learning*), is a failure to understand what spirituality means or could mean in the context of public education.

John Dewey, the father of progressive education, had little to say about spirituality in his writings about education and knowing, a possible blind spot for which he was criticized by Ron Miller in his perceptive treatise, *What Are Schools For?: A History of Holistic Education*. But despite the efforts of Moffett, Miller, Palmer, and others to expand the horizons of learning based on an expanded conception of spirituality—to move beyond the idea of learning as a mechanical input of information into the mind, and toward the development of the whole person—progressives in our secular culture have typically been reluctant to address the idea of a spiritual source of energy animating students, and human consciousness in general, toward insight and creativity. Paul Tillich called this source "the depth dimension" of human experience, not something apart from our concrete physical existence but integral to it.

As I see it, this view of spirit comports well with Moffett's. And although Suhor was not "with him" in the '90s he was "just a few steps back." This, I take it, refers to the fact that he wasn't immersed, as Moffett was, in world spiritual and esoteric traditions. Being only "a few steps back" made him able to take inspiration from Moffett, though unable to wholly identify with Moffett's spiritual orientation or the argument that spirit is of central importance in a progressive agenda. But Suhor remained "with him" (at least intellectually, I suspect) in turning away from the objectivism that dominated educational politics at the time, toward creativity, originality, and community as core values that progressives perennially prize as the goals of education.

The struggles in the progressive decade were carried on with little explicit reference to the spiritual dimension of the learning process. But as Moffett and Palmer and others have observed, education can be operationally approached as a "spiritual journey," with "spiritual awakening" as its goal, and "spirit" as the non-objective force at the heart of experience that makes learning itself possible in the lives of teachers and students. This possibility includes the "expanded" forms of learning that Suhor spent his life promoting.

Creativity and Chaos is an excellent read—for the drama of its storytelling, its wit, and its strong judicious reasoning. I recommend it highly.

Contributors to JAEPL, Vol. 27

Madeline Crozier (she/her) is a PhD student in English (Rhetoric, Writing, & Linguistics) at the University of Tennessee Knoxville. Her research interests include composition pedagogies and literacy studies, with a focus on the nexus between writing assessment and social justice. She has presented at conferences including CCCC, CWPA, and MLA. (mcrozie2@vols.utk.edu)

Mariya Deykute, M.F.A., is an instructor at Nazarbayev University in the Republic of Kazakhstan. She teaches fiction writing, poetry, rhetoric and composition, and public speaking and co-edits the trilingual literary journal *Angime*. Her writing has appeared widely in both English and Russian. Her research interests include multilingual creative writing pedagogy, postmemory, and creative writing across the curriculum. (m.deykute@gmail.com)

Naomi C. Gades is an assistant professor of English at Frostburg State University, where she teaches first-year writing. Her research interests include the intersection of modernist poetry and science, which was recognized with the Fathman Young Scholars Prize from the T. S. Eliot Society, as well as college pedagogy. She has contributed to *The Robert Frost Review*, *JMMLA*, *The Imaginative Conservative*, and *JAEPL*. When she has spare time, she enjoys engaging in outdoor activities, playing video games, and composing questionable poetry. (ngades@luc.edu)

Jamey Gallagher has been teaching at the Community College of Baltimore County since 2011. He has a PhD in Rhetoric and Composition from Lehigh University and an MA in Writing Studies from Saint Joseph's University. His writing has been published in the *Journal of College Reading* and *Learning and Teaching English in the Two-Year College*. (jgallagher@ccbcmd.edu)

T J Geiger II is Assistant Professor of Technical Communication and Rhetoric in the Department of English at Texas Tech University in Lubbock, TX. He studies religious rhetorics and feminist rhetorics. He is the author of *Faithful Deliberation: Rhetorical Invention, Evangelicalism, and #MeToo Reckonings* (2022 University of Alabama Press). His publications also include articles in *College English*, *Composition Studies*, *Rhetoric Society Quarterly*, *Rhetoric Review*, and *Peitho*. (TJ.Geiger@ttu.edu)

Jay Hardee is a PhD student in Writing and Rhetoric at George Mason University, with a graduate certificate in Women and Gender Studies (Mason), MA in Literature (American University), and BA in History (Tufts University). Previously, Jay spent twelve years working in small professional theatres in and around Washington, DC. (jhardee2@gmu.edu)

K. Shannon Howard is associate professor of English at Auburn University Montgomery. She analyzes the use of material tools and spaces in writing classrooms and in popular culture narratives. Her book *Unplugging Popular Culture: Reconsidering*

Materiality, Analog Technology, and the Digital Native was released in 2019 by Routledge. (khowar20@aum.edu)

Kandace Knudson is a professor at Sacramento City College and helps faculty and students thrive in the online learning environment. Because she really loves college, she earned masters' degrees in English, Liberal Arts, and public health; and a PhD in Education. (kmknudson@gmail.com)

Michelle LaFrance is Associate Professor of English at George Mason University. She is a feminist critical ethnographer, who teaches courses on community writing, feminist methodologies, writing studies, and critical pedagogy. Michelle's current work has her investigating urban communities, studying discourses of volunteerism and belonging at Historic Congressional Cemetery in DC. (mlafran2@gmu.edu)

Erika Luckert is a poet, educator, and PhD candidate in Composition and Rhetoric at the University of Nebraska-Lincoln. Her research is in creative writing and composition pedagogies, with a focus on writing workshops. Originally from Edmonton, Canada, Erika received her MFA in Poetry from Columbia University. Her poems have appeared in *Indiana Review*, *CALYX*, *Tampa Review*, *The Rumpus*, *Epiphany*, *Boston Review*, and elsewhere. Her research has appeared in *Writing on the Edge*, *Journal of Creative Writing Studies*, and *Dangling Modifier*, and is forthcoming in several edited collections. (eluckert2@huskers.unl.edu)

Matthew Overstreet is an assistant professor of English at Khalifa University in Abu Dhabi. Originally from Kansas, he has taught writing and writing pedagogy on three continents. (matthew.overstreet@ku.ac.ae)

James Ryan is an assistant professor of Writing at University of Alaska Southeast, Ketchikan campus. He is a founding member of Creative Writing Studies Organization and served as Editor-in-Chief of *Journal of Creative Writing Studies* from its inception to 2021. *Recovery Writing*, which presents James's research on writing and healing in the context of Twelve-Step recovery fellowships, will be published by Lantern Publishing and Media in 2023. His book, *Beyond Craft: An Anti-Handbook for Creative Writers* (co-authored with Steve Westbrook), is available from Bloomsbury. (williamj35@gmail.com)

Amanda E. Scott is currently pursuing at PhD in Creative Writing at Western Michigan University, where she also serves as an Assistant Director of the First-Year Writing program and Editor-in-Chief of *Third Coast*. Her articles have appeared in *Technical Communication Quarterly* and *Cuentos & Testimonies*, among others. (amanda.e.scott@wmich.edu)

Stan Scott. (stan.scott@maine.edu)

Christian Smith is an associate professor of English at Coastal Carolina University where he teaches courses in writing, literary theory, and film studies. His work has recently appeared in *Dappled Things* and *Ruminate Magazine*. (csmith8@coastal.edu)

Joonna Smitherman Trapp is the Director of the Emory Writing Program and the Writing Across Emory (WAC program). She is finishing a book on the Southern Lyceum Movement and does work in the areas of faith and learning, creative nonfiction, and American gothic. She enjoys acapella music and is a frequent choral singer. (joonna.trapp@emory.edu)

Steve Westbrook is an associate professor of English at Cal State Fullerton, where he teaches courses in creative writing, composition-rhetoric, and cultural studies. His scholarship has appeared in a range of journals, including *College English, Computers and Composition,* and *New Writing: The International Journal for the Practice and Theory of Creative Writing.* His book, *Beyond Craft: An Anti-Handbook for Creative Writers* (co-authored with James Ryan), is available from Bloomsbury. (swestbrook@fullerton.edu)

Heidi M. Williams is an Associate Professor at Tennessee State University, an HBCU in Nashville, Tennessee. She specializes in Rhetoric and Composition, Technical Writing, and Research Writing. Her research primarily reflects on various aspects of accessibility as the term relates to higher education. (hwillia4@Tnstate.edu)

The 26th Annual Conference of the Assembly for Expanded Perspectives on Learning of the National Council of Teachers of English (after a Covid-induced hiatus of three years!)

Empathy and the Teaching of Writing
June 18-21, 2023
Y of the Rockies, Estes Park, CO

Keynotes:

Lisa Blankenship, Baruch College, NY

Eric Leake, Texas Tech University

Organizers:

Bruce Novak, The Foundation for Ethics and Meaning

Liz DeBetta, University of Michigan

PARLOR PRESS
EQUIPMENT FOR LIVING

Now with Parlor Press!

Studies in Rhetorics and Feminism
   Series Editors: Cheryl Glenn and Shirley Wilson Logan

Emerging Conversations in the Global Humanities
   Series Editor: Victor E. Taylor

The X-Series
   Series Editor: Jordan Frith

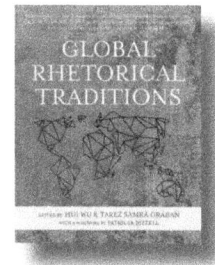

New Releases

Global Rhetorical Traditions, edited by Hui Wu and Tarez Samra Graban

Rhetorical Listening in Action: A Concept-Tacticc Approach by Krista Ratcliffe and Kyle Jensen

A Rhetoric of Becoming: USAmerican Women in Qatar by Nancy Small

Emotions and Affect in Writing Centers edited by Janine Morris and Kelly Concannon

MLA Mina Shaughnessy Prize and CCCC Best Book Award 2021!

Creole Composition: Academic Writing and Rhetoric in the Anglophone Caribbean, edited by Vivette Milson-Whyte, Raymond Oenbring, and Brianne Jaquette

Check Out Our New Website!

Discounts, blog, open access titles, instant downloads, and more.

www.parlorpress.com

JAEPL **Discount:** Use CLJ20 at checkout to receive a 20% discount on all titles not on sale through December 1, 2022.

www.ingramcontent.com/pod-product-compliance
Lightning Source LLC
Chambersburg PA
CBHW031322160426
43196CB00007B/625